# DODGING THE DEVIL

MARTINDALE—
In fond memory of George Gowthorp Martindale,
"Normanby", Dimboola, late 5th Batt., A.I.F.,
who passed away April 1, 1922.
A true friend.
—(Inserted by Ettie Dawson)
Notice from the Melbourne *Argus*, 2 April 1923, p.1

# DODGING THE DEVIL

Letters from the front

## GEORGE MARTINDALE

Commentary by
Nicolas Dean Brodie

**hardie grant** books

Published in 2016 by Hardie Grant Books

Hardie Grant Books (Australia)
Ground Floor, Building 1
658 Church Street
Richmond, Victoria 3121
www.hardiegrant.com.au

Hardie Grant Books (UK)
5th & 6th Floors
52-54 Southwark Street
London SE1 1UN
www.hardiegrant.co.uk

All rights reserved. No part of this publication may be reproduced, stored in a retrieval system or transmitted in any form by any means, electronic, mechanical, photocopying, recording or otherwise, without the prior written permission of the publishers and copyright holders.

The moral rights of the author have been asserted.

Copyright letters © Paul Cunningham
Copyright text © Nicolas Dean Brodie

A Cataloguing-in-Publication entry is available from the catalogue of the National Library of Australia at www.nla.gov.au
Dodging the Devil
ISBN 978 1 74379 215 5

Cover design by Nada Backovic
Typeset in 12/16 pt Centaur MT Regular by Kirby Jones
Cover image courtesy of AWM G00963
Printed by McPherson's Printing Group, Maryborough, Victoria

The paper this book is printed on is certified against the Forest Stewardship Council® Standards. FSC promotes environmentally responsible, socially beneficial and economically viable management of the world's forests.

# CONTENTS

| | |
|---|---|
| Preface | 1 |
| Part One: The Journey to Egypt | 15 |
| Part Two: Mena Camp, near Cairo | 31 |
| Part Three: The Gallipoli Peninsula, Turkey | 69 |
| Part Four: Following Aeneas | 93 |
| Part Five: The Western Front | 117 |
| Part Six: Convalescence | 131 |
| Part Seven: France, again | 171 |
| Part Eight: Holding the Line | 181 |
| Part Nine: Dismissed | 193 |
| | |
| Appendix One: Explanatory Notes | 199 |
| Appendix Two: Family and Friends | 223 |
| Notes | 243 |

Private George Martindale (centre) in a photograph taken by Captain Charles Bean (war correspondent) in May 1915 on the Gallipoli Peninsula. (AWM G00963)

# PREFACE

'I suppose the censor will not pass this letter', George Gowthorp Martindale wrote to his father, because there is 'too much truth in it'. Corresponding from Egypt in January 1916, George was a long way from his hometown Dimboola, in western Victoria, and had passed through one of the great moments of his nation's history. A few months later, when 'Anzac Day 25th April came round again' he and only one other man in his company stepped forward when an officer asked for those who had been at the landing. 'Certainly a quieter day than last year', George quipped to his father.

George might have become one of the great writers of twentieth-century Australia. Landing on the Gallipoli Peninsula at Anzac Cove on 25 April 1915, fighting Lone Pine, enduring Fromelles, and suffering Bullecourt, George's war experience reflects something like a litany of the nation's hallowed trials during the Great War. Certainly, George described some of these actions for members of his family in the letters he sent home, forming a collection of his writings that is the basis of this book. But unfortunately, George's literary output remains incomplete. Unlike a fellow veteran of D

Company in the 5th Battalion, Albert William Keown, who wrote and published a history of the war in the years following its end, George suffered and lingered and died in its wake.[1] George's diary, which he kept during the conflict, is lost. Other letters, to which he makes reference in those that survive, are, at best, dispersed. And the inbound correspondence from home, which he said he treasured while in the dugouts and trenches, and which served as his greatest inspiration, largely went the way of his diary. In the confusion following his unconscious evacuation from the front his letters and writings were, perhaps appropriately, most likely lost to the contested earth in the general neighbourhood of no man's land.

Yet not all was lost. Fittingly, his words survived in Dimboola, where his mother and father and sisters and brothers read of his adventures and tribulations. They passed the pages between them, and wrote back to George in turn. The Martindale family conversed across oceans and continents, months and years. In doing so, they produced a history from the war like no other. It was a time that was not just about warriors. It was about chickens in backyards, local gossip and shire politics, the weather here and there, meeting old mates in foreign locations, and of course the many sacrifices the war demanded and the people endured. All of this, in its complexities and contradictions, George articulated with a distinct style. His expression was both indicative and unique, capturing and challenging the prevailing zeitgeist. His frames of reference often diverged, as he strived to embody certain characteristics of Australian soldiery, while also criticising the falsehoods of a deliberately fostered national mythology. He expressed antipathy towards 'the Hun', but sent kind wishes to the old German settlers back home. He read the Koran, quoted the Bible, enjoyed poetry and slaughtered his foes. Before he was a name on a plaque or part of a collective legend he was a son, a brother, an uncle, a friend, a discerning observer, a witty companion and a compelling correspondent.

PREFACE

'War has been declared against all surplus stock & usual prices', advertisement heading from *Dimboola Banner*, 25 August 1914[2]

George signed his 'Attestation Paper for Persons Enlisted for Service Abroad' on Friday 21 August 1914.[3] He recorded Footscray as his birthplace, gave his age as twenty-seven years and five months, and affirmed he was 'a natural born British Subject'. Standing over five feet and six inches tall, George had brown hair, blue eyes and a 'florid' complexion. The unmarried carpenter recorded that he belonged to the Church of England and put his mother down as his next of kin—Mrs Martindale of Dimboola, Victoria.

Electoral records reveal that George was living in Brighton for at least some of that year, working as a carpenter. This is why his attestation was initially completed in South Melbourne. Once preliminary information was gathered he was examined by a medical officer and formally appointed to the Australian Imperial Force, 5th Battalion, H Company. George was given a service number—901—and the rank of private. The whole process was completed that day.

Within a few days George's enlistment was public news in his hometown, courtesy of the *Dimboola Banner and Wimmera and Mallee Advertiser*. 'Another volunteer for the expeditionary force who has been accepted', the paper noted 'is Mr George Martindale, of Dimboola.'[4] The *Dimboola Banner* recorded the collective enthusiasm of a town hectic with recruitment fever. There had been a great deal of 'patriotic fervor' displayed for Dimboola recruits as they headed off for service in small batches. Only on Thursday evening, the day before George signed up, the local recruiter had arranged a social gathering at Howard's Hotel for 'the third contingent' of Dimboola men. During the night the king was toasted, speeches were given and applauded, and the mood was generally vigorously patriotic. Then towards the end of proceedings Captain Crebbin, the recruiter, stood up and turned to the volunteers.

Now, lads, you are leaving your mothers, your fathers, your sweethearts, your sisters, and your brothers. On every opportunity that you get, write to them. You will be in the midst of excitement. They will be waiting anxiously and looking for news from you. Write loving words to them. They may not see you again, although I hope that they will. You may depend upon it that they will hand those letters around among their friends, and that they will be read with interest.[5]

Then the night drew towards its end. The party continued a little while, before the men 'were escorted to the rail-way station by a large crowd, who sang patriotic songs, and shouted them hoarse in their enthusiasm.' The ten volunteers boarded the express train, scheduled to depart from Dimboola at 2.18 am, and headed towards their training camp at Broadmeadows in outer suburban Melbourne. Whether this was the turning point for George he never revealed, but the timing is at least suggestive. More likely he was still in Brighton and missed much of the Dimboola pageantry. But the fact that the event was chaired by 'Mr R Martindale'—George's father—probably reflected a wider compulsion for George. Mr Robert Martindale, 'Dad' to George, was a prominent local timber-merchant, builder and plumber who had helped build much of the material fabric of modern Dimboola. As a Justice of the Peace, Mr Martindale was also one of the town's leaders. George's family were therefore socially situated in the midst of a busy country town, where, sometimes working with his father as the local undertaker—another side of the business—George was well-placed to know most, if not all, of the town's main families. He certainly knew some of the men boarding the train.

Recruitment within Dimboola was closely linked to some of the town's inner circles. Among those to first enlist, attracting much public attention as he did so, was the local Shire Secretary, Henry D'Alton. His surname ensured prominence on the first lists of local recruits, but so too did his social standing.[6] At the farewell function for his departure,

One of the recruitment posters appealing to patriotism and fear for family. (AWM ARTV01149)

held on Monday 17 August, a few days prior to the other function, and at the start of the week in which George enlisted, Henry was given a standing ovation when he rose to respond to the toast and well-wishes of the townsfolk. On that night Mr Martindale had expressed himself 'very proud' of Dimboola's response, asserting that 'we would be less than human—we would be craven slaves—if we sat silent and let someone else fight for us and what we had inherited from our forefathers.'[7] In response to the adulations, Henry spoke on the volunteers' behalf. He and the others were, he said, doing 'nothing more than their duty in volunteering'. They would, he concluded, 'do their best, and try to return to Dimboola.' He and his companions were walked to the train, and cheered as it departed. The following night, a similar party and railway fanfare saw off another group, then on Friday George seemingly quietly volunteered in Melbourne. It was a hectic week for the young men of Dimboola.

Certainly, many of the recruits, like Henry and George, were or had been members of the Dimboola Rifle Club, and felt themselves capable of contributing effectively to the Empire's fight. More than simply shooting societies, these organisations were close to paramilitary organisations, a sort of citizen-led militia force, and were very common in Australia in the years leading up to the First World War. In a localised way, these clubs reflected the wider arms race and growing militant nationalism of the empire in the early twentieth century. The Martindales were certainly very active members at Dimboola. 'Captain' Robert Martindale was club president during June 1914 when, in distant Sarajevo, the Austrian Archduke Franz Ferdinand was assassinated. By late July, when Austria-Hungry made a series of demands on Serbia, the nation accused of having responsibility for the killing, Mr Martindale was secretary. And like his father, George had been an active club shooter for some time.

Quite probably George had also been a cadet, drill marching as a boy under the command of the headmaster of the local school,

'Captain' John Thomas Crebbin. Such junior military institutions also reflected the general nationalistic militancy of the period, as civilians like Crebbin adopted military 'ranks' and marched Australia's youth into preparedness. Unsurprisingly, such phenomena overlapped. George potentially manoeuvred in formation under Crebbin's orders, cadet or not. Hoping 'to make themselves more efficient if called upon for active service', the Dimboola rifle clubmen had 'requested Captain Crebbin to drill them.'[8] On Wednesday 12 August, with 'twenty-two out of the full strength of thirty-nine attending', the men marched about the school grounds, even as the major powers of Europe were mobilising their forces. In late July Austria-Hungary had declared war on Serbia, and with triggering alliances, opportunistic positions, demands, counter-demands, declarations, and counter-declarations, the European powers cascaded into a general conflict. When Britain declared war on Germany in early August, Australians assumed they too were at war, and rallied to defend the empire. Within days of the official declaration it was being reported in Dimboola that the 'Dimboola Rifle Club, has been notified by the Commonwealth military authorities that the club will be called upon to supply its first quota of twenty-five members for the 73rd Infantry regiment'.[9]

The war agitated Dimboola, literally seeming to spur many of its inhabitants into rapid action. While George possibly helped his father conduct the burial of old Mrs Graf on Tuesday morning, or continued his carpentry in Melbourne, by the close of Friday he was a soldier.[10] This rapid response was partly due to the imperial enthusiasms of the period, but also actuated by a very real sense of the war's rapid progress and reports that the enemy was committing atrocities. Great movements of troops, and heavy engagements by English and French against German forces, presented a complex and distant front. The people of Dimboola had, like most Australians, only been able to follow the war's great European movements in snippets, blipped and bleeped throughout the world in electrical pulses that were reconstituted into words and sentences. Yet the people of Dimboola did not just receive information passively. They responded to the fluid international situation with various relief funds, especially through the agency of the Red Cross, avid attention to the war's progress, and actively recruiting men from within their community.

Complementing its reports of recruits being sent-off, the *Dimboola Banner* gradually turned its attention towards covering the story of the Dimboola 'boys' in the training camp at Broadmeadows. George's departure for service was, a little surprisingly considering his father's standing, not met with any major press attention. While electorally he was in Brighton in 1914, he was also listed living in Dimboola, perhaps confusing officialdom and posterity alike, but affirming continued closeness to his hometown. But his quiet slipping away was, perhaps, simply a result of the paper's narrative shift from recruiting to training. Having boarded early morning trains, chugged towards Melbourne, and disembarked, the Dimboola boys disappeared from the easy surveillance of country town life. So, to keep their families and friends up to date, the boys wrote home.

If George wrote home, which he probably did, the letters have not survived or passed into the main surviving collection of his war writing. Fortunately, however, Henry D'Alton and others did so in those early days, and parts of their letters were transcribed into the *Dimboola Banner* for the benefit of the wider community. One such missive from Henry, received in Dimboola on the day of George's enlistment, reveals the first steps recruits took on the transition from civilian to soldier: 'We (the volunteers) went out to Surry Hills and were sworn in. We were then dismissed and required to be in barracks by 7.30 pm. ... We slept last night on the ground, with only a water-proof sheet and one blanket.'[11] In a Victorian August, this was hardly a pleasure expedition.

Another of the Dimboola volunteers wrote on 19 August to Captain Crebbin, describing the Dimboola boys coming in to camp in batches, and being 'treated with great courtesy by the officers'.[12] He described how 'we started to rough it there and then, some walking the floor all night, and some sleeping in straw, like fish packed in a tin'. Apparently their first night 'was a terribly cold one, and tried the men to the utmost.' Having thus originally gathered at Surry Hills, once sufficient numbers had arrived the recruits headed for the Victoria Barracks, and 2000 of them marched 'between eleven & twelve miles' to their training camp at Broadmeadows, cheered by the schoolchildren and public of Melbourne.

A Dimboola resident, having visited the camp the Sunday after George enlisted, also provided the paper with an account of the trainees and their situation.[13] Apparently the trains from Melbourne were packed with visitors, making the trip out uncomfortable and disembarkation slow—such was the public interest in the soldiers and the desire of friends and family to observe and communicate with them. The correspondent walked from the station as part of a large crowd disgorged by the overcrowded train, gradually arriving at the camp. It was 'prettily situated on rising ground, and the numbers of white tents extending over acres of green fields made a fine picture'. Once in, he 'soon found the Dimboola tent', and met a number of the Dimboola recruits, including Henry. The Dimboola boys were given messages and letters from friends and family, as well as some copies of the *Dimboola Banner*, where they could no doubt read accounts of their own recent departures. Then the correspondent re-boarded a packed return train, and left. 'They are all in the best of health,' he noted, 'and are enjoying the camp life.'

Within a week, another report had come through courtesy of a letter to Crebbin from one of the volunteers. The trainee reported that there had been 'three men down with sickness,' from among the Dimboola boys, 'but they were well again, and were resuming duty.'[14] George may have been among them, as he admitted to his mother that he got ill in his first fortnight at Broadmeadows, before enjoying good health for the remainder of his training. 'The boys all join me in giving three hearty cheers for Captain Crebbin and good old Dimboola', the corresponding trainee concluded, adding that 'We all hope to come back victorious.'

So much was there an *esprit de corps* among the Dimboola boys, in fact, that they wrote home asking for a dog to be sent to act as their camp mascot.[15] While New Zealand occupied German Samoa, and France started to consider the possibility of a German attack against Paris, the townsfolk of Dimboola sought out a suitable animal. They also pooled some resources to send a hamper to Broadmeadows. Crebbin continued to drill members of the Rifle Club, and more recruits were 'dispatched from Dimboola by Captain Crebbin.'

Crebbin's capabilities as a recruiter put him in relatively good stead with the military authorities. He managed to negotiate with them that a contingent of the Dimboola boys should all get leave at once, such that they could be feted in their hometown, before departing Victoria for active service overseas.

The Dimboola boys returned home on the Saturday night express. There were crowds at the railway station in expectation of their arrival and as the train pulled to a halt it was greeted with cheers. The men stepped onto the platform and were met with 'hearty handshakes', while the Dimboola town band 'rendered patriotic airs'.[16] The band then accompanied the crowd as it walked back into town, and the soldiers dispersed to their homes, families and friends. On Sunday, they rested.

On Monday morning, 7 September 1914, there were 'unprecedented scenes in Dimboola' as the volunteers prepared to leave.[17] At 10.00 am the town turned out to witness their departure, as they marched through the town in formation, under the guiding hand of Crebbin. The town band led the soldiers from the Masonic Hall to the railway station. Henry D'Alton was at the forefront of the soldiers, marching with their new mascot, 'a collie-puppy—decked out with the Union Jack and the Australian flag'. As the soldiers entered the railway station, they passed through a 'guard of honor' composed of the schoolchildren lined up in formation.

The 'boys' boarded the train, and a short speech was made for their benefit. Henry responded on their behalf, promising they would do their duty, and thanking the town for the mascot. They would return the dog if possible, he added. Then, with 'tears in many eyes' the train pulled away from the station to the tune of 'God Save the King'. The people cheered, children flanked the line, and the soldiers left their families behind.

In Dimboola, newspaper attention returned to local concerns like a regional election and the state of the 'Aborigines Camp' near town. But news continued to come in detailing the fighting in Europe, and the tens of thousands of men killed, wounded or captured in various engagements. The *Dimboola Banner* also reported that there were rumours of naval engagements between Australian and German ships closer to home, gave an account of the Victorian contingent of soldiers marching through Melbourne, and noted continued drilling of riflemen by Captain Crebbin. Moreover, the paper published the first letters from a Dimboola boy on active service: Jack McKinnon's accounts of life at sea, the heat of Queensland, and the taking of German Rabaul in New Guinea, revealed how during September and October 1914 Australia begun to actively contribute towards winning the war.[18] Meanwhile, the Martindale's had started their wartime correspondence …

## An editorial note on the correspondence

What follows is the surviving correspondence between George Gowthorp Martindale and select family members contained in a single family collection. The letters are arranged sequentially, as George read and/or wrote them. As such, two disparities may stand out. Firstly, George was receiving mail weeks or months after it was written, so for the purposes of narrative cohesion it is most appropriate to place the inbound letters proximate to his reading of and responding to their content. This produces a lack of total chronological exactitude, in favour of an approximate experiential one from the perspective of the soldier whose correspondence forms the bulk of this collection. The second disparity, reflected in a few instances, concerns George's tendency to compose two sorts of letters—brief updates and longer descriptions of battles. The latter of these were often composed in multiple writing sessions, sometimes weeks apart. These letters have been included in the collection by the date of completion, rather than first conception, meaning they may at first glance appear to 'pre-date' some of the shorter 'update' letters. Moreover, readers should be alert to the fact that George's commentary on a particular action can be written considerably later than the events concerned.

The letters have been divided into sections, based on the main locations from which George was writing—the Indian Ocean, Egypt, Gallipoli, France and England—and a short introduction frames the broader context of each batch. These segments are intended to provide greater narrative coherence, such that the letters can be read sequentially with relative ease, without burying the letters with too much introduction. An appendix provides more specific commentary on each of the various letters and their content. Here readers may find some further explication of references to specific people or events mentioned within the letters. Another appendix specifically details the core service details of soldiers that George refers to and which have been identified.

In this collection George's main correspondents were his older sister Maggie, and his mother and father. He also wrote some letters to his younger brothers, Bob and Peter, although only a few have survived into this collection. One other letter to George's father has been included, even though not actually from George, as it forms part of the Martindale collection and illustrates the wider correspondence networks that have not survived in full into the present. Similarly, a letter from George to a family friend has been included, having been published in the *Dimboola Banner*, which is probably quite typical of another body of correspondence that has not survived. Inbound correspondence to George in this collection is exclusively from Mr Martindale, although George's other family members also wrote to him regularly, especially his mother.

Finally, George's letters have been edited to reflect the manuscript originals, with some allowances being made to assist modern readers. George infrequently separated out the text into paragraphs, for instance, and some editorial selection has been made to break up the original text. Paper shortages meant George was generally making effective use of all available space. Moreover, George had an idiosyncratic approach to punctuation, meaning again that some editorial selectivity has been required. What is presented here is generally as close to the original as possible, although some changes to the text have been required based on George's style. Modern editorial interpositions are contained in squared parentheses, but have been deliberately kept to a minimum. George's tendency to leave out full stops when ending a sentence at the margin of a page has been corrected for convenience, for instance, without adding brackets. Given the hurried circumstances of much of his composition, it is remarkable how clean the originals were. That his letters could also be entertaining and well-written highlights that he was every bit as capable as writer as he was as soldier.

Australian soldiers on board a troopship being farewelled by family and friends. (PB0840)

PART ONE:

# THE JOURNEY TO EGYPT

*'Old men with war medals on for the occasion and women held their children up to see and to wave their hands.'*
Great Australian Bight, October 1914.

*'This war had to be, as you know, I always said I could see it looming up.'* Egypt, January 1915.

After some basic training George travelled from the Broadmeadows camp to Port Melbourne. There, he boarded HMAT *Orvieto*.[19] This was a passenger ship turned troopship, one of the largest in the combined fleet that was preparing to cross the Indian Ocean. Massive crowds cheered the soldiers as they travelled through Melbourne by train, were marshalled at the docks, boarded and departed. On the afternoon of 21 October 1914 the *Orvieto* left Melbourne, with a contemporary film capturing the scene as civilians and soldiers waved their goodbyes.[20]

On board, George reflected on his departure, and described how well he adapted to life at sea. He captured the fleet's main narrative arc only in passing, referring to bits of news he knew his family had likely long since heard by the time they read his letters. The fleet converged at King George's Sound near Albany at south-western Western Australia, from which thirty-eight ships filled with Australians and New Zealanders headed across the Indian Ocean on 1 November 1914. They had a relatively close encounter with the war while at sea. A naval battle was fought near the Cocos Islands between the HMAS *Sydney* and the SMS *Emden*, where the Australian ship effectively pounded the German ship into submission. German prisoners were taken on board the *Orvieto* after their ship had been scuttled, giving George his first contact with the enemy.

Arriving at the old port of Aden, George took the opportunity to obtain a postcard, which he sent soon afterwards. It was something he would often do, but only a fraction of which survived into the family collection. He also kept a diary—similarly now missing—which helped him to remember details in the letters that he had already begun writing and sending home.

Dimboola
30th Sep 1914

Dear George
            Just a line of farewell which
you may probably get before sailing. I have
just got off Tuesday night's & press train going to
Port th... by the return train. I went out to Colden
on Saturday morning & returned 11 oclock Monday
night. Mr C is able to be up & about but I don't think
he will be any good again. Fred, Elsie & Daisy & Daisy
young ... are doing the best they can with the dairy
farm. Mrs C is writing to Eva & I gave her one of your
cards which she is enclosing. She wishes you to call & see
Eva & Winnie if you have an opportunity. Tuesday morning
I went to Port Melbn thinking I might see you embarking.
I saw several transports. I believe you the 5th are going in
the (Orvieto) A3 she is ... the railway .... the 1st one
on the right hand side. ... the Shropshire A 9 & the
Wiltshire A 18 at the Town pier, The ......... Ororata A20
Orvieto A3, and Benalla at the Railway pier, and the
Rangatira A 22, and Star of England A 15 at the new pier.
The last two came in on Tuesday morning with
Queenslanders on board, one of the guards told me the
saw some cruisers outside about 2 oclock that morning

Dimboola
30th Sep 1914

Dear George

Just a line of farewell which you may probably get before sailing. I have just got off the Tuesday nights xpress & am going to post this by the return train. I went out to Cobden on Saturday morning & returned 11 o'clock Monday night. Mr. C is able to be up & about but I don't think he will be any good again. Fred, Elsie & Daisy & Daisy's young man are doing the best they can with the dairy farm. Mrs. C is writing to Eva & I gave her one of your cards which she is enclosing. She wishes you to call & see Eva & Winnie if you have an opportunity. Tuesday morning I went to Port Meln thinking I might see you embarking I saw several transports. I believe you the 5th are going in the (Orvieto) A3 she is at the Railway Pier the 1st one on the right hand side. There are the Shropshire A9 & the Wiltshire A18 at the Town Pier. The Hororata A20, Orvieto A3, and Benalla at the Railway Pier, and the Rangatira A22, and Star of England A15 at the new pier. The last two came in on Tuesday morning with Queenslanders on board, one of the guards told me the[y] saw some cruisers outside about 2 oclock that morning.

    I spoke to Mr Menzies on Tuesday morning & he said he thought you were being detained waiting for the New Zealanders. I think the Orvieto is the best passenger ship there & if you go on board her you will be lucky. I think you will do well to look Sergt Smith up (8th Batn) as I think him a man of sterling character. He has a farm at Lower Norton outside Horsham with a wife & family. He was connected with the Rangers for a long time (as sergt). He joined your lot as a private but I see he soon advanced. I don't think there was a more soldierly looking man in your Co than yourself as you marched out of the park on Friday and I hope you will look after yourself well. Mother is still very bad with Influenza but all the others are well.

Its time I was moving so I must say good bye. You are now going on an expedition wherein you will be called on to look grim death straight in the face and I wish you to accustom yourself to the thought so that when the time comes you will not be unprepared for him but will tackle him with a good conscience. I have full confidence that you will put up a good fight and hope we may all have the pride & pleasure to welcome you home again after a duty well done. Be patient and give ready obedience to your officers and as Kitchener says let Duty be your watchword. Do that and I leave you with confidence in Gods care.

Your affectionate Father

> Troopship A.3.
> "Orvieto"
> Great Australian Bight
> Sat 24th October 1914

Dear Bob and all at home

We're off at last: this is my first essay at writing aboard ship. It's about 5 o'clock in the afternoon here, our time is put back about 25 minutes daily so it will be about 1/2 past 6 at Dimboola. There are so many things to write about that I'd better start at the beginning. First of all "Reveille" at Broadmeadows on Wednesday morning 4 am and away from there about 1/4 to 10. The 2nd Contingent turned out, bands and all & gave us a great "send off", as each Company passed they would get 3 cheers and after we (H Coy last) were all past they started all clapping—"Auld Lang Syne" at the station—our engine was decorated with flags & flowers, the Kangaroo and Emu in front and the funnel with a soldier painted thereon with the word "United" inscribed underneath. All along the route (we didn't stop except at Flinders St) people waved hats, flags, handkerchiefs shirts aprons or anything that came to hand, there were people out in front of almost every house. Old men with war medals on for the occasion and women held their children up to see and to wave their hands. At the warehouses & offices in the city the windows were crowded with people. I sent Mother a wire "goodbye" from Flinders St—asked a lady to transmit it for me.

At Port Melbourne we waited about 11/2 hours on the pier & it was very hot. There was a great contrast between our fellows who were all sunburnt and the fellows on the ship who have very white skin. They have very long hair—all ours have their hair cropped close allover. We embarked about 1/2 past 12 & went below to our messes. Our company is complete on G Deck—the bottom one—the signallers also are on this deck. The floor of this deck only is of a material which is harder than cement—and looks like plain brown linoleum—all other decks are of wood—the top or boat deck of oak—we carry two 4.7 inch guns but they are not mounted. A hold runs right down to this deck & there is a space in the centre about 14 ft square hatched over, its a well about 30 ft deep. The mess tables are arranged around this, 15 tables to this company—6 men in ours all out of the same tent so we are lucky in this respect at least. When there is a small number of men in a mess we have smaller joints of meat. Consequently they are better cooked or browner—Suits me alright we all like the meat pretty brown.

Each mess is numbered—there are hammock hooks and racks—at night the hammocks are swung over the tables from which latter one can get into them. I have not taken to the hammock yet I've discovered a nice place under a big ventilator shaft where I spread out the hammock a canvas one then a blanket & another blanket over me. They are single blankets—using my greatcoat as a pillow—haven't wakened during the night once—notwithstanding that I sleep just over the screws & can hear the steering gear at work. Theres a fair bit of vibration this part of the ship—we are Aft. Starboard side—cannot open the portholes—sometimes they are above water sometimes below—Lying at Port Melbourne the water was about 1/2 way up them (they are glazed with very thick plate glass) & we could see shoals of small fish about 6" long swimming past. We are living below the water line.

The arms that is rifles & bayonets in scabbards are arrayed in racks all over the place. They look very nice—the bayonets looking like teeth in a giant comb. As the ship rolls so do the rifles like so many marionettes. I'm getting out of sequence. After the final inspection of the ship at Port Melbourne we had dinner & were then allowed on deck—I got a most uncomfortable position. 1 foot jambed on a rope in one place the other dangling most of the time one arm round a big hot water pipe & the other round a rod—but I saw what was going on. Everybody was yelling on both ship & quay some singing & some crying some waving arms like semaphores—others clutching ribbons of paper multi-colored ones—If they had been strong silk ones some fat old ladies would have been dragged after us into the sea when we sheared off—by jove they did hang on for grim death—most of the ribbons broke at about 20 feet but 2 or 3 held for about 50 or 60 ft & one long red one floated away up in the air & right over the ship—When we backed out the screws churned the mud up for hundreds of yards away perhaps 400 or 500 yards radius. It looked like a dirty Duck pond.

 I got along to the stern & looked up—there she was—the blue ensign at the mizzen—starred with the Southern Cross. She furled and unfurled nicely in the breeze. There was hardly a perceptible move in the bay, but as we entered the rip for a few rolls & pitches I thought I was gone. I only thought—others <u>didn't think</u>. We got out of sight of land on Thursday morning Cape Otway I think.

 So far we have had very good weather. The food is good and plentiful. We appreciate it after B$^d$ Meadows where towards the last the "grub" was scandalous it was filthy & not improved by the filthy cooks!? Save the mark—it wasnt fit for a self respecting dog & most of us wouldn't eat it. On board we have had about 4 Roast joints of beef—potatoes—pumpkin, carrots and 6 nice loaves of fresh cooked bread daily. Beautiful crisp crusts on them, more like home made than anything. Porridge for breakfast no milk of course & no sugar—tea plenty of it for breakfast & tea with sugar & milk—condensed milk only I expect. Raspberry jam, plum jam (good too) and marmalade—quite as good as Maggie's make too & that's saying a lot—for every meal.

 It's now Sunday morning & we are past the Recherche Archipelago & 5 or 6 hours run to Albany. Theres a pretty good swell up now I'm writing this on a brass ventilator & going up & down about 20 feet and enjoying it—I've felt A1 on board & can eat like a horse & am always hungry no matter how much I eat. Don't feel hungry at present just had a good breakfast of lambs fry & bacon—bread & butter & marmalade & 2 mugs of tea & am having a smoke. Theres not a "white horse" in sight but its like on the heath only in water up & down & smooth allover. There are scores of things I would like to write about happening all the time—but I've got to shave & get into uniform for Church Parade. We are mostly clad in blue dungarees, I washed mine in camp but even so I'm quite blue allover where they touch me. I had a bath yesterday, but you cannot get up a lather with seawater & it was a bit of a failure but it made my legs a very pretty color a kind of eau-de-mil down to the top of my socks where they were flesh color!

Of course you know that this is the flagship of the fleet & carries all the "nobs" from General Bridges downwards. There are I should say about 1600 or 1700 men aboard and about 20 horses—they are beauties—especially two of them—each of these has a separate stall about 11 ft square with big cocoa nut mats on the floor and a groom each to look after them—I'd like to change my quarters for theirs they are up on the main deck amidships. These 2 neddies shine like satin.

We have "Reveille" (get up) at 6 am breakfast, sweepers & swabbers parade & to work—parade till 11.45 Dinner 12 noon parade in afternoon till 4 Tea at 5. Lights out 9 pm so don't get much time to ourselves. I've been mess orderly more than ¾ of the time on board only two of the six of us being fit. Some of the fellows have been pretty sick—I was looking over the rail & a chap each side of me started feeding the fishes but it didn't affect me. It's a novelty getting up & down stairs with boiling water, tea, soup, etc. I can foresee a few being scalded. You may not have noticed it but we sailed on Trafalgar Day the 21st Oct. The first day out we sighted whales & porpoises one whale almost got run over by the ship. We could see them spouting in the offing. The little glass comes in very handy.

We're running into a rougher sea now. Last Thursday we saw a ship in front & gained slowly & passed her in the night we found out afterwards that it was the "Miltiades". On Friday morning the "Melbourne" our cruiser appeared behind us, and soon got abreast & passed us—you were aboard her you'll remember on your last trip to Melbourne. She looked low in the water but she has a good turn of speed—she looks efficient and would I bet be a nasty customer to tackle. Our first day out till noon Thursday we travelled 246 miles. To noon Friday 299 miles. To noon Sat 290 miles. We should be at Albany about 3 this afternoon. I get up in the bows sometimes and gaze over. The waves she throws up are very pretty—it looks like a big pail of frothy milk spilt over a blue satin cloth. Whilst over the stern where the propellers are going the sea resembles greatly a giant Seidlitz powder, white & bubbly & spray rising straight up like rain and opalescent. At night the water astern is quite phosphorescent. It's remarkable how many hues the water assumes sometimes white sometimes like black ink & all in the space of a few seconds. Often a beautiful light green & often various beautiful shades of blue. 2 of our mess have been orderlies nearly all the time—I think I wrote that before—the others are a bit seedy. It's worse below than on deck & rather close! When the stern dips & the water covers the porthole it's like looking at a blank film passing on a Kinematograph.

I forgot to say we get plum pudding sago rice etc for dinner daily & I can smell cauliflower cooking now. Nearly all the fellows on board are wristwatchy! On a bright day on shore they look like so many Heliographs. They vary in size from like a 6$^d$ piece to your town hall clocks. There are albatrosses following us from 2 to a dozen at times—they are cunning gentlemen. How did you get on with the mutton hounds at the show? I came across Alan & Clem Cordner in camp they are big fellows and one is in the A.S.C. & the other in the 6th Bn A.I.F. Tell Maggie I hope Miss Menzies had a pleasant time at the show—but she shouldn't have had the escort she did—not much class. If Val married all the girls he has had he would be either in Turkey or Pentridge—We had a few words re the war by wireless but nothing of any moment. If I get near the Germans I'll put a few of them out of circulation. Start a few of them practising the scale on the harp!

I'll be wearing my wrist out writing so I'll have a spell till after dinner, also this is the end of the paper I have at present. The chaps are singing this ditty, have you heard it—they are playing cards—I'll go one said Russia, I'll go two said France, I'll go three said Belgium, I'll take a sporting chance, I'll go four said Germany and wipe them off the map, But they all dropped dead when John Bull said: I'll go 'nap'—Yes I wrote to Mrs Browne tell Maggie.

## THE FIFTH EMBARKS.

*The Fifth Battalion, Australian Infantry, under the command of Col. Wanliss, embarked on board H.M.A.T. "Orvieto," A3, on October 21st, 1914, for Active Service Abroad.*

By MICHAEL DWYER.

The month was October—Nineteen Fourteen;
　The sun it shone brightly o'er that martial scene,
For one thousand young heroes, Australia's pride,
　Were embarking that day for a land o'er the tide.

"Orvieto, A3," was the name of the ship,
　That was taking so many on their maiden trip,
And while some said "Good bye," and others shed tears,
　The bold Fifth embarked amid loud ringing cheers.

Just picture the trooper, so stately and grand,
　And the brave lads embarking to the strains of their band
Their mothers and sweethearts and sisters also,
　And you'll find out their feelings regarding the foe

Boasting or bragging was heard from no man,
　"They're bearing it well" through the crowd quickly ran
You may talk of those Uhlans, and the great Prussian Guard
　But to beat those young fellows their job will be hard.

When the big ship moved off, and the shore became dim,
　From many a heart came a prayer unto Him,
To protect and to guide those leaving their home
　To go to a war that was none of their own.

It's not often, thank God, that we witness such scenes,
　Except just in fancy or perhaps in our dreams;
But may He who has said "*On Earth Peace & Goodwill*,"
　The hearts of those brave lads with courage may fill.

*Alex 25 Nov: 1914*

> Flagship "Orvieto" A.3.
> Gulf of Aden
> 24th Nov 1914

Dear Mother

Just got an idea that there will be an Eastern & Australian mail forwarded from Aden so will send a few words on the chance—daresay there will be one from Port Said for sure. It's a quarter past 6 pm now and I've just finished washing up. Being mess orderly isn't all it's cracked up to be by any means. Up and down 2 flights of stairs & steep at that & one has to force ones way through a crowd of struggling humanity to dump the refuse which consists practically of all the "food" (?) which is thrown to us. I thought I had seen a few fairly rough things in Australia but I'm satisfied now that I've seen nothing—that in these things I was a baby.

You'll think that the thoughts of food obsess my mind as I've mentioned it a few times before, but really its beyond a joke—an ordinary everyday self respecting pig wouldn't tackle it and I'm sure that Billy Ross's pedigreed ones would have a fit at the sight of it. After these eminently mild remarks I feel a bit relieved—our collective remarks right here on the spot are <u>not</u> mild.

At 8 o'clock this morning we left the main armada (about a dozen boats had preceded us from Colombo) and are now making about 14 knots an hour (nearly 16 miles) being aft and close to the propellers the vibration is fairly considerable—like a train running at a fair speed on the Rainbow track & its a bit awkward writing. So far we have had very calm weather. Today especially the water was as smooth as the proverbial millpond, it was and looked just as smooth as a piece of glass. There were dolphins & flying fish in plenty. I daresay you will know by now we have some prisoners of war on board 45 of them including a nephew of the Kaiser's—the Captain of the Emden who is a prince. They're a nuisance but are

## THE JOURNEY TO EGYPT

well treated—better than we in the ranks are. Sentries with loaded rifles & fixed bayonets prowl round and we're in hourly peril of our lives—a club would be more suitable for most of them—they would feel more at home with it, I'm sure.

We had a close shave with the "Emden" its now known that she was within a very short distance of our transports (about 6 miles) she passed in front of the "Orvieto" but as we were showing no lights she didn't see us. Had we been showing lights I don't suppose I'd be writing this—but probably practising the scale on the golden harp. I saw the official report which says that "had she passed astern of us she would doubtless taken toll of our ships with her torpedoes". However a miss is as good as a mile. When the "Sydney" connected with her it was "goodnight" Emden. (a few verses by an Irish Sergeant enclosed, a bit of a curiosity it will be). The Germans lost killed 134 men—wounded 50 men—prisoners 104 men and 45 who were looking for the cable escaped—escaped capture pro tem. When the "Emden" was making north towards us the Melbourne and Ibuki (a Japanese) started off to meet her but only got 4 or 5 miles & stopped. We could see it quite clearly. Our 2 cruisers & the Jap were a picture—all new ships. The "Sydney" made over 27 knots, about 31 miles an hour—same as on her trials. They reminded me of sheep dogs round a flock—but didn't the smoke pour from their funnels. The "Melbourne" and "Sydney" each have 4 funnels the "Ibuki" 3. The Germans (several of them speak English) were astounded at the accuracy of our gunfire. I fancy they will get a few more surprises yet. I'm keeping a bit of a diary and will send it from England, it will give you a fuller idea of life on a troopship. We've a brass band, a bugle band & bagpipe band on board but since the advent of our guests—and I fancy the big majority are not unwilling guests—no patriotic airs are to be played or sung or whistled or even thought of. I wonder if the position were reversed if they would refrain from whistling or playing <u>their</u> national anthem or patriotic songs.

Most of us sleep on deck at night. I'm keeping well—was vaccinated 5 or 6 days ago. I don't think it will take, it's got to be done again: Some of the men have very bad arms—and they get more knocks than halfpence. We will be at Aden in the morning. This will be the first time an "Orient" line boat has called there. One chap has been coming to Australia via Suez for 20 years and has never seen Aden!! I've sent a few people at Dimboola post cards for Xmas—just a few. Must ring off now: I hope all are well at home. Hope to get a letter or note at Aden. With love to all from your loving boy.

George

THE JOURNEY TO EGYPT

Flagship "Orvieto" A.3.
Red Sea Nov 28th 1914

Dear Mother

Landing in Egypt in a few days—all hope to spill a few gallons of Turkish blood—just as a hors d-oeuvre to a German feast. Vaccination took "successfully" and quite satisfactorily so far as I'm concerned. Don't think it will leave the slightest scars. Typhoid inoculation (twice) was much more severe. Quite well & hoping you all are the same. Writing again on landing—Much love from your affectionate son George

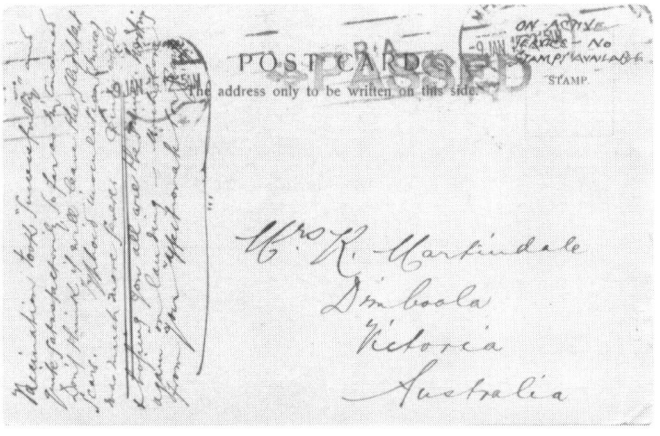

The main Australian training camps in Mena, Egypt. (AWM H03083)

PART TWO:
# MENA CAMP, NEAR CAIRO

'*In short Capt Bean is a liar.*' Cairo, February 1915

'*I can assure you that some glories are about to be added to the history of Australia & N.Z.*' Cairo, 16 April 1915

After disembarking in Egypt, George underwent further training, parts of which he described in letters home. He was based at Mena Camp, several miles to the west of Cairo. As such George had the opportunity to explore the city and surrounds, clearly indulging in some antiquarian interests while doing so. Yet a notable proportion of what George focused on when detailing his adventures really concerned information coming into Egypt from outside. Through the proclamation of the military authorities and the British press, for instance, George learned of reports from Europe of German atrocities, which he conveyed to his family back home. Through this, a sense of the righteousness of the British cause against Germany was being furthered, even while the Australians increasingly suspected they would be sent to fight against the Ottoman Empire in the first instance, which had joined the conflict against Britain.

George's commentary from Egypt also reveals quite a lot about home. He reconnected with people he knew, fostering that sense of the Dimboola boys being at war together, despite his being in a different battalion from a number of the prominent early recruits. He continued to express the sort of bravado that featured back home at the war's outbreak, and anticipated the Australians making a good showing when they got a go at combat. Linked to this, George made popular cultural references that his readers knew well, which reveals how the war inflected and affected cultural output at home and abroad. In another example of his strong emotional link with home, even while experiencing foreign territory, he mentioned the ready devouring of a comfort fund pudding sent from Australia.

Yet George also turned his mind to contentious matters, as did Henry D'Alton in a separate letter to George's father. These Dimboola boys became outraged at reports they read in the Australian press that painted their time in Egypt in a less-than-wholesome light. The Australians were not only writing and sending reports to home, they were receiving and reading letters and newspapers from home. Through this, some of the Australians were enraged to see some reports by Charles Bean, who had been appointed as an official war correspondent, which suggested Australia's reputation was at risk through the misbehaviour and debauchery of some soldiers. In one report, for instance, Bean made some remarks about the misbehaviour of Australian soldiers in Egypt. He asserted 'that there are a certain number of men in those who were accepted for service abroad who are not fit to be sent abroad to represent Australia', suggesting some of these were veterans of the South African war and were 'given to the very childish habit of showing off'. Bean thought there were 'in the Australian ranks a proportion of men who are uncontrolled, slovenly, and in some cases … dirty'. He then referred to men being sent home 'because they have contracted certain diseases'. This same letter, when printed in various papers, was matched with a series of titles that furthered the sense of public scandal. 'Australia's Name. A Passing Shadow' ran above the letter in the *Ballarat Star*, 'High Jinks at Cairo. "Do All Australians Drink so Much"' in the *Gippsland Standard*, and 'Conduct of Some of the Men Bringing Discredit Upon Australia' for Hobart's *Mercury*.[21] Upon reading this and similar assertions, George and Henry were clearly infuriated, especially as the soldiers' habit of sharing papers increased the exposure of the story within the camps.

The Australians, however, were not merely there in Egypt for convenience and training. Strategically, their presence helped serve bolster British strength in Egypt against an attack from the Ottoman Empire. In the event, the expected attempt on the Suez Canal was relatively easily beaten off by British forces at the beginning of February 1915, with a single day of fighting serving to prove that the Canal was well-defended. George took no part in this, but it had important ramifications for him. With Egypt secure, the Allies could more confidently make their own assault on Ottoman territories, including Turkey itself.

Mena Camp
Cairo 14th January 1915

My Dear Maggie
I suppose you will get this along with other letters & postcards I have written as the mail from here to Australia goes weekly—so far I have had no letter from home but one from Uncle George and this morning one from George Tilley (both single page ones). Mr Tilley says he got your letter and is taking my things to John Ward's—I'm sure John will put them where the sea air will not rust them—if any of you see him perhaps he wouldn't mind oiling my tools—there is some Pike's "Stonoil" in my basket also some raw linseed for the wooden tools planes etc. etc. I may not need them again in this vale of tears, and again, I may D.Y.

When you hear that I'm coming home you could get my blue suit out and have it cleaned & pressed—it's pretty good but there's a stain on the coat lapel. I'll most likely come ashore with my kit only and these are certain to be inhabited—at any rate a big percentage of the chaps here have live stock some in pairs some in scores and some in hundreds—they are off the Arabs and I suppose I'll get my quota before long. It will be a great treat to get a good hot bath and into clean clothes again, not that I'm anxious to doff the Kings uniform, which I'm prepared to cleave to as long as necessary.

Now there are so many things to write of that I hardly know what to say first and my time is ever limited—both day and night. But we were out in the desert a few days ago and I made a mental resolve to describe an early morning scrap, it may be of interest to you. We were turned out at 2.30 am or so and fell in—no lights or smoking and orders to be given in undertones. It reminded me of meeting the express (2nd) only 'twas more dismal & ghostly. No talking, just here and there a mutter or chatter of teeth. Had anyone permission or the inclination to sing I think Harry Lauders song

MENA CAMP, NEAR CAIRO

would have been most appropriate "When the snow is falling, and its murky overhead—It's nice to get up in the morning—But it's <u>nicer</u> to be in bed". This song has a great vogue here—in fact it's one of the favorites. We got away quietly & quickly and were soon plugging along into the desert—Pat Kenny's tramps are nothing to ours—throwing out a vanguard and scouts in front and either side—I and two others were with the first Lieutenant. After covering about 5 miles (which seemed like 50) we got in touch with the enemy & sent word back to the main body—just before dawn we all separated, I going straight in front and then making a detour, the enemy scouts spotted me and lay down—I spotted them too! but pretended not to have done so—in a few dozen paces I got to a fold in the ground and bending double took to my heels and after a few hundred yards lay down near a rock. Soon their scouts passed quite close to me arguing as to my whereabouts—When they got over a bit of a rise I kept straight on and soon heard the enemy entrenching themselves. I got up close enough to know that they were in considerable numbers and then I made a masterly retirement er hem! got back to our vanguard and reported what I had seen & we occupied some trenches, and when the enemy attacked at dawn we mowed them down. Our lieutenant & the two other scouts were captured as was also a party of 10 men & a sergeant. The decision was all in our favour. When we got out of the trenches we did look scarecrows—worse than usual, rifles & uniforms & faces covered with red earth & frozen almost stiff—we were all too cold to smoke even—I might say here that cigarettes or cigars are not to be smoked whilst out on the march—It's a bit rough on some of the chaps who are not too well marching till they are perspiring freely & then to lie down (without overcoats too) on the wet sand & stones (for the dews are very heavy) for perhaps an hour.

    The stars here are beautiful and its really wonderful how a lot of fellows here seem not to notice their beauty—perhaps they consider beauty to be only a skin disease. There is the morning star like a young moon it looks very close & a greater number twinkle here than in the Southern Hemisphere, of course we have no Southern Cross. Gazing up at them makes one think—<u>and stop thinking</u>! The dawn is also most beautiful—something different—in the foreground the Pyramids loom grim and solid and robing the earth is a beautiful pale blue mist that looks like the sea. Then gradually the mist fades away and daylight prevails.

We form up and each man has his breakfast or part of it—3 small S & A biscuits which are issued overnight—that is provided he didn't scoff them immediately he got them, like I did: then off we start for camp, marching "at ease" in the morning sun which raises the spirits which have been nearly down to zero. A song is struck up—"Fighting the Kaiser" or "It's a long way to Tipperary"—this latter is destined to become a classic! We now forget Harry Lauders song and a song we (you and I) learnt at school from Miss Jones or Miss Jessop occurs to me as being appropriate: Oh! Who will slumber in his bed, when darkness from his couch has fled, and where like diamonds in the light, Dew drops sparkle bright. I don't think we sung it since we were kiddies at school together.

On arrival back at camp we have breakfast—dry bread and tea—and not too much of that—I suppose they are training us to exist only—to live a perpetual fast! I could do a real good dinner now like we have at home. I lost my original webbing belt and got another which met with difficulty round my waist. It meets with tolerable ease now—<u>perhaps it's stretching</u>! Anyhow its consoling to know that Wilhelm the Mad will have to take up a few holes in his belt if things go on as they are at present—and even then he will eventually be like Humpty Dumpty.

A great many Egyptians & Syrians are very anxious to enlist in our ranks—fine fellows too but there's no chance of joining us. I think a separate regiment or two will be recruited here shortly.

## MENA CAMP, NEAR CAIRO

They are as anxious to be "at" the unspeakable Turk as we are to be "at" the superlatively unspeakable Hun! I'm keeping fit—I say this with a certain pride and satisfaction—it's a soldiers duty and one of the first to be fit. I don't think there is a man here more ready than I to go straight to the front—it takes a fairish bit of care here and I am exercising that care!

The old H and F Companies have been incorporated in one Company of 4 platoons which is now known as D Coy—so that instead of eight companies to the battalion as formerly there are only four companies. The old F Coy consists mainly of Public School boys and includes in the ranks chaps such as McIlwraith (McIlwraith and McEachern) the ship owners—McCracken of Brewery fame—Gordon Hope owners of George & Georges—Marshall (son of Dr Marshall of Scots Church Collins St [)] etc. etc. This old company averaged 5ft 10" in height and 11st 9lb in weight for 119 men—not too bad!

We bought some butter from Khartoum a few days ago 2/- per lb it wasn't up to much. We were out rifle shooting yesterday from 5 am to 7 pm on one small roll of bread and a small tin of cheap sardines (they would cost about 3d at home) amongst 3 men. This is how they dispose of the 6d extra per man per day that is allowed for service in Egypt. It was a hard day—quick or rapid firing 15 rounds per minute and the bolt and magazine full of sand. It is what we term the "mad minute" and from all accounts the Germans cannot equal it or stand against it. "Lights Out"—Goodnight!

Friday Evening 15th Jany

Got a letter each from Dorothy & Warrack also "Weekly Times Annual ["] from each Father & Warrack—I expect to get Mother's soon. Others are getting "Leaders" ["]The Age" "The Argus" and local & provincial papers from both England & Australia. There is great excitement when the mail is being dealt out—on return to camp there is a stampede to the company color sergeants tent—the chaps all covered in dust so that they look like niggers—they go at it like a hart at a waterbrook. If there is "anything doing" they march off wearing a grin—the mouth (inside) and teeth being the only clean parts visible. If they get nothing they slope off dejectedly.

You cannot appreciate how we all look forward to news of home—I think the fellows with girls are the worst—some of them write every few hours & we have to stop them sometimes when an extra violent spasm occurs. It's then that we take away their ordinary razors and hand them a safety one which tears up their faces like a ploughed field. I am posting an "Egyptian Mail" and a couple of other papers. The former is supposed to be a very big good paper here it costs a 1/2 piastre (1 1/4 d) and doesn't even equal to the peerless "Banner"—Oh by the way—So ____[22] is to be married "tomorrow". All I can say is—serve 'em both right! Had she lived in Melbourne perhaps she could have got the hangman— glad to know that you were not invited. Do you remember the night he had the desperate encounter with the "Gib Mac"—I have emitted a guffaw about a minute long as I picture it in my minds eye, and others have looked up and enquired in a startled voice if I felt unwell!

Hope you & Bella had a real good time when she was up home! Do you still hold the palm at talking? I must write to Mrs Brewer soon, she's not a bad old sort! We have had a route march (12 miles) today—the whole division was out—duty men sentries etc excepted—Artillery, Machine Guns, Transports, water carts, all ranks paraded—in full marching order—greatcoats, messtins spare boots & socks towel soap razor field service dressing (First Aid) spare shirt etc. all crammed into knapsack—food in haversack—with a rifle a fairly considerable load. There would be about 20,000 men on parade and many thousands of horses & vehicles. The procession covered several miles in length—we marched along the road to Cairo for a few miles (You will see the road in one of Mothers letter cards—it's an avenue) & then turned north & passed along a kind of bank with vegetable gardens and maize fields on either side.

The natives draw water from the irrigation channels in the same manner as the Chinamen—also by a water wheel, or wheels, cogged, and all of wood & turned by a buffalo cow. We passed through a couple of villages & the population turned out "en masse" to behold us—I imagine the sight opened their eyes a bit. I could hardly open mine for dust which rose in such dense clouds that we couldn't see more than 3 or 4 yards ahead. The niggers are indeed vile and have all sorts of vile disease. If a fellow doesn't develop something from all the dust he has swallowed here—he ought to.

A couple of English girls came out here in a motor car to see some friends—they enquired the way of me—you cannot realize what a treat it was to see and hear them speak. And they were neat & clean and not dressed like the heathen here. I will have to stop again for tonight anyhow as time is nearly up.

I took this out with me today thinking I might have time to write a bit when halted but I went to the Light Horse Lines & met Mr Domeyer—Machine Gun Section, he looks well & fit & like the rest has his horse (a fine big bay) trained like a dog (it doesn't attempt to get away like our curly short legged black one did) it's as gentle as a sheep & when he says "get down" the horse sinks down saddle and all & rolls gently on its side and lies its head flat on the ground & not a move. Then he gets on & still it doesn't move till he says quite gently "get up" then up she gets. She will get down whilst he is mounted, its wonderful how quickly they can do it—he doesn't move his feet from the stirrups but just moves his near side foot sideways and rests it on the ground. Nearly all the other horses are as tractable, it was nice to see the horses and men all lying down together. Sometimes the man lying with his head resting on the horses head and sometimes with the horses head in his lap and fondling one another. You would think that the men would get their corns trod on when they were all getting up—but they didn't! We had some good yarns & the time slipped past very quickly—we laughed over "White Wings" falling on me—the black dog—"Gus" Sallmann Walsgott and Co. chicken shooting in the back yard etc. etc. Then blest if Jim McCallum didn't come up—he's in the 4th Light Horse & we had a good yarn. They both wish to convey to you all their kindest regards.

I'm pretty tired tonight. The Major said on our arrival in Egypt that it was recognised that 1 hours work here was equal to two at Broadmeadows, at that rate we work about 30 hours a day. But then perhaps they say that 1 hours sleep here is equal to two at home, and a half holiday (we have not had one yet, except Xmas day in the afternoon) is equal to a whole one, or that 1 slice of bread and jam is equal to 2 slices of the same home. They are "the limit" in their lines of argument—they say that the farriers, artillery men, A.S.C., Light Horse, in fact <u>every</u> arm of the service other than infantry (who by the way are the hardest worked of the lot) should be better fed and accommodated because they are fewer. We contend that the food etc. should be the same. However, in the future we will laugh over it and treat it as a huge joke.

This last week I have taken to underpants, they stop chafing & where the water bottle and bayonet & haversack rub. I sleep with my pants on too as its bitterly cold o' nights. I have also got a sack to put over my feet which get very cold. I've grown a bit of a moustache which is pretty incipient and looks as though my eyebrow had slipped—I think I'll sacrifice it tomorrow as its a harbor for germs. I want to darn some socks tomorrow if possible—I've got a nice round stone to do it on if no one pinches it. My boots are pretty bad too—I have a corn and have a plentiful supply of corn cure so it will be alright in a day or two. Our uniforms are also fairly disreputable.

Saw Jack Armstrong about a week ago, he is as fat as can be, I should say he has put on about 3 stone in weight, he is a farrier in the Army Service Corp. "Lights out"—Goodnight!

MENA CAMP, NEAR CAIRO

Sunday Evening 17th Jany 1915

Just come off quarter guard which extends over 24 hours generally and comprises 4 reliefs of 2 hours each per man, and one gets very little rest even when off on account of guard rounds, visiting rounds and falling out to all officers of the rank of Major and higher, also to all armed parties and being fully clothed and equipped (ammunition and all) <u>all</u> the time: it's very tiring!

However we had a good breakfast this morning, porridge (Quaker Oats) and we sported a tin of condensed milk and 6 doughnuts from the canteen—this three of us consumed—my share 1/3rd of the milk neat into my porridge and a bit in the tea, the first time since on board ship! A good stew and plum pudding—which was "more-ish", this latter being donated by the "Daily News" Army & Navy Christmas pudding fund—I'll send you the <u>label</u>!

The 5th brass band is playing in the next mess room (C Coy's) Cardinal Newman's "Lead Kindly Light". It's a change from the bugle bands which seem to always brazen forth defiance and aggression. Yesterday we had a rough day on the desert. It was windy and the sand was stifling & blinding.

A couple of weeks ago a chum woke with a very sore eye and was going to parade sick before the doctor (?) but I persuaded him to place himself in my hands. I gave him some Egyptian Eye Salve one application did the trick, his eye being quite alright in the afternoon. I have been fortunate so far in having no occasion to use it myself. I don't want to take chances with my eye, having in mind how helpless (and useless) I was a couple of years ago and its a very rare exception for the natives here not to have some dreadful affliction in regard to their eyes. The Salve is made in Cairo—I have seen the place!

There were a lot of Territorials, on leave, out here this afternoon: it's believed they will be moving very soon. Some say tomorrow—but not to France there are 22,000 of them here, 30,000 of us (Australasians) 29,000 Indians (Sikhs & Gurkhas)—& others. We could put 100,000 men up against a possible attack on the Peninsula of Sinai (by the way I saw Mt Sinai when on board ship—the place where Moses lost his temper & broke the tablets containing the Ten Commandments—I also saw the spot on the Nile where Pharoah's daughter "found" him in the bullrushes but the bullrushes are now gone—So is Moses).

We all expect to be transferred to Ismailia before long and hope to have a bit of a practice at fezzes just by way of whetting the appetite. Of course you will have heard that the Turks under German officers, have accumulated large stores and thousands of camels for transport—they have seized—with violence—right and left everything they could get their paws on, and are supposed to be on the way here. However the "bird men" will soon let us know what they are doing—they will get a surprise packet and a mighty rough mauling when they arrive—it will not be a "flower show" but the cold meat wagon for theirs: also a few of us will be slabbed at the morgue.

The Royal Engineers have had a very pleasant month or two over there preparing the way for them. "I go to prepare the way for thee" (St John 14-2) I don't suppose you could realise what a machine gun can do—I've seen em at it and I can just about—it's just like turning a hose on and slewing it round. Sounds like a sewing machine being pedalled by a maniac. They are pets!

Just got Mothers letter of 7th Nov brought in to me and more than pleased to get it and glad to know "all's well" I have been looking for it for days now it's short, literally, but long—and contains more, to me, than quires of some letters could hope to. We, too, hope for peace which will be concluded eventually, but it's absolutely imperative that we should have what we set out to have, and what we mean to have, and that is immunity from the German menace. This war had to be: as you know, I always said I could see it looming up. If you could hear the official accounts of the atrocities

MENA CAMP, NEAR CAIRO

committed by the Germans (they are read out in orders) you would know why they must be rendered innocuous and incapable of engaging in another war. There is a Red Cross nurse with both hands cut off. A party of 400 Germans abused the use of the white flag and murdered a major and a score of our men who were going to accept their surrender, they fired on them with the white flag still on the bayonets. Within 5 minutes they were wiped out to a man—a bloody but just reprisal! They use explosive and dum-dum bullets—it's proved beyond question and it's official. We don't want and will not have such people (or any other people for that matter) master us.

The Tommies here today as on other days have their meals with us and vise versa. They cannot hold a candle to the Australians as horse men, if a horse kicks up a bit they fall off. I intended to try and get some scarabs (stone beetles with ancient characters on the bottom of them. The beetle was evidently venerated or held sacred in some way same as the hawk and the crocodile) today but couldn't get away. They can be used as a scarf pin, ring & seal, or as ear rings—I've seen some 6 or 7 thousand years old and genuine.

Just got word that that the mail bags are being closed now so must dash off with this or you will have to wait a week longer. Hope things brighten up in the Wimmera and Australia generally.

With my love to you all at home from your loving brother.

George

Will write for next mail too Geo.

DODGING THE DEVIL

Cairo<br>
20th Jany '15

Dear Mother,
Yours received two days ago & most glad to know all is well home. The view on "tother" side depicts an Arabic Cemetery—on the march one recent Sunday we halted for a rest under the big trees. I'm O.K. With love from George.

MENA CAMP, NEAR CAIRO

>3 Platoon A Coy
>8th Battn
>2nd Inf Brigade
>1st Aust Division
>Mena Camp
>Egypt
>27–2–15

Dear Mr Martindale
Your letter dated 20.1.15 arrived here today I've handed it around to all the Dim lads. They all wish me to thank you for your greetings. We have all read Captain Beans reports and think that he was wanting in tact in writing such report, especially when he admits that there are only a few wasters, but then the said gentleman seemed to delight in scandal. If I remember correctly it was the same person <u>who</u> made such a row about the cricket trouble. The troubles he reports are just as prevalent amongst the New Zealanders & Terriers[23] and according to what I hear it is the same in every force throughout Europe. Did Capt'n Bean think he was with a legion of saints or what did he expect. The majority here are disgusted with his report and there is a big meeting of South African soldiers tonight. I'll try and hear the result. There is one thing I can mention while on this subject and that no Dimboola boy has had to answer "Defaulters" Capt'n Crebbin will explain how much that means. The people of Cairo do not seem to think the Australians a disgrace, I've sent the mater papers with their remarks concerning us. Before I close I wish to congratulate Bob Budde & yourself in your finish for the Dim trophies. I coveted that trophy myself and intend to place that score against Kaiser Bill. Good luck for the present year & future.

>Yours sincerely
>Henry

DODGING THE DEVIL

Mena Camp<br>
Cairo Egypt<br>
Sunday Feby 28th 1915

Dear Mother

Your letter of the 13th Jany also one from Father I received a couple of weeks ago and have been <u>going</u> to write but didn't. It's the same old tale, no time or when I got back to camp would lie down "just for 5 minutes" & that would be the end of it: we don't have much time on our hands, when we do get an hour or two we do a bit of washing & mending & then to sleep, no sleeping draughts required here! The men just flop down, some flat out face downwards (my style) others head pillowed on their web equipment & are snoring in a few seconds; we aren't particular where we sleep, or how: some fellows flat out on their backs & the sun beating down onto their faces. But this is a mere trifle. When they are wakened (and it's surprising how quickly they are fully awake) you can see the impression of the webbing, buckles etc. on their cheeks; this too is a mere detail.

Yes, we have done a lot of tramping on the desert, it gets on the nerves month after month, the same thing day after day Sunday included & night after night, for of course we are on duty 7 days a week and 24 hours a day. We have covered many hundred miles & worn out a few thousand pounds worth of shoe leather. I'm glad to say that my feet are alright & my corns are giving me no trouble in fact they have disappeared!

You will remember Father advised me to try for the Light Horse as he was apprehensive lest my feet would not stand the strain (it is a big strain and an infantryman is only as good as his feet). We had a foot inspection yesterday, we wash our feet periodically in permanganate of potash. I have no sign of a blister & my feet are not tired. We are <u>all</u> splendidly shod and everlastingly being warned to take the greatest care of our feet. <u>Feet</u> <u>first</u> <u>face</u> <u>after</u>! This doesn't mean that we are to wash the former first and the latter last but that the greater care should be taken of the feet! I'm well equipped with corn cure and eye salve.

You will have seen the articles by Captn Bean in "The Argus" & I suppose also "The Age". He has spoken out of his turn! His foot slipped & I imagine he is in the mud, and not deep enough to get the frogs. There are those here who say that when they see him they will spread him over the landscape. I have had evening leave I suppose on an average of once a week and though no one will deny that a few hoodlums have made the pace a welter his articles convey an absolutely wrong impression. I must say I'm surprised (and agreeably so) at the forbearance and good conduct of the men in every respect. In short Capt Bean is a liar. The officers of the higher ranks are very indignant at his remarks—and make no bones over saying so.

An individual named Byers of our section wrote to "The Rechabite" paper published in Melbourne. Private Anderson's brother saw it and wrote to his brother here: he showed it to others; I was away at the moment—Byers left in a hurry for the rest of the evening for the good of his health (he lived in the same tent as myself). When I returned Anderson showed me his letter and when Mister Byers sneaked in at "Lights Out" and started to hurriedly disrobe I was rude enough to ask him to keep <u>all</u> his clothes on as being a fine night I would like him to accompany me for a little stroll. I don't think he was over anxious to come but he didn't like to refuse (he showed a certain amount of discretion here).

Now it so happens that all the dirty water from the 5th Regiment is run into a hole resembling an underground tank and covered with a cellar-door-like flap—greasy dixie water, soap suds etc. etc. the water being about 4 feet deep. He was very demure, trembling visibly as taking his arm I led him gently along, the rest of my company following. My understudy without undue tarrying removed the lid, and with the aid of a couple of assistants I projected him through the opening. He is fairly heavy and made a grand splash. Peering down into the darkness I could hear a sound like waves rippling against the side of a ship—then the swimmer—like a seal coming to an air hole in the ice—appeared. I had a factotum stationed handy with a bucket (kerosene tin) full of <u>exceeding dirty</u> water. He was a very good shot. I couldn't have done it better myself!!!

This Byers is a dirty dog—a big mouthed Jew—when he smiles it is like a dredge bucket opening out. I hope he smiled as the buckets contents connected with him, but I'm not very sanguine about it! We then went back to our lines and threw his blankets & kit bag out. He camped out and didn't appear for breakfast. I told him I would be cross if he showed his nose inside the tent in his dirty condition—which was chronic—inside. In the morning he wrote a rambling letter to the aforementioned paper: it is a work of art indeed, he admitted that he was an embroidered liar—with frills. A score of chaps gathered round him and told him what they thought of him—and what they <u>didn't</u> think of him—and his seed forever as Dorothy would say. He was after a bit of cheap notoriety—and he certainly got it.

We went on the march at 2.30 pm and bivouacked for the night. We had a great discourse on tar and feathers—it's uses—methods of application etc—also its various discomforts; various methods of plucking or scraping the mixture off, some advocating lard mutton fat, dripping, kerosene, turps etc. It was generally agreed that the tar would remove the hide of the interested party. Of course none of us addressed Mister B.—but he has brought listening to everything that concerns himself or others to a fine art. I wouldn't have been in his shoes for all the tea in China and half the rice: I think we made it plain to him that we were displeased with him!

Capt Bean writes of the various bodies of men here. The Territorials, Australians & New Zealanders etc. I can safely say

## MENA CAMP, NEAR CAIRO

that as men and soldiers the former are like the boy that fell out of the balloon, not in it. The N. Zealanders and Australians are very much alike though the Australians are smarter at drill & on parade etc. The N.Z.'s have red pipings & facings in their uniforms & hats, black boots—polished brass buttons and badges, rather more showy than ours. They are armed with the long M.L.E. rifle and short bayonet. We have the short M.L.E. rifle and the long bayonet.

Talking of bayonets, I was in Cairo the other night & met a Sikh—he asked me where was my bayonet I told him we privates were not permitted to carry one when on leave; he seemed surprised: put his hand down and patted his. I asked to see it so he unsheathed it (his scabbard was polished up with boot polish). He passed me the "knife", the <u>short</u> bayonet and <u>short</u> rifle is their weapon, evidently they like to get nice (or nasty) and close. He had it sharpened up so that it would shave and had a point like a needle and was liberally smeared with vaseline. He was mighty proud of it—I wouldn't like to be the German he comes up against, he was about 6 ft 4 high & broad & straight as a rush—a bonzer! And there are countless thousands like him.

The Gurkhas are small about 5 ft to 5'2" high and like Japs—when fighting on the canal at the end of a charge they dropped their rifles & bayonets & got out their "Kukris", a short curved knife—they're rotten things to be up against, they can lop a mans head or arm off without effort—just a twist of the wrist or they can cut a piece <u>clean</u> <u>out</u> of a mans chest. When they kill goats or sheep it's just the same—they cut its tail off behind the ears and its considered a disgrace to make two hits.

The Australian uniform is the most sombre of all, nothing showy, just the drab khaki a sad yellow, brown bone buttons, dull copper badges & no colors in relief. Nothing shiny to catch the sunlight, but this dull uniform looks much more business-like than the others. I don't think you could find a finer looking body of men anywhere in the world as fully equipped they march along, every leg and every arm swinging in perfect unison. We have a new sergeant in our platoon Sgt Marshall a son of Dr Marshall of Scots Church Collins St Melbourne.

I was on Quartermasters fatigue a couple of days ago; getting bread, meat, vegetables, corn & other stores, firewood etc., it's work but its a change and more like play. The Arabs grind the corn & barley for the horses by hand between 2 stones like small grindstones the top one having a handle near the rim & a hole about 3" in diameter in the middle & they drop the barley in in handfuls & keep revolving the top stone, it cracks or breaks the husk: After finishing I went to Mena House and had a swim—there is a marble swimming bath about 60 ft long x 25 wide & from 4 to 8 ft deep, and a row of sugar gums growing alongside—they are very homely.

I suppose you will have heard all about the fighting on the canal long before now. I am sending some souvenirs home I daresay by the time you receive this that we will have been in a scrap or two. A lot of new daily papers have started in Cairo. Well I'm blest! A chap has just touched me on the shoulder and asked me what I was doing at Mena on Wednesday, I said having a bath & he showed me a snapshot he had taken and I'm in the middle of it. I'll send one if possible tomorrow.

I bought a black baby the other day for 1/2 piastre—but wouldn't take delivery of the goods.

We had a bit of a menagerie at the cooks lines about 20 rabbits white, yellow but no grey ones, a dog that would eat lucerne & grass because the rabbits did, 2 monkeys and 2 snakes; the rabbits were killed, the snakes died, but the dog & the monkeys are like "Johnnie Walker" still going strong. We took our mascot "Doris" the bull pup on the march a couple of weeks ago but she blew out and we had to carry her, she is a fat lump but a nice pup—the Captain carried her a couple of miles on horseback.

MENA CAMP, NEAR CAIRO

Dug up a skull when digging trenches & a fellow took a snap of me holding it. Skulls will be common before the war is over. We have struck some at least of the seven plagues of Egypt. Locusts in clouds have passed over. Lice abound, everybody has em! Dust storms are pretty severe one can hardly breathe & it gets between the teeth. I have the Koran— translated—and have read part of it, it is interesting.

There is a chap with a cornet outside playing Home Sweet Home and the others are "counting him out". These songs are not allowed here. We also catch fellows pulling out girls photos and having a look at them on the sly. This is against the rules but when they make excuses (as they all do) we let em off! Poor devils! Some of our fellows looked a bit sick when we left Port Melbne when a brass instrument somewhere with ghastly playfulness struck up "The girl I left behind me".

It's getting a bit late and I want to write to Maggie & Father & Bob and others. I expect this is the last letter you will get for a few weeks perhaps as we are under orders for embarkation, one brigade having moved off today. We don't know where we are going but many think it will be to the Dardanelles and Constantinople. Others think it will be Marseilles but no one will know till we are away. I daresay we will be gone within the week. We are all set and sharpened and ready to start in with the scythe and do murder on one anothers' sinful bodies. Before long Germany will be in a turmoil—her emperor at the best of his wits, is imbecile; he will

51

find his much vaunted empire in tatters: the horns of France in one flank, the teeth of Britain in the other. Italy is a menace to him & Russia an open wound. They have called the Kaiser here "King Herod the baby killer".

I hope you are all keeping well at home and am always looking forward to news from and of you all. I know Bob would like to be here, but I don't think he would be able to stand this life. You know he used to have "growing pains" or something when he was younger and how he used to get up at nights shivering also a lump that came on his heel—also he gets sore throat somewhat often. These former things point to Rheumatism and a fellow with even a trace of this is better at home—at least as yet. A great many of those being invalided home have rheumatism and tonsilitis, these being the cause of the greatest number of invalids. A soldier has to be in good health to stand an ordinary campaign but this one will be extra ordinary. I think that I will stand it alright as I have not as yet (with the exception of once at Broadmeadows in the first fortnight after enlisting over 6 months ago) paraded sick and have not missed a single parade!! It's not many that can say that. So if there is no bullet made with my name on it I should with luck scrape through.

I notice by the "Banner" that [xxxxx is still in Dimboola[24]] it must be nice for [Miss xxx[25]] to have a lover <u>almost</u> in The Army. His mother won't let him go, so I am told. Bah! Good people are scarce. War is no doubt intensely horrible, but those it slays die <u>men</u>. "And how can man die better?"

I've dreamt of home once or twice lately—it's alright! I'm sending Peter my presentation knife—a Joseph Rodgers—from Geo Reid, also my chocolate box & some other things. Lights Out has sounded, I must get up early & try to write a few short letters. My kindest regards to all my friends in Dimboola, Mrs Deneys, Mrs Campbell Bennett etc—and to yourself all my love—Your affectionate boy George

MENA CAMP, NEAR CAIRO

Mena Camp
Cairo 28/2/15

Dear Maggie

Your letter also Bob's of the 27th Jany to hand a few days ago and needless to say I was very pleased to get them. I had an idea that there would be a hot summer—Sorry to know also that it was so dry, and all that entails: We got our share of heat & dust here with very cold nights. No wonder that Harkins youngsters have come to grief—its a wonder they have escaped so long—<u>lights out</u>! Must finish in pencil.

 Tell Peter he can use my shotgun (if you care to let him) & he can have it for his own if I'm detained here permanently—under the ground! I have had some jolly good times on the heath—I suppose it will soon be mushroom time by the time you get this. There is a good spot near a corner of a paddock about 100 yards from the river bank back of Klinge's—Dorothy & I had a good time there a couple of years ago. I'm very sorry to hear Clarence Jaehne death—poor old Jaehne has had more than his share of trouble. "Nigger" is just the stamp of horse they like for military purposes. I have had a good look round Cairo during my 3 months stay here. There are some great sights. I put in a whole afternoon (about 5 hours) at the museum. Saw Rameses II, III & IV—Thiya King & Queen etc—pitiful objects they are, these mummies—they lie there under a glass case—observed of all—defeating their own wishes when alive. There are some wonderful granite figures there, old boats 5,000 years old, old tools, jewelry & gold—it would take months to go through properly. The building itself is a very fine structure next door to the Kasr-el-Nil barracks—I was on guard over the artillery 36 guns (18 howitzers) there for 2 days and a night.

 I'm enclosing a few leaves of bougainvillea Cairo is fairly robed in it—also a sprig of Uganda verbena from Giza Gardens.

It's Monday morning & I have to get this away to the post & have very little time—my fingers are cold. I suppose you will get the most meagre news of us now for a while as we are under orders to move any minute. I hope to be able to give you news of a fight next time I write—Constantinople is whispered! Must stop now—my love to you all at home.

From your affectionate brother<br>George

Won't have time to write to Bob & Father this mail—my congratulations to them both on their wins in Rifle Shooting & hope Father has a good old time in South Australia—it should be very enjoyable. Also congratulation to Bob (&son). Suppose Peter will be next!! All Dimboola boys are well—none going for promotion as yet—later we may—most men are handing their stripes in color sergts, sergeants corporal etc—but things will alter later & promotion will be rapid—I got Bob's letter tell him.

## MENA CAMP, NEAR CAIRO

> Mena Camp
> Cairo
> Sunday 28th March 1915

Dear Dad

Your post card—bulldogs—arrived duly—we had one somewhat similar on the "Orvieto", also one letter from mother dated 23rd Feby enclosing a spray of verbena—it smells alright. Also one from Warrack 24th Feby, these arrived here about 5 or 6 days ago. I was very pleased to get them all—we would all go without a days tucker for a letter from home.

I've just come off quarter guard 24 hours & its been a frightful day a sandstorm passed over the camp—last night was muggy & a few spots of rain fell not a hundredth of a point—the wind got up blowing from the north about 9 am and turned round by the afternoon—in fact it blew every way. I was on duty outside the guard tent facing Infantry Road & had to be on the alert all the time—looking out for field officers, OC's, Brigadiers, General Officers Grand Rounds, visiting rounds etc. & my eyes were nearly cut out by the driving sand and pebbles. The ground looked like it does under a very heavy driving rain and at times I couldn't see 5 yards away & the tents were completely blotted out and scores of them blown down. About 4 pm a signalling officer brought me a pair of amber goggles they were alright.

The wind had a pretty high velocity—a Union Jack which has been flaunting on a building a couple of hundred yards away for the past 6 weeks was showing no signs of wear this morning—tonight it is indeed a "tattered rag", flapping away in a dozen strips. The sling of my rifle was flapping like a halliard (or halyard) against a flagpole & the wind repeatedly made me lose my balance. Tonight 8 pm there is not a breath of wind stirring.

We have been getting some "hurry up" during the past few weeks a lot of long marches and a lot of night work. Last week we were away from camp overnight 6 nights out of 7—skirmishing & trench digging, its tiring work—pick & shovel—one raises a sweat and then has to lie down do a perish till an hour before dawn: the pebbly ground is hard and cold & we are generally speaking, insufficiently supplied with cover and doze in gooseflesh & formless dreams the night through.

When we wake cold shivers slant up & down our back—bones 4 deep and we're simply beehives swarming with pains—then theres a rush on the enemy (imaginary) and then a rush back to camp (<u>not</u> imaginary) and the usual starvation promenade—the rations still hardly pay for the wear & tear of digestion. The porridge (Quaker oats) is not too bad & sometimes we get some red herrings—these are as salty as Lots Wifes' elbow. This morning I had 2 eggs (pigeons I think) and yesterday a chap gave me a slice of <u>bread and butter</u> butter actually—I'd almost forgotten what it looked like let alone tasted like—I think he pinched it from the Officers Mess.

The flies here are a plague & bite savagely—its necessary to smother up to keep them off and a work of art to see that they don't eat <u>all</u> our dinner—I've not seen any blowflies yet, but mosquitos are making their appearance—I find that sleep in daytime is not very refreshing & would rather have 4 hours sleep at night than 8 in the day.

We are supposed to have completed our course of training & to have had our last night's bivouacking—but we'll see! We are to have a march past Sir Ian Hamilton tomorrow. I suppose he will pronounce sentence on us, fit or otherwise—I'm satisfied we will never be more fit than we are at present—been here over 16 weeks, nearly four months now.

I fancy we will go to the front in a place other than France & Belgium. There's a lot being said re the Dardanelles now and we'll probably go there. If the Allies put a strong army in the Balkans it will undoubtedly give Serbia renewed confidence in herself and us and it may also be the means of persuading Italy Greece Bulgaria Roumania & Coy to "inject" their forces into the brawl. The Allied fleets are already banging at the door and from all accounts (which are very meagre here) are putting large quantities of the Unspeakable out of circulation. By the way what a smack in the eye for Germany our having the "Queen Elizabeth" (8—15" guns) over this way, saying in effect that we can manage the German Navy without the help of the most powerful ship in the world.

Monday Evening

I went to sleep over this letter last night, so now continue. This morning we were reviewed by & marched past Sir Ian Hamilton—early it was a fine morning but at 8.30 when we marched out to the assembly ground the sand was driving unpleasantly. We took up our allotted positions 1st & 2nd infantry brigades—about 8,000 men. The General arrived about 10 o'clock—'twas a great sight to see him gallop up accompanied by the staff—a mounted man (a private soldier) being with them & carrying a lance with 2 small red streamers attached. A blast on a bugle & the 2 brigades "presented arms" & the band played the General Salute—there were scores of niggers up on the cliff overlooking the parade ground watching the proceedings—I don't suppose they have seen a sight like today's before.

Sir Ian (he wore 3 rows of ribbons on his breast—and clothes too of course) then inspected us—then we marched past—or to be precise 7 regiments did—the 5th scrambled past & we all feel savage and disappointed over it as it was not our fault. The other regiments brass bands played them past whilst a nondescript push of pipers inflicted their—er—dashed music (?) on us. The saluting base was on Infantry Road and we marched 8 abreast.[26] 4 men marching in column of route <u>on the hard metal road</u>, and 4 men ditto on (or through) the heavy sand—the men on the road were marching at a nice sharp quick march so those (I was amongst them) on the sand had to get a move on to keep up—heads and bodies forward and down. I never heard such a din as the person with the big drum made—hopelessly out of time—a tin Kettling is music compared with it. I believe we, the 5th, are mentioned in orders as having made a poor march past and my company—D—the last, as being particularly bad—the worst of the 32 companies that passed by!

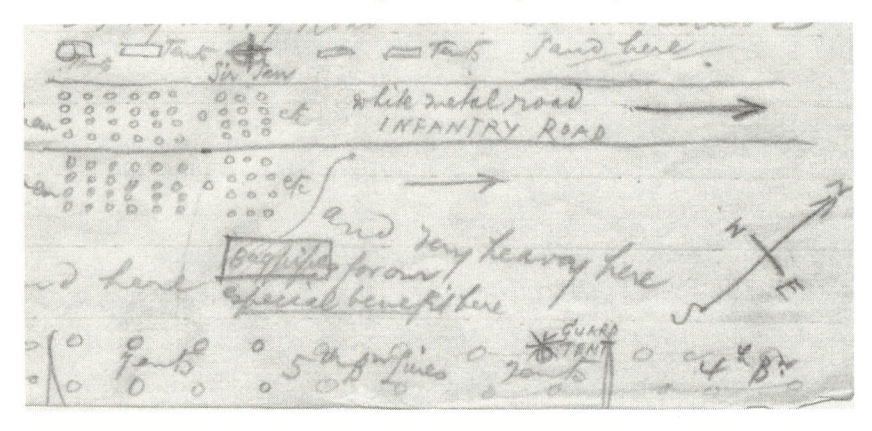

The 5th Transport (horse vehicles) was on the contrary particularly good, it's a mercy horses don't have to keep in step. The whole regiment "counted out" the pipers on returning to our lines and immediately got up a petition which was signed by 95% of the men by 2 o'clock pm asking the O.C. to abolish the use of bag pipes (not smoking pipes) on the march. We couldn't hear the beastly things till we were within about 40 yards of them and then there was no step to pick up. He will be a daring man—and a fool—who has the temerity to blow the pipes within our hearing for some considerable time to come. Some of our chaps have dug a grave in readiness to bury the first bagpipes seen or heard in our lines, and the piper will be thrown into the dirty water in the pioneers well.

We feel doubly wild because we believe and <u>know</u>, that the 5th can march better than any other regiment in the division, and we consider that our Company is the best in the regiment. (we also have the best brass band)[27] The 8th Battn think they are "the ones"—

but they "aint"! They're best—after us—You'll see we know how to swank here. The 8th are a good lot of fellows—from the country districts almost exclusively, I fancy I could get a transfer thence if I wished, but much as I'd like to get with the fellows from home and thereabouts, I wouldn't like to leave the 5th. We have been a lucky regiment, so far, in having had only one death amongst us during these 7 1/2 months we have been in being.

<u>Tuesday Morning</u>—The nigger lamp tender put the lamp out abruptly last night so I had to stop—but I have a whole holiday today. I intend to go down to the Light Horse Lines to see Domeyer, Rupert Moon, Williams C. E., Wilfred Robinson this afternoon— I've seen both Clem & Alan Cordner. Alan is a military policeman in the 6th Bn—so I see him frequently—I saw Colin Cromb the other day but was going on guard to the Quarantine Hospital, so didn't have an opportunity of speaking to him—he is I believe in the Army Medical Corps.

There were several cases of scarlet fever, any amount of measles cases, and a fairish lot of small pox—this latter however is now well in hand all being right again now. It was funny to see the M.P.s (<u>milty police</u>) rounding up the niggers in camp & fetching them up to be vaccinated—they yabbered a bit but to no purpose—they had to be "done". So far I have heard of no cases of typhoid or cholera amongst any of the first contingent though I believe there are some cases of the former among the later arrivals. All of the first lot were inoculated against typhoid & cholera on board ship in addition to vaccination against small pox. I consider this speaks volumes for the wisdom, yes, <u>necessity</u>—of these precautionary measures—The flies which are daily becoming worse amounting now to almost a plague crawl over and into <u>everything</u> regardless of what or where it is and in the ordinary course of events half of us should be down with fever. The doctors consider that a person who has already had typhoid doesn't run much risk of a second attack—Other cases of a different nature are enclosed within barbed wire entanglements and are in strict quarantine—yellow flags being fixed on the fence—Not a pleasant place to be on guard.

Roy Sandow who was baking for "Old Jim Baker" and Hopkins is in the 5th—I was speaking to him last week. I also met a chap who used to drive a cab for Bye. Len Morrow who was a clerk in the Railway booking office at Dimboola is attached to our company as signaller—he is a very smart chap and has had a good experience in the Morse Code. There are also 2 chaps who worked for the same firm at Hampton as I did, they are very decent fellows—one a L/Corporal & one a M.P. both of the 5th. I also saw a chap who worked for some farmer near home, I can't remember who & I can't remember his name though I often saw him—I've been puzzling over it for a week. Its remarkable how one runs across fellows he hasn't seen for years perhaps.

I'm told that young Wallsgott (don't know which of the tribe) on being asked why he did not enlist said "he paid other fools to do his fighting"! May God make us all, in time of our country's need, fools, such fools as we! We have also got wind of another individual who spoke out of his turn, to wit, Fred Gersch. I imagine that when we get back he'll stand a good chance of getting a bit <u>bent</u>. Henry D'Alton says he'll look as though he had been in a railway accident if he catches him.

By the way I'm enclosing a cutting of one of Lord Londonderry's jokes—you might show it to Mr D'Alton, it will amuse him, I think it very good. I suppose it's one of the penalties of greatness to have dirty tykes of this type in our midst but I don't think you at home will let them yap too loudly unless it's when they're scratching gravel with their tails between their legs as it were. They're hardly worth bothering about, however, they will never do anything very good and aren't game to do anything very bad.

I've received all the "Banners" Bob has sent me I think & have read them with great interest (& passed them on to Henry)

## MENA CAMP, NEAR CAIRO

especially the Shire Severance news. Shire politics home now seem to be a <u>vocation</u>—usually, I think, they are a <u>vacation</u>. Hoffmann may be big hearted in little things—in big things he is small.

<u>Tuesday afternoon</u>—I expect to get a "Banner" next mail giving an account of your trip to Keith SA & to the Little Desert—I should think you would have an enjoyable time. D— the flies. I've never known them so numerous and persistent before. Another night march tonight—evidently the Brigadier thinks that the edge of duty is apt to become blunt without daily observance to keep it keen. We should be able to march the Kaiser off the face of the earth after our training—our usual gait even on the sand is that of a man going for the doctor or as though he were 20 minutes late for a flower show or garden party. D— the flies, I'm fumigating the air with smoke but it doesn't deter them. You said in one of your letters that you were loading Gus Petschel's wagon after tea. I'm surprised at you trading with the enemy!!

Pay day tomorrow when I'll be forced to take pit 68 1/2—14/- today a 100 piastre note seems about the dimensions of a tablecloth and a 20 pit piece about the size of a windmill or a merry-go-round—we are all "mafish valoush" today—don't think there are 5% with any saved up currency. Pit 5 seems a fabulous fortune—last pay I saved 18 piastre—3/8 ['50' written above]—but on Saturday I made a miscue and flashed the boodle on the tent circle—I was mighty soon pried away from my cart-wheel & the bold bad dagoes soon had it in cold storage & now I'm solvent to the extent of P.t. nil—Next time I'm going to see how much of my stipend I can segregate and isolate and set apart for later use.

I've just been told that cholera has broken out in a native village about a mile from our camp & that there are 40 cases so far. Its strange that I should have just mentioned that it had not made an appearance—so now the sooner we get to the front to fall on the Teutons or Turks the better. When anything crops up here it generally goes the whole hog and is a plague, there is a Locust plague on at present—great yellow (canary colored) four winged insects 3" long, nearly as big as sparrows in huge clouds—countless millions of 'em they actually cast a shade over the ground—this is literally true. They perch on the telephone wires till they look like ropes an inch in diameter swung from pole to pole.

So we will be glad to get to where the battles are no longer sham and the cartridges no more blank and where <u>we can tune our souls to the raw facts of war</u>. It takes a <u>chap a while to re-adjust his mind</u> to an altered universe which has suddenly changed from <u>tameness to menace</u>. War has its virtues too: it has gifts for those who become warriors—it makes of them <u>men</u> who can order themselves, who can force themselves <u>uncomplainingly</u> to do what they must do. The tasks are <u>generally arduous</u>—<u>always responsible</u> and <u>often dangerous</u>. The real soldierly spirit expresses itself in supreme patriotism—the ideal with which it <u>inspires a man</u> is that of willing self sacrifice for the welfare of the state and for the good of his fellow citizens: to this ideal should the occasion arise the <u>soldier must be faithful unto death</u>. It will also give him the tenacity of purpose which will enable him to overcome great difficulties, to persevere in the face of disaster, and at all costs to be faithful to himself and to his cause to the end. <u>If he be not of</u> that metal, <u>then it breaks him and casts him aside</u>.

Some people affect to think that Germany will be beaten to her knees & eating out of the hand within a few months <u>but I harbor no such optimistic views</u>. The riflemen here have done some very good shooting. This proves of what value is the training they received whilst members of Rifle Clubs—not just a superficial knowledge which enables them to scrape through the musketry course here, but which enables them to hit the mark "every time". A pal of mine in the same section and a member of the Prahran Rifle Club put <u>all</u> his shots in the black. It couldn't be beaten, if equalled, in the Brigade!

## MENA CAMP, NEAR CAIRO

I shot well & lacerated the bullseye pretty severely I consider this <u>one</u> of many good reasons why every <u>man</u> should enrol himself in a rifle club and so become efficient. A soldiers best friend here is his rifle and he should have so much control over it as to become almost part of himself. A first class marksman cannot (with few exceptions) be produced in a few weeks, certainly not in the very limited course of musketry which we receive here. Ammunition is of more value now than in time of peace.

Most of the men from the country districts of Victoria know a bit about a horse: which side to get on and all that. Sorry I can't say the same of a few of our officers—some of them dismount either side—the deciding factor being the horse. One thing about them they're expeditious and don't waste time unduly in getting down to good old Mother Earth. At such times it's not a good policy to smile. Yes! I think the time is not far distant when a military system such as obtains in Australia will be made universal in the Empire. We are British subjects, and today we are face to face with the consequences which are involved in that proud fact. We have long enjoyed the benefits—today it's our duty and our privilege to accept the responsibility & the sacrifice. Nowadays a man should be a patriot first—anything else afterwards. The work in hand—not the workman—is the matter of supreme importance. To quote poetry "We know whereon our hopes depend, we serve the hour, and wait the end!" I think after this war that the nations will be rather chary of treading on The Lions tail. I often sing about him and the more I do so the more I think how peculiarly appropriate the words are—"His foes at best are knaves confessed whose malice from envy springs". In my minds eye I can see the "Blucher" going down. "And great & small, <u>down down</u> they fall 'neath the storm of his iron hail" & curiously enough it was H.M.S. Lion that was passing them the goods! The "Swiftsure" was in the canal as we came through also some French Cruisers. She gave the impression of having great power, looked as though she could eat the lot. She is now at the Dardanelles—perhaps at the bottom—perhaps through them by now. Who knows?

    I think I had better stop now or my fund of gossip will run out and I want to write to Mother & the girls Bob & Peter. I wonder if the few curios I sent home arrived safely? They weren't much but were at least genuine & thats something coming from Cairo where most things are fraud. I sent Peter a knife. I also posted Maggie 19 snapshots last mail. All the Dimboola & District boys are well. Warrack said in his letter that you were all OK and I trust this still continues & that things are on the improve generally. Dispense my kindest to those who would like them also my love to you all at home from your affectionate son.

George

<u>I got Peter's letter</u>

5th Battalion pack horses
with picks & shovels
Pyramid of Mycerinos in
the background. Note
the small pyramid (one of
several surrounding the three big
ones) The king's daughters are
or were — buried here

Note my will in my pay book—"Mother All" / George

Got the two Banners re Dimboola Downs, I've had some good times there

British Soldiers' Café<br>
Cairo, Egypt[28]<br>
April 16th 1915

Dear Mother

I got yours, Bob's & Maggies letters of the 10th March & one from Dorothy on each 3rd & 10th March. The little Cecil Brummer—my birthday present—was intact and the perfume was quite pronounced. I am very pleased with it—also Maggies narcissus & the leaf Bougainvillia I think—from Dorothy. A letter from home—and a rose—a bit of a day dream—and thoughts & associations of the past clutch my heart like the voice of a loved woman—at such times I'm happily miserable—a strange mixture.

I very often look back over the past. I've been wrong in many things & was slow in another: however I was at least not slow in getting where I am now—a man's place at last & for the present I'm content. Things might easily have been different but—! they weren't. In the future—if such is permitted me—'twill not be too late to begin rebuilding. I had my jam first & then the pill was left—I had that too. But we can sit by old tombs in the dark too long. I'm ready for anything that crops up now and fully intend to "make the pace a welter" as the saying is, when we get with the enemy.

I'm glad to know that Peter is doing so well with the rifle—he's only fulfilling my expectation that he would uphold the tradition of the family in this particular. Why he'll be a better shot than I was if he sticks at it, as I'm sure he will & will be giving Bob & father points. I have partly written a letter to Walter Gamble but was told that no letters could be sent—however I will try to get one off to him. I wrote a short note to old Suhr & wonder if he got it alright?

Give my kindest regards to Mrs A. C. Bennett—she's a grand little woman and to Mrs Deneys—she's a good old soul—she won't mind me calling her that I'm sure—and when you or the girls are writing to Brewers please convey to them my reciprocation of their good wishes for my welfare. But hold a moment! didn't Bertha send her <u>love</u> underlined—to me—oh! yes. By all means <u>return</u> it. I 'aint in the matrimonial market & my resolutions re celibacy are rather confirmed at present—in fact have been for some time.

So Bert Wilson has made the plunge—he was balancing on the brink last August when I enlisted. He should make a good soldier. I'm sure Sam will. In my minds eye I can see Sam & Henry calmly marking and picking off their man—they will not miss many at anything like a decent distance say 600 or 800 yards. Now is the time that the great value of Rifle Club training will be demonstrated. Johnson isn't here—apparently he's too busy scraping up a few paltry shillings or pounds on various ranges. He evidently considers that good people are scarce & that discretion is the better part of valor. & we never know the day that will be our last as sound men—it will soon be that each step may be the last one we will take as unbroken men.

I can assure you that some glories are about to be added to the history of Australia & N.Z. we will soon start now to hit meat. I've only had a note from Mrs Browne but I send Val a post card or two. Is he still as much addicted to ladies as ever I wonder? I must stop now—I could write on for days—describing my impressions and the events that have happened—but <u>censor</u>. I'll have some good yarns to tell if I get back home. This is doubtless the last you'll get from me for some time—<u>but you will see the papers</u>—However, as I said before I'm quite ready for anything—everything. My kindest to all my friends in Dimboola and elsewhere when you see or write them & trusting all is well with you all at home—My love to you all from your loving boy George

Poppies enclosed—red & black our regimental colors for <u>good luck</u>

The first boats laden with Australian soldiers landing on the Gallipoli Peninsula at 8 am.
(AWM J03022)

PART THREE:

# THE GALLIPOLI PENINSULA, TURKEY

'*As a matter of fact a great many never fired a shot*', July 1915

'*It's a most bloody engagement.*' 10 August 1915

The 5th Battalion landed on Gallipoli on 25 April 1915. George's company was part of the second wave to go ashore at what came to be called Anzac Cove. Quite noticeably, the volume of his correspondence diminished. When he had time to write home about it, George recorded the action of that and subsequent days for his family. This included the initial landing and advances from the beach at Anzac Cove, being redirected in support of the main Allied landings on nearby Cape Helles, and fighting the lengthy battle in August that unsuccessfully tried to break a strategic stalemate—Lone Pine. The surviving correspondence makes minimal explicit mention of his rising in the ranks. George was appointed Lance Corporal on 9 May during the Cape Helles action, and promoted to Corporal on 18 August following the battle for Lone Pine. Like others similarly thrust into positions of command, George was filling positions depleted by high casualties, and pointing to his own battle experience. On 30 September he 'Reverts to Ranks at own request', as his service record put it, for reasons that remain unclear.

George's descriptions of his time on the Gallipoli Peninsula, and in particular the various battles and actions, were all framed in part by his retrospective. Similarly affecting his account, George was not just describing what happened, but also responding to queries in letters he had received from friends and family, but which do not seem to have survived. By his own account he kept a diary, which helped inform the details within his letters, but his attitudes and comments reflected more than the happenings in the trenches. As time wound on, and the campaign stalled, George's attitudes became more ambiguous. In subsequent months, as he reflected on the experiences and meanings of Gallipoli, his feelings were often mixed. Writing for his family, in the midst of a great conflict, George was conscious that he should try and live up to the expectations and aspirations of his family, town and nation.

It is probable that George sent more short letters than survive of a sort similar to that to his mother on 13 May. He asserted he would write to his father the following day, for instance, even though no such letter survives. This and two other letters from Gallipoli, one each to his mother and father, was the sort of thing that George clearly wrote with some regularity, keeping his family abreast of his health, and giving brief news of the Dimboola boys or other acquaintances. One to his mother dated 6 August was written in the moments before George's company was due to go into action. This chronological fact, as much as anything he actually said, highlights his immanence to the war. The following letter of 10 August places George writing to his father even while the battle was still being fought.

But George's missive dated 26 July 1915 has a different tenor and purpose. Here, in a letter written in at least two parts, because it was completed on or after 25 August 1915, George provided a longer narrative account of the Gallipoli campaign. That he intended to write it in parts is indicated by his enumeration of this letter, thus writing a sort of serialised account of the conflict for his father, perhaps also on behalf of the Dimboola boys. It is fascinating not only for its focus on his own actions, and his comrade's exploits and ends, but for engaging with a wider narrative of the war developing at home in Australia. With weekly letters from home, some local and metropolitan newspapers to read, and the soldiers' companion 'rumour', the men at the front were not entirely unaware of the way their exploits were being recorded back home, albeit with some delay. And, perhaps surprisingly to modern readers, George's letters carry a note of concern in this regard. Painfully aware that his battalion was seriously depleted, and that the campaign was not an unmitigated success, George tried to uphold the standards of soldiery he expected of himself, and saw in many of his comrades. He had lived the battles, and took pride in reflecting the traditions of the 'fighting fifth'. Yet, he was acutely aware that Gallipoli had taken on great national significance and that some stories of heroic conduct were mythologised for effect. It enraged George that false and hypocritical stories of ardour and talent proliferated, because this phenomenon diminished the credit due to those who fought and died, and were fighting and dying still.

Regards to Mr & Mrs Deneys & other friends

13th May 1915

Dear Mother,
Just a word to say I'm still in the land of the living—at present watching "Jack Johnsons" tearing up the earth about 600 yards away. It's a glorious uncertainty—one never knows where the next will hit. Been in all the brawls so far—so have had <u>some</u> experiences. Mr Bean (war correspondent) took a snapshot of me standing near a "fragment" (?) of 15" shell—it only weighed about a couple of hundred weight lbs—it may be republished in say "The Australasian" or the "Weekly Times"—there was 3 of us there. You'll know me—in the centre—laden like a pack mule of infantryman—an awful wreck I look. You will of course have cabled news of us. I lost my belongings yesterday spare clothing shaving tackle etc—a good thing in a way—less to carry—started to grow a beard but it got too prickly, so got it off. I'm writing this under difficulties—got a "gammy" hand—dropped a box (1000 rounds) of ammunition off my shoulder—fell in a creek—it dropped on the back of my hand & has strained the tendons I think—did it 4 nights ago—very sore—keeps me awake—but will be alright in a week or so I hope—otherwise I'm O.K. Sam Wilson is alright & camped nearby. Looking forward to a mail from home—wonder if those curios reached you safely—have just been down for a wash in the sea—it was alright & very acceptable—I trust that all is well at home & will write to Father tomorrow if possible.
    My love to you all at home from your loving boy

George

THE GALLIPOLI PENINSULA, TURKEY

Anzac Cove<br>
Turkey in Europe<br>
<u>6th August '15</u>

Dear Mother,
Just a few words on the off chance I get an opportunity of posting this & that you get it. It's afternoon—a hot clear day—and we're just crouched ready for a swift spring on "Abdul"—been here nearly 16 weeks a perpetual grind—and are now going to take it out of his hide—or try to! I'm back again to almost the same spot I dug into on Sunday night the 25th April. Everything is prepared, a new firing line all ready to be opened up, only a crust of earth remaining over same—we all have broad white bands on either arm & a big white patch on the back for identifying one another as there's sure to be a mix up with the bayonet—The artillery has the range to a yard—literally. Observers and telephone operators ready with receivers strapped to ears—wires, scores of miles of them running in every direction—back to batteries etc. Got a pint of water each worth its weight in £5 notes—hope they will not take it away from us for the water jackets of machine guns this time. A lot of torpedo craft cruising around in the Gulf of Saros—expect soon to see a few battleships standing in over here—oh yes! there's something doing! Just saw Domeyer and some Stawell chaps. Domeyer is well but thin and tired like the rest of us, but we're better than the Turks & Teutons even if we were twice as bad—and then we would be dead.[29] I'm about the last of our push remaining "in the ring"—it will take a shell or bullet to put me out too. I think I'm the only one from D'la who has been here all the time without any holiday or rest and who has not gone sick!!! Don't suppose I will be able to post this—in fact I'm sure—so will put it in my pay book in case of accident—as Arthur Ladner says—here a fellow doesn't know what minute will be his <u>last</u>! Haven't heard from home for

about 3 weeks—hoped I'd get one before today however—Dum spiro spero!![30] Hope you will not let Peter come here till he's at least 19 years old! He's too young yet—and Bob couldn't stand it—they should boot along Arthur McRae and some other kindred carcases who are so consistently posing as ideal young <u>men</u> (?) and bidding for cheap notoriety at home.

Your loving boy George

I don't mind fighting for women young old or incapable people but it riles me doing it for shirkers.[31]

The busy beachfront crowded with troops, tents, stores and equipment. (AWM H03500)

## THE GALLIPOLI PENINSULA, TURKEY

<u>Dimboola Fallen</u>
Mother Country, land and sea
Yield strong sons who die for thee
Grant that through the years that we
Worthy of thy fallen be

Tues 10th Aug 1915

Dear Dad
Yours of 30th June also Maggies to hand this evening, enclosing recruiting pamphlet—I don't go nap on people who are <u>forced</u> to <u>volunteer</u>(?) by public opinion, agitation—If their offers are not spontaneous and actuated by patriotic sentiment they can never be "volunteers" in the true sense of the word—they are forced men as surely as those recruited under conscription, public opinion the all powerful forces them. I learned today that Eddie D'Alton is killed in action—by our own howitzer—a faulty fuse perhaps—it occurred a couple of days ago—things have been moving since Friday a big prolonged battle—Who's next? Who knows? Australia must send more men—We <u>must</u> emerge from this conflict victorious—otherwise—if every efficient man does not come—he will have died in vain—<u>this cannot be</u>! As I write I can hardly breathe on a/c of the stench of dead men—they are lying about in hundreds—we have taken 3 lines of Turkish trenches, ammunition, machine guns, hundreds of prisoners etc and will hold them, they have made most desperate efforts to bomb us out, but we will not yield—The Turks are lying 3 and 4 deep in trenches. Saw Domeyer today he's well. Sam and I are about the last now. Fighting enemy only 10 feet apart and less. They don't like the bayonet, but are very game. It's a most bloody engagement.
    Regards to my cronies & others—George

Dugouts constructed on the slopes where they were a difficult target for the Turkish artillery.
(AWM G00942)

THE GALLIPOLI PENINSULA, TURKEY

Anzac Cove
Turkey in Europe
Monday 26th July 15

No. I

Dear Dad,

I've received a couple of letters from you since landing here. One from you signing yourself "satisfied & affectionate". Thanks. I also got mothers weekly letter: it's something to look forward to. We don't get much news of the outside world here. "Banners" also from Bob arriving regularly and are much appreciated—I pass them on to Sam or to Eddie D'Alton.[32] A good many Dimboola boys are either killed or hors de combat now, but as long as there's one of us left we will endeavour to keep our end up for the honour & glory of the old town—the Dimboola contingent are a fine lot of fellows & good soldiers all—Egotistical but nevertheless a fact! We were always proud of being citizens of Dimboola, and we will not disgrace it at this time. Henry D'Alton died as he lived, a brave man and a gentleman. I know that he would wish—if the Almighty decreed it—such a death, not an end—for his memory will live as long as we—longer than some of us most likely. I was entrenching about 10 o'clock on Sunday night 25th Apl when I heard some chaps moving up behind me— they were speaking to one another, I paused & listened & said to myself—that's Henry D'Altons voice. I enquired & this proved to be the case.

In the morning I found that most of the chaps near me were of the 8th Bn. Eddie & Henry, Sam, Clements, Hutchinson, Hermann, Jim Bond, Baldock from Jeparit, Tony Fisher etc. had all dug in within 100 yards of me. We had some sniping 700 to 900 & 1400 yards on Monday morning. Henry was hit about 10 am—I didn't know for some hours afterwards. Jim Bond was killed in a trench about 40 yards in front of one of our 18 pd field guns on Tuesday. They say not but I'm certain it was our gun that killed him. I found the spade he was using when he was killed—it was smashed to matchwood and had the marks of leaden shrapnel bullets all over it—he was riddled. You will remember he was firing on the Adelaide to Melbourne express the night Young Watkins was run down on a tricycle & killed—Bunting was with him that night (he Bunting[33] was in the 7th & is wounded) and jumped off in time to save himself—Len Morrow bought a wreath & dome case—he is also here signaller in the 5th H.qrs and is so far alright. Young Lauchs is in the next dugout to me & made himself known to me tonight—Do you remember old Lauchs & the water pipes—"You are the one"! He made kind enquiries re old Gebert er hem! Arthur Anderson is wounded—not seriously—in the head—Jim A is in Manchester Eng.—I saw him on afternoon of 25th Apl he looked very bad—had influenza badly & was invalided.[34]

Now to write coherently its necessary that I should start at the beginning, say Mena on 1st April last. I'll endeavour to give this necessarily short a/c in sequence as far as possible though one soon becomes hazy as to day and date and I'll no doubt be distracted perhaps for a day or two as I go on—so will proceed as exigencies permit.

On the 1st Apl Thursday my birthday we had a divisional "scheme" on the tapis and had a hard day of it chasing the horizon—2nd Good Friday a fairly easy day—Saturday morning 3rd on the parade ground the colonel addressed us briefly—"Men—Your period of training is finished—Your period of fighting is about to begin—we leave tomorrow!["] Hurrah! Hurrah! Hurrah!! Our feeling of jubilation could not be repressed. Then was seen a mighty burning—we took only absolute necessities—everything else was given to the flames—I went down & saw C.E. Williams of the Light Horse & asked him to post home "The Life of Napoleon" I noticed it arrived alright. Cameras, walking sticks, letters, photos, a million and one things were destroyed and when we eventually marched out on Sunday evening—no bands playing the instruments being packed away & stretchers taking their places. We left the desert as clear and clean as on the day we arrived there 4 months previously. Mr Murray, our platoon lieutenant, who was on the sick list and unable to accompany us, got out of Mena House Hospital somehow & met us on the road as we marched past. We gave him a good cheer and rumour has it that he shed tears of chagrin at being unable to march in his place at our head. We had great faith in him! I think he could justly feel proud of the men of his platoon—as indeed he could of the whole of the First Australian Division—as they marched away—He was with us at Broadmeadows from the first—and what a transformation—from a rabble to admittedly the finest body of soldiers in the world! and in 8 months. They were certainly a most business like looking body—with the short stubby rifle at the slope—the one khaki colored uniform & equipment—even to the mens faces & arms—"With never a speck of crimson perhaps it would make us vain"—as the sparrow said.

 Arrived in Cairo & into the Central Railway yard—and reclined for a couple of hours in about 3 inches of impalpably fine dust. So fine that when I put my boot on its surface I could not feel it; it offered no resistance but just rose like smoke. At daylight we were nearing Alexandria & were a pretty spectacle. Just the whites of our eyes being other than dust color, except when one would grin and then his mouth would look like a ____ bucket opening out. We detrained early on Monday morning at the docks & some of us had a wash—going down some steps to the sea. Others attended to the inner man. Had a look (my first) at a 6" Howitzer, squat little big fellows whose bite is much—oh very much, worse than their bark—they only use a small propellant charge but when the missile 'bursts' there's something doing. We used the Leyland liner "Novian" as transport to Lemnos Island & Gallipoli Pen'sla—4096 tons—about 1700 men & 330 horses and transport—we were aboard her for 20 days <u>and</u> nights we did <u>not</u> have a cabin each as you can readily imagine. Anyhow there was no room for drill—a mercy.

On the way to Lemnos it was a bit rough and most aboard were sick—I rather enjoyed it, the trip I mean. The deck upper was iron and I slept above all except 2 nights. A greatcoat (anything but waterproof) a blanket and a waterproof sheet 6 x 3—The nights were cold, bitterly so some nights, and it rained frequently but these are mere details—I can sleep on an iron deck with rivets & seams sticking into my back, or on a coil of rope, with a soaking wet blanket round me & the boat rolling & pitching, with the greatest comfort. You only need to be dog tired, the rest is easy! I never slept sounder in a feather bed. A fellow will have to sleep on the floor when he gets home for a start. We rowed ashore once (2 boatloads) to bury a horse and had a run round for an hour or so to stretch our legs—gathered some flowers and had a race back to the ship. The exciting part being getting a start from the land—there is no beach, there were about 30 in each boat & the other one got off first after half our number had got out & were up to their necks in water pushing her off—I gave them a great deal of encouragement—from the boat. I was on one of the oars, 2 per oar, great sport dragging them over the side when we were afloat like half drowned rats. The other boat had about a quarter mile start, and one sport in the stern waving adieu but he made a miscue & fell overboard—we gained a couple of hundred over that lot and after a good go got back first—you would have thought the race was for a sheep station.

The harbour was full of transports of all sorts, store ships repair ships and warships. You will know the composition of the latter lot—from the little swift torpedo craft to the mighty "Queen Elizabeth"—the latter lies low in the water & is very broad—would just about fit in Lloyd St. If she were there she could demolish

Horsham, Nhill, W'Beal & Jeparit without moving. French battleships with their bulge on the water line & the Russian 5 funnelled "Askold"—By the way I saw the last of the "Triumph"—torpedoed off Gaba Tepe on Tues 25th May about noon—watched her turn over after about 10 min and then sink. She had stuck to us well throughout and was always ready with her 10" & 7.5" guns. "Sadly missed" Now and then a battleship comes up with a dash with a score and more destroyers as a screen around her. Up goes the balloon & aeroplanes and then the thunder starts, tongues of flame & orange colored clouds of smoke belch from her 12" guns and as we watch a kind of thunder cloud appears <u>slowly slowly</u> rising where her target is—this is lyddite tearing up the plot. Sometimes Maidos gets it, sometimes Chanak. The former must be burnt out by now as it has been heavily on fire, a great plume of smoke floating along the straits as far as one can see. I'm getting ahead of myself.

On Saturday afternoon 24th Apl we were told that we were to force a landing on the morrows morn and each received 200 rounds of ball ammu'n & 2 days iron rations, so called from the biscuits which were like iron & many a score of teeth did they break. A water bottle full of water 11/2 pints. We had no sleep that night (Satdy). Here's where the newspapers take up the tale, and where the chaps who were wounded the first day start writing. I've seen a lot of their effusions in the various papers & mostly they would make you sick—Some are written by "Beach Combers" who never attempted to leave the shelter of the cliffs near the water's edge. They tell with gusto of how they charged the Turks with fixed bayonets and of the numbers they slew. As a matter of fact a great many never fired a shot. They tell of how they scrambled out of the boats waist deep—so we did—but there were no barbed wire entanglements and no pits with sharp spikes in them. We made a place for Australian soldiers among the top notches of the worlds fighters & the very big majority of our chaps were splendid but unhappily there were some who had severe attacks of cold feet. These jellied spine creatures should be taken well out to sea and jettisoned, they're not fit to exist. We all feel the most profound disgust and contempt for them. These, generally speaking, are the ones who rushed into print, and were photographed and foisted on the world as "Australia's Heroes"—It's abominable—I would rather be killed a dozen times than resort to their crawling tactics to keep out of the firing line, the way they schemed is almost unthinkable. They will crawl home & brazen it out and take their pay, but those of us who get home will have something to say to them and about them. Nearly always they were fine big (physically) healthy fellows with an overweening regard for their filthy hides. Oh I'll leave this subject it makes me sick at the stomach!

When we landed and a couple of shrapnel shells burst over us with one accord we got our heads well down to the ground, I don't think many prayed though. If they were all like me they were in a variegated funk. Things weren't too bad till about 10 or 11 am and then the brawl got going properly. A lot has been said and published about the 3rd Infantry brigade (Q., S.A., W.A., Tasmania) landing under heavy fire, this is not a fact—a section mate of mine has a brother in the 9th Bn who was in one of the first 3 boatloads. He says only one shot (the first) was fired before they landed, when they were only 200 or 300 yards from the beach—evidently by a sentry. I don't consider there were 500 Turks within rifle range till about 10 am, but towards evening we were certainly very much outnumbered. As a pal of mine wrote in his diary they had us beaten by evening had they only known it. We bogged in all day, up to our knees in mud in the small valleys, our arms &[35] hands torn by prickly shrubs, which also tore our puttees off. Of course we had no meal times, and as we had been enjoined to be very careful of our water I didn't touch mine all day, though it was very hot, and towards evening it was taken from us to fill the water jackets of machine guns, the water from same having gone as steam. Hard times—water <u>was</u> water then—but we poured it out with good grace, willingly, but with plenty of "roaring"—a soldier's only privilege, which the unwritten law says must be exercised on <u>all</u> occasions.

We got well inland but the line was too long and reluctantly we had to fall back bringing our wounded with us. The "Fighting Fifth" were I think furthest in and we suffered severely—It's an awful job getting the wounded back, first getting his rifle bolt so as to render the rifle useless and one cannot be too tender, we were afraid, after hearing blood curdling tales of Turkish atrocities on wounded men, to leave them behind poor fellows with smashed bodies & legs were dragged along like a sack of rubbish leaving trails of blood behind. They would groan but <u>never</u> complain. I had cut away a chaps sleeve & was just about to bandage it to stop bleeding when bang! came a 15 pdr over our heads 5 feet away—I didn't fix him. I didn't try to overtake him—oh! he did scratch gravel down hill. It was almost ludicrous I suppose he got in alright the velocity of a bullet is only 2300 ft per second. I've read of battlefields running red with blood and thought it was farfetched, but now having seen what I have I'd believe anything. In places the blood was so much spilt that we would slip back in it, and it was spattered over the bushes in all directions. There were some altogether shocking sights, 3 of my 9 lieutenants were killed that day. And so we slowly fell back to the main ridge and dug in. Here I must record our admiration for and appreciation of the stretcher bearers—they were superb—with a few rare exceptions of those whose hearts failed them. Many & many a V.C. was earned, and well earned that day, though not awarded.[36] <u>But</u> <u>we</u> <u>know</u>, and are proud of the race that breeds such men—proud to be members of it! All that day I didn't hear a single complaint—it was always, always, "Go on! Go on! Never mind me!" One officer wounded in several places was staggering back crying not for himself but "Oh! My poor men, my poor boys"

Yes! they had us beaten <u>nearly</u>. I felt very anxious about 4 or 5 pm as we retired fighting a rearguard action. I was afraid lest some should start to run and the others might join in.

 I slipped back with my old Captain (Walstab) and 8 men & we dug a bit of cover & fired about 100 rounds each till things got very hot and they put a couple of machine guns on us. They are wicked almost splitting ones ears as they emit their hideous crackle—They are almost human—They "traverse" a section of ground with their 600 shots a minute—the bullets make a sound like swishing a piece of fencing wire back & forth through the air. When they got within 300 or 400 yards of us we slipped back over a bit of a precipice & crashed down into the gully, more than half falling. We left a bit of meat behind as several puttees & some pieces of clothing but caught up the main body all safely. We were lucky—a bullet went through the front of my hat—along the leather lining & left a red mark across my forehead like a cut from a whip though it didn't draw blood. I thought I was hit & was surprised to see no blood. Another half an inch would have just about have started me practicing the scale on the harp a good job my head was no bigger. About this time the warships closed right in, so did transports & every available boat. They were afraid we couldn't hang on. It was like throwing a man who couldn't swim into the water and saying "Sink or swim!["] With us it was hold on & fight to the last or be butchered on the beach. The warships opened up a violent fire over our heads the moral support was invaluable for we hadn't a single field gun ashore only a few Indian mountain batteries which are taken apart & transported on mules. I would have been pleased to see the enemy get in amongst the cravens who were shivering on the beach, they would have been slaughtered lying down. The Indians fought well but were hopelessly outclassed by heavier metal. This force the First Australian Divisions 1st, 2nd & 3rd brigades bore the brunt of the fighting all day; at evening we had a couple of battalions of New Zealanders on

## THE GALLIPOLI PENINSULA, TURKEY

our left (all infantry—"the queen of battles"—mark you) we stuck to it till Thursday when we were given a rest (or change) from the fire trenches. Personally I had no sleep for 4 days & nights continually, how I did it I don't know.

Later other battalions arrived also light horse (dismounted) the latter impudently arrogating to themselves achievements they did not achieve. They had the cheek to describe to us the landing and subsequent fighting. We soon dug in on Sunday night and when at 2 am Monday the Turks attacked they got a bad mauling & we took some prisoners. They said then that we were "more terrible than the Bulgars". The 25th Apl was essentially a soldiers battle—a second Inkerman, everyman for himself & the Devil for the lot of us. On Monday morning there were 31 dead Turks lying in front of our section of trench. I went out with a party & got some trophies & 7000 rounds of ammunition, a Russian officers uniform overcoat evidently from the Caucasus, I still have some buttons from it, they will make a nice brooch for mother. I lent a chap a spade to dig in with & thought he had gone to sleep so I shook him—but he had been shot dead a bullet through the head. I had been lying there a few minutes previously. It's better to be born lucky than rich.

The Turks when charging yelled Allah Mahomed—Allah Mahomed—It gave me cold shivers which slanted up & down my back 4 deep & my hair stood on end like an angry dogs bark—I wasn't a bit scared but it was so uncanny. A lot has been said re men going into action and feeling great elation and being imbued with an overwhelming desire to Kill—I didn't feel that way & none of the others I spoke with did. Just a feeling of utter indifference permeated me. I kept racking my brain for the forgotten name of an author etc etc. There were not many men in the firing line on Sunday night but those that were there were there for keeps. When an artillery officer crawled into my trench about midnight & asked us if we could undertake to hang on till daylight when he would have guns with us we said we would not fall back for old Nick himself. Righto he said to me, you stay here till dawn and I'll be here with guns—It put new life into us and sure enough he didn't fail us—the guns were in position & ready for action by dawn. I never heard such a lovely sound as when their adamantine mouths crashed out the 18 pr shrapnel. I Tangoed, I Turkey Trotted, I sang a Te Deum. I adore guns—when they're ours, and hate them with a hate bitterer than the bitterest of bitter beer when they "aint" especially machine guns. I know these well—I've no desire to know them worse. It rained Sunday night and we were wet through.

As I expected when I started this I didn't finish it, it's now 25th August—4 calendar months since we landed—nearly all the original 5th chaps are gone & we have up to the 6th lot of reinforcements with us. Don't expect too much of the good old regiment now—it's not the same by a long long way, there are some damned wasters amongst us now—a lot of unemployed by their own admission and a lot of <u>unemployable</u>. I took a batch along to a sick parade about 10 days ago, they were all 5th & 6th lot of reinforcements there were 16 of them—some had only been here 3 days and had cold feet. It's wonderful how they value their useless persons whilst a decent man will "play the game". One was tired (Oh Lord!) one had "nerves" others suffering from excesses two with self inflicted injuries, fingers shot off the right hand, this is too common an occurrence altogether. Shooting off the trigger fingers foresooth. <u>Pte Cameron—Geo Barmby's cousin was one of these beauties I paraded</u>—he, and all the rest will get attention here and a court martial. I consider they should be punished—advertised—and forfeit all their pay, if they are found guilty of intentionally doing it. They never by any chance put a bullet through their bodies or heads oh no. I enquired in the 8th for Sergeant Smith—asked Eddie D'Alton about him also Sam W. and others—their opinion of him is most unenviable—he has cold feet—badly!

Relieving troops arrive. (AWM A00847)

I think I am now the only Dimboola chap left here who has not had a rest, the 8th battn had 4 or 5 days at Imbros Island—out of sound of the guns—I've only been out of rifle range twice—once on H.M. Destroyer "Basilisk" on which I went to Cape Helles and H.M. Destroyer "Reindeer" on the way back—about 4 hours altogether & then we were under fire from the Asiatic forts & batteries. I've never gone to sleep without the sound of firing in my ears once—it's quite incessant day & night—artillery & rifle fire the former, machine gun & rifle fire & bombs & grenades the latter. At night when a machine gun opens up it emits a blue flame quite continuous exactly resembling a Vesuvius or Ætna burning off camp. The bombs, about the size of a cricket ball are wicked and do a lot of damage, they are hollow & are filled with a couple of handfuls of high explosive & when they explode the cast case flies to fragments everyway like a high explosive shell—Shrapnel exerts its energies all forward fan or funnel shaped—There has been some wonderful gunnery here at 3 or 4 thousand yards they (and we) can hit the same spot exactly ad infinitum.

I'm getting ahead of my tale again. I could write a book on the experiences of the first days—German officers we captured in our lines dressed in our uniforms & speaking excellent English. Turkish snipers, very game, were behind us and hard to find—These all got short shrift, a lunge with the bayonet and Finis! By the way I had the unique experience of assisting to drag our first gun into position & helped carry its ammunition to it, it was right in our midst in the firing line 30 feet away from me. This is the gun that killed Jim Bond, as the shells were set at zero and when fired burst almost at the guns muzzle—a glorified blunderbuss—Whilst here a list of killed was passed along the trench in which I was included—I just added "Liar" and initialled it. I was also reported killed at Cape Helles. When I rejoined my regiment with others on Thursday my pals thought it was my "shade" as 3 of my tent mates swore they had seen me lying dead shot through the head. There was great rejoicing when I turned up—for with all modesty I may say I'm a bit of a favourite with my company. One grabbed my rifle another my equipment and a couple helped me up into a dugout as I was just about exhausted—they made me a cup (or dixie) of tea. I had had a very strenuous & trying time. I'm rather proud of how I can "stick it"—I feel tired—but I can <u>force</u> myself to do what I must do.

To be continued

George

Mrs R. Martindale
Dimboola
Victoria
Australia

Nothing to be written on this side except the date and signature of the sender. Sentences nor required may be erased. If anything else is added the post card will be destroyed.

I am quite well.

I have received your 4 parcels

Letter follows at first opportunity.

I have received no letter from you lately.

Geo G Martindale
17 Sept '15

NOTHING to be written on this side except the date and signature of the sender. Sentences not required may be erased. If anything else is added the post card will be destroyed.

I am quite well.

~~I have been admitted into hospital~~

{ ~~sick~~ } ~~and am going on well.~~
{ ~~wounded~~ } ~~and hope to be discharged soon.~~

I ~~am being sent down to the base~~.

I have received your ~~letter dated~~ _____
~~telegram,~~ _____
✓ parcel ,, _____

Letter follows at first opportunity.

I have received no letter from you

{ lately.
{ ~~for a long time.~~

Signature } *Geo. G. Martindale*
only.

Date *17th Sept 15*

[Postage must be prepaid on any letter or post card addressed to the sender of this card.]

(9625) Wt. W3497-293 1760m. 3/15 G.A.T.

# AUSTRALIAN MILITARY FORCES.
## AUSTRALIAN IMPERIAL FORCE.
### Attestation Paper of Persons Enlisted for Service Abroad.

Duplicate Correct copy

No. 901  Name Martindale George Gowthorp
Unit 5. Batt.
Joined on 21 Aug. 1914.

**Questions to be put to the Person Enlisting before Attestation.**

1. What is your Name? — Martindale George Gowthorp
2. In or near what Parish or Town were you born? — in the Parish of ... near the Town of Mooroo in the County of Victoria
3. Are you a natural born British Subject or a Naturalised British Subject? — Yes N B
4. What is your age? — 27 5/12
5. What is your trade or calling? — Carpenter
6. Are you, or have you been, an Apprentice? If so, where, to whom, and for what period? — No
7. Are you married? — No
8. Who is your next of kin? (Address to be given) — Mrs Martindale, Dimboola, Victoria
9. Have you ever been convicted by the Civil Power? — No
10. Have you ever been discharged from any part of His Majesty's Forces, with Ignominy, on an Indifferent and Worthless, or on account of Conviction of Felony, and a Sentence of Penal Servitude, or have you been dismissed with Disgrace from the Navy? — No
11. Do you now belong to, or have you ever served in, His Majesty's Army, the Marines, the Militia, the Militia Reserve, the Territorial Force, Royal Navy, or Colonial Forces? If so, state which, and if not now serving, state cause of discharge — No
12. Have you stated the whole, if any, of your previous service? — Yes
13. Have you ever been rejected as unfit for His Majesty's Service? If so, on what grounds? — No
14. Do you understand that no Separation Allowance will be issued to you either before or after embarkation during your term of service? —

I, George Gowthorp Martindale, do solemnly declare that the above answers made by me to the above questions are true, and I am willing and hereby voluntarily agree to serve in the Military Forces of the Commonwealth of Australia within or beyond the limits of the Commonwealth.

And I further agree to allot not less than two-fifths of the pay payable to me from time to time during my service for the support of my wife, or three-fifths for the support of my wife and child, or wife and children.

Date 21/8/14     Signed Geo. G. Martindale
Signature of person enlisted.

PART FOUR:

# FOLLOWING AENEAS

*'I tell you it makes me mad—we're supposed to be fighting for justice and that is just what is denied us.'* Egypt, January 1916

*'I saw 13 mules killed by one shell.'* Egypt, June 1916

In early November 1915 George was admitted to hospital on Lemnos Island in the Aegean Sea. He had been transferred off Gallipoli because he was suffering from influenza, an illness that disabled him for about a month. He was therefore in hospital when the strategic decision was made to withdraw from Turkey, and when the evacuation operations commenced. George rejoined his unit at Lemnos only a few days before the final Allied units left their positions. Then, in early January, he was shipped to Alexandria on the *Empress of Britain*. George spent a few weeks in Egypt with the remnants of the devastated 5th Battalion before being transferred briefly to the 57th Battalion, and then to the 59th Battalion as part of a wider reorganisation of Australian forces. The old Gallipoli veterans were distributed among the new battalions, the idea being to disseminate their experience.

With his letters increasingly focused on recording battle actions, George left off part of his experience. At Lemnos, for instance, a series of infractions were recorded on his file, noting things like absence from parade. When he arrived in Egypt he was sent to the Tel el Kebir 'Detention Camp' for fourteen days punishment. The charge in this case revealed a suggestive context—he was being punished for 'Drunkenness at Sarpi Camp Lemnos 1/1/16'. The date of the offence reveals that he celebrated the end of 1915 and the start of 1916 with some panache.

As he settled into his new battalion and undertook training duties George continued his account of the Gallipoli campaign in letters home. He was again promoted to Corporal on 17 April 1916, only days before the anniversary of the Gallipoli landings. Before leaving the training camp at Moascar, however, he again 'Reverts to ranks at own request'.

Focused on his experiences of 1915, George was also replying, in a very real way, to correspondence from home concerning how the front was represented and the stories his family had read or heard. George therefore wrote of Gallipoli just as the Anzac tradition was being used to effect in a nationwide recruitment drive, believing that parts of the narrative were misrepresentations. He expressed annoyance at storytelling coming from people with limited claim upon the campaign. Yet George in many ways literally embodied the ideas of Australian soldiery that were being propounded. He criticised the lack of vigour among many Australian recruits, while memorialising the service to the Empire of men like Henry and Eddie D'Alton. The Dardanelles campaign was, he revealed, a contestation point of Australian identity where tensions between idealisms and realities were being played out in fact and in fiction.

George mourned the losses of the 'fighting fifth'. Even though the 5th Battalion was reinforced and sent to France, George knew it was not the same body it had been a year beforehand. Turning his attention towards the western front, to which his new battalion was also headed, George anticipated finally getting his encounter with the Germans. But he also learned something from home that further revealed the complex ambiguities in his attitude to the war and its prosecution. By the time he finished writing home from Egypt George knew that in late March 1916 Peter had signed up in company with a couple of other Dimboola boys.[37]

Tel-el-Kebir
Egypt 23rd Jan 1916

Dear Dad

I've had several letters from home at varying intervals since I last wrote the last being one from you dated 13 Dec & one from Mother dated 20th Dec containing cuttings re Miss Pankhursts attempted speech, Bgr. Gen. McCoy's speech etc—also parcels of sox, Lam Buk, cigarettes, Hd'Kerchiefs, Eucalyptus, mufflers etc, a parcel of ginger, sweets etc. 2 weeks ago Freddy Cooper who stayed with Mrs Regent in South Yarra called to see me, I was on quarter guard, gave him half the ginger—he's in the artillery & looks very well—his regards.

 I've not written before as there was some uncertainty as to letters being sent, and also I've had very little time—we get no rest. Instead of giving us old hands a spell, who have born the heat & burden of the day, the later reinforcements are the favored ones & is the cause of a great deal of dissatisfaction—I've not had leave at all for nearly 10 months now, been right through a campaign & a gruelling one at that. Fellows who have never been on the peninsula can get leave however.

 As to pay—altogether mine is about £108 to come to date. After arrival in Egypt in Dec 1914 the authorities informed us that we could only draw up to 2/- a day—this they would pay—at that rate I should have been able to draw £18 on arrival here a couple of weeks ago—I applied for £10—and got the princely sum of Pt. 100 = £1-0-6! This doesn't go far when one has to buy his own food, for if we relied on what is issued to us we would just about starve. For instance we get about 1 2lb[38] loaf of bread once a week—1/2 a lb every second day about. We are entitled to 16 oz meat a day & get about 4 oz not that very often—the jam? (The Lord forgive me for calling it such) is fabricated here in Egypt—a self respecting pig wouldn't eat it, so I don't. And I'm not too fastidious now I can assure you. Tea 1 pint twice a day, 1 small spud & a teaspoonful of cabbage complete the menu, ugh! I don't want or expect 7 course dinners, napkins etc but reckon we should get at least the regulation army ration and the pay we are entitled to. I wonder, with others, if people at home know how things stand. I know men in other corps who can & have drawn £15 in one hit. If they can get it, why shouldn't we? I tell you it makes me mad—we're supposed to be fighting for justice and that is just what is denied us. I'm still wearing the same trousers I've worn for 9 months, they have never been washed. The malingerers who got back here without firing a shot, and the cold footers who stayed here are dolled up like sore fingers. They've drawn money & even wear uniforms tailored to measure. To look at some of them you would think they were at least generals. I can see myself with black eyes & skinned knuckles for 6 months if I get back home.

How do you fancy creatures who eat cordite to raise their temperature—parade sick—<u>and get away</u> on it. Sometimes they have a good dose of soap & froth at the mouth the while they implore the M.O.—the Base, Doctor, the Base! I know 2 of my Coy who did this, the same day, just after Lone Pine, and it worked. Over 5 months elapsed and Lo & behold one of them rejoins wearing 3 stripes on his arm, 4 or 5 days ago—trots up to me with his luncheon hook extended—Oh no! says I. I don't shake hands with a ____ like you, I told him and incidentally the crowd about—why, anyhow he lost his stripes the next day.

I suppose the censor will not pass this letter—too much truth in it. If he's a sport, he will. I'll write to mother the girls Bob & Peter—I don't feel in the mood for writing today & when I feel in the mood is when I'm doing something else & have no time.

We're camped on the battlefield of Tel-el-Kebir where Arabi Pasha got his, from Sir Garnet Wolseley. I picked up a few empty Martini-Henry cartridge cases—they are solid drawn ones. I'll send 'em along as a curiosity—also a piece of driving band from an 8.2 shell that was pitched in Lone Pine from Chanak on the Asiatic side.

When I can settle down to it I'll continue that letter, as you seemed to think the first instalment good—that one only covered about a fortnight after landing—before the Cape Helles stunt—I'll have to leave off—as the books do—"just as he's catching the bear". Also my old hat with bullet holes in it—and a Turkish Fez, Backsight of Turkish rifle etc etc—I've also got another hat band for Maggie. Glorious weather here—nights pretty cold & heavy dew.

Love to you all at home<br>George

[3 June 1916]
Moaskar Tel-el-Kebir

Dear Dad,
I'm going to make an attempt to resume that brief epitome on our doings in Gallipoli as promised—there is a "to be continued" letter you got posted about last August I think, but I don't quite remember what ground I'd covered but imagine it was to about May 5th—anyhow that will do. Now on 5th May we were lying in reserve in Shrapnel Gully in Dugouts & getting our fair share of attention from Abdul. Late in the afternoon we were moved off to near the beach & lay down & got nicely frozen—then we were shaken up—not awakened it was too cold to sleep—and issued with 48 hrs iron rations (bully & dog biscuits) and moved right onto the beach & loaded like so many cattle into barges—no lights or smoking of course—here the Navy took charge—Middies of 14 ordering all & sundry about without respect of persons or rank. They would stand no back chat from anyone, not even a General if he'd been there—It was quite a change: no hurry or bustle or confusion—You see we were in the hands of the Navy! The picquet boats towed us out & aboard—by us I mean the 2<u>nd</u> Brigade—I found myself on board H.M. Destroyer "Basilisk"—now about 4.am—and away we went, it was bitterly cold night & by good fortune I got a mug of cocoa from a "sailor-man"—they don't like being called "sailors" & oh! such cocoa—hot & with milk <u>and</u> sugar—milk! There was about a pint & I divided it up with 3 pals. I won't forget that drink in a hurry. They were all very decent to us, couldn't do enough for us. The destroyer was crammed & there's not much space at the best of times.
 Arrived Cape Helles after daylight & disembarked—were sorted out and started off along the cliffs in companies or so. Approaching Seddul-Bahr some Turkish batteries on the Asiatic side gave us a welcome—we would much rather have dispensed with this—they

didnt do much damage but made a lot of noise & smoke. Near Seddul-Bahr proper we came on a couple of 10" guns that had been knocked out by naval gunfire, they were in a proper mess—here also were ammunition vaults which would defy almost anything—even an earthquake. Round stone cannonballs of about 18" diameter were lying about, relics of prehistoric times they appeared to us after seeing what modern high explosive shells can do. I daresay these would play havoc with a sailing ship. At Seddul-Bahr was some French artillery posted among the ruins countless thousands of tons of masonry lying about & pieces of huge shells.

We now turned inland—to our left—and passed through lanes flanked by hedges, through almond & olive groves, walnut & fig trees—a very pretty locality but rather unhealthy at this time. Here we came across batteries of the famous French 75s lighter than our 18 pdrs & faster—French native troops, Senegalese—giants these average height perhaps 6'2" & big withal, dressed in navy blue & blue fez & nearly all wearing war ribbons: they were as black as sin even their tongues were a purplish color—good teeth & when they smiled which was nearly all the time they would remind one of a piano keyboard and a dredge bucket opening out all in one. Their eyes were bloodshot like a bulldog's. They carried long rifles &—I was going to say <u>longer</u> bayonets—but that's going too far. Anyhow the rifle with fixed bayonet was as long as they themselves so they could reach a long way—I looked at my rifle 3'8½" long & thanked my stars we were not at loggerheads, see! They could reach a fellow 10 or 11 feet away. These regiments of Jack Johnsons weren't too bad in a scrap provided it wasn't too hot, but they would <u>not</u> "stick it". They might hang on to a position during daylight but at night they would crawl back. It was said that we were to be put with them to stiffen them—no not that—we veterans (?) of a fortnight—Then we came across French white troops—some in the picturesque long blue tunic & red trousers & blue & red cap—The officers were in the new sky blue uniform which is very smart, but to my mind the old khaki takes beating.

Oh! I forgot to say that from near Seddul-Bahr we could look out over the plains of Troy. The 75s were busy & kept firing briskly, as we got to the site of our bivouac. This was by the side of a gutter about 8 ft wide & 3' deep. We at once proceeded to dig in—dugouts about 3 ft deep—these were little wells by the morning on a/c of the soakage and about as comfortable as a horse trough. Therein we would doze the night through in goose flesh & formless dreams. But we had the gutter to wash from and water from the holes we dug to drink & we appreciated that. I was dog tired that first night but was too cold to get much sleep so next day I dug up a couple of old Turkish knapsacks an old door & some straw in a piece of hessian from some Indians. I had a better sleep next night with a sock on one hand & part of a puttee round the other, my head in one pack & my feet in the other. Hunted round in the almond grove but there were no almonds but the second day I found a piece of bacon about 1 1/2 or 2 lbs, "it had been rather knocked about but it was good still"—It was near the crossing to the gutter & plenty of horses passing, so appearances were slightly against it, I'll admit. I invited the other chaps in the dugout to share it but they declined—Good Lord! eat that? No fear! I got to work & washed it & trimmed it up, cut it into rashers, ~~pinched~~ acquired part of a biscuit box made a fire & fried it. When they smelt it they soon changed their opinions & I hardly got a look in—they went at it like a hart at a water brook. "Bite bigger "Robby" bigger yet", you bet they did. We were kept on mighty short rations at this time—always seeking what we might devour.

On Saturday (8th May) morning we got orders to move up toward the firing line, so within a few minutes we were on the move and kept going till we came to a creek—about the size of the creek at Dimboola, this we followed for a while & then got orders to dig in. A few of our chaps stopped stray bullets here—we had dug for a couple of hours & I was just beginning to think of boiling the dixie when all of a sudden—fall in!—fall in! leave your packs!, 2 minutes & we were off—the Great Charge had commenced—we advanced for a while in artillery formation that is in columns of fours at 50 yards interval and 200 yards distance. I was in the front 4 of our platoon on the directing flank so had a good view of what was doing—Presently men began to fall fairly often, so we extended & kept on being now about 1200 yards from the enemy. Just before opening out I had the toe of my boot shot away—I was looking down at the time & saw the spurt of dust, my foot being on the ground. It amused me I remember. Now we come to trenches occupied by the Manchesters & jump over them—Good day "Choom"! our fellows shout—have you got any kangaroo feathers? have you got half a piastre?, have you got an Australian sovereign?, I'm saaving em oop! a rusty one will do! They reply in kind I suppose:

Then we come to the Ghurkas squatting in their trenches & moving their hands up & down meaning us to lie down. We jumped over their heads & boxed on to the front trench & had a couple of minutes Breather—then Come on Australia! The Brigadier Colonel McCay was there with a walking stick in his hand—right up with the front line. There was no hesitation whatever here—the cold foot push had made themselves scarce at Anzac on the Lond Sunday, and were at this moment in Egypt writing of the exploits they had never performed. Those who had no stomach for a fight had on one pretext or another managed to get away—the scum & dross had gone & left pure metal, if I may put it so—our field guns & naval guns were pouring tons of metal over our heads onto the Turkish trenches the French 75s doing some wonderful work. I was told afterwards by a Frenchman that 34 batteries of these guns alone were in action that Saturday afternoon 136 guns of one class alone! We are now as far ahead as any of our troops had got & now for the final rush. We ran at a trench held by the Lancashire Fusiliers off we go & them for machine gun fire. They seemed to have m-guns posted everywhere. We made straight for the town of Krithia & kept going for about 500 yards. Our right flank was now exposed & the Turks tried to turn it so we were forced to stop & dig in & make good the breach.

So dig we did, clawing out the hard ground tooth & nail & trenching tool, it's wonderful how quickly you can dig when you like. From time to time we would pause and hand 'em over 10 rounds rapid. Then darkness began to fall & the guns eased off & we were soon down a couple of feet. The enemy machine guns & rifle fire was going all night & our chaps started quarrelling as to which way the bullets were going some contended that it was our own troops firing over our heads—but it wasn't. About 3 o'clock on Sunday morning I went back with others for ammunition about 1/2 a mile back & several were hit. I got a box & was carrying it back when a bullet smacked right into it near my ear—It wasn't very nice, they're such lazy bullets, rather go through than round you. I'll never forget that trip it was an awful experience, hundreds of men lying about dead & wounded. The cries & groans of the latter were heartrending—scores died through want of immediate attention, though the stretcher bearers were splendid & toiled like slaves. On the way back I came across a chap—a tent mate—who was shot high up through the thigh—He was in great need of a cigarette so I made one from the leaf of my notebook & putting a discarded tunic over my head, lighted it & gave it to him. It was a bit of a struggle to leave him there (he had the field dressing on) but its against orders to take wounded to the rear so I went on with my box—it was just after this the bullet hit it. I saw a photo of this chap the other day—his leg was off at the crutch.

All this time star shells were being fired—they burst like a rocket & light up the landscape for about a minute or more. At dawn on Sunday the naval guns had a cut at the Turks trenches & made some excellent shooting. Achi Baba looked as though a bush fire was raging. When a lyddite shell bursts it sends up a cloud of smoke yellowish green & earth like a huge cauliflower & the concussion is very great. I had some of the "Goeben's" 11 inchers burst within a hundred yards of me, its quite near enough thank you. I remember this Sunday morning a pal of mine named Kelly was squatting down lighting a cigarette when a bullet went close to his ear; his indifference to these little varmints is usually such that we were not a little surprised to see him leap nervously to one side—apology was offered as he settled down again "Sorry" he said "I thought it was a wasp"! Then of course I had to have a look around & was watching what didn't concern me—namely some big shells bursting on our left front—and got my eyes filled with sand kicked up by a bullet for my trouble.

And so Sunday passed fairly quietly considering—one chap in my trench would be wakened for his relief at observing & he would straightaway waken <u>his</u> relief—but its not my turn yet, surely—have you been on an hour? No! Why? I don't like observing; I might be shot!! He was evidently carried along in that charge against his will. We were relieved from the trenches on Wednesday night & went back to our old bivouac. A small party of us were taken in town by the Fmen of the Royal Naval Air Service—& were given some hot rum—it was a bitterly cold night—tobacco jam etc. There was an aeroplane place near our bivouac several machines being kept there & Abdul was always trying to get them firing great shells, some of which came our way. I saw 13 mules killed by one shell.

The roll call after this action—129 men[39] left of 1160 in the 5th Battalion. No wonder the poor old Colonel wept. He was a fine game old chap & a gentleman Lt Colonel Wanliss. I went with a fatigue party along the creek which runs from Krithia—it was a very pretty view poppies, red & black, mignonette, daisies & mauve marshmallows in great profusion & a beautiful perfume—then all of a sudden we would come on a dead Turk about 4 ft high—a most obscene object. I was lying in my dug out one morning at about 4 oclock & it was raining—I was awake—& I could hear some one moving quietly near me I just peered through quarter opened eyes & here's a Tommy appropriating my water proof sheet which was over me—He had it right off me & felt "home & dried" no doubt when I sat bolt upright—Oh! Good morning, chum! do you want this? no answer—Oh! Sorry chum, I didn't think you wanted it. Still I kept mum—he then spread it back over me, said goodbye & walked off—Talk about cheek—that knocks anything even I heard of. Oh! I was going to say about the amount of Turkish gear in the creek near Krithia we got thousands of rifles & bayonets & there must have been millions of rounds of small arm ammunition lying in the creek, one could walk for pretty well a mile stepping on this gear all the time. About 3 oclock on the Monday morning I had the bad luck to slip & drop a box of ammunition on my right hand & had a pretty rotten time for several weeks with it.

The first night back in our bivouac a chap came along and said we <u>must</u> find room for him, well, we did—then he started to cry about the cold—had no greatcoat etc—he kept up his whining till about 10 pm—my hand was very painful & I couldn't sleep so I damned him roundly & said here! take mine, taking it off & throwing it <u>at</u> him—he took it. I just about froze—I would have done so had I sat down but I kept on the move all night. There was ice everywhere in the morning—ugh! The reason he had no overcoat was because it was "too heavy to carry"—he came in without even a rifle & bayonet. I suppose he's back in Australia now—a "Hero of the Dardanelles" (?) The men on service are not heroes—they are only doing their duty—<u>But</u> those that shirk their responsibilities are cowards—there's only one reason why they don't come—fear of injury to their precious hides!

And so on Sunday the 16th May we left Cape Helles—passing the light house a heap of ruins & embarking on H.M. Destroyer "Reindeer"—we passed down the pier of boats & planks alongside the "River Clyde" the transport which was deliberately run ashore on the Lond Sunday. This is where we saw some horrible looking barbed wire entanglements—spikes an inch long & close together. As we pulled out the crews of the battleships & cruisers gave us a great cheer also the Tommies and Frenchmen ashore. Their bands played & I could feel a lump in my throat. People at home have no idea of what a cheer can be under these circumstances—we felt amply repaid for the rough time we had had & the privations we had endured during the past 10 days—we had fought with such men as the Dublins, Inniskillings etc regulars of the 29th Division & we surprised them all. The Gurkhas were a big bit doubtful of us before—but afterwards—Bahadur—Australia—& they would bring us chupatties & ask for badges—anything—a bamboo cigarette holder or an old knife—as mementos.

It was at Cape Helles that I saw dead men lying about all with their clothes half burnt off—evidently set alight by shell fire—as one walked along the creek he would see arms & legs & heads sticking out of the ground telling of hurried burials—just a bit of earth scraped over them—there were hundreds of such burials as Sir John Moore's at Corunna. Smashed Turkish rifles were used as firewood for boiling dixies & bayonets as supporting bars—I lost my pack here—The English Tommies had a right royal time looting them whilst we were in the firing line—at least I got my pack back but it was empty save for a pair of holey socks which were lying near—There were scores of these super sneaks around where we left our packs. They're a miserable crowd, generally speaking—they were some of "Kitcheners Army"—<u>not</u> men of the glorious 29th Division—than whom it would be hard to find a finer lot of fellows—they're regulars.

[40] So we landed back at Anzac on the night of 16th May & went into supports straight away—on the 19th May I got my first stripe. This is the day that Enver Pasha and Liman Von Sanders ordered the Turks to take our trenches—they tried but failed losing over 3000 killed alone & about 9000 wounded—our losses under 500 killed & wounded. Armistice on the 24th May, 8 hrs—8 am to

4 pm—We counted 400 Dead Turks in a space of 100 yards x 80 yards in mule valley. They lay in places 4 & 5 deep & we didn't like the wind to put us in their lee.

And now follow months of hard work, next to no rest—nights running into days & days into weeks & weeks into months Sundays & all—everything forgotten except the job in hand—wounds, sickness & death on every hand and no one knew which minute would be his last as a sound man—but after all it's the work in hand and not the workman that is the matter of supreme importance. We would be

The temporary armistice to bury the dead of both the Turks and the Australians. (AWM P02649.009)

shelled by day & get rifle fire by night—and one has to be vigilant & very much on the alert when the enemy is only a few seconds away—I was for 14 weeks continually on duty—<u>not one day or night off all the time</u>! 3 hrs on & 6 off—that is I could lie down handy but not leave the trench & could not remove my equipment 150 pounds, bayonet (this was always fixed from sunset to sunrise) water bottle haversack & entrenching tool—Slept in this harness day & night until it became almost part of me—If an alarm was given or a "Stand To" as I stood up Id automatically seize my rifle—always had it very handy—slept with it between my knees usually—I could sleep through heavy bombardments—& could lie down & go to sleep in 1 minute.

 Some nights I would feel uneasy—get an idea an attack was coming—then I would stay on the fire step all night with the other non-coms. It was a case of as Joffre said "Fight and Endure"—its easier to fight than to endure—If we were on the Peninsula now I believe I would be there—I counted & hoarded up the days like a miser does his shekels—at one time when I was off color an A.M.C. chap took my temperature 103°—he called me several kinds of a fool but I <u>would not</u> & <u>did not</u> parade sick—though I could hardly stand.

 I got a cutting from you re a sniper of ours and a Turkish officer—You said you wondered if I was the sniper. Now it's a funny thing, but I had an experience exactly as detailed (a "Herald" cutting it was). For 2 or 3 mornings just after dawn I had noticed through a powerful Telescope a couple of officers—(Germans I reckoned them) who pushed their frames up to scan the landscape o'er—I quietly and at my leisure got the exact range—700 yards—and was at my post betimes next morning—They didn't appear till it was just a nice light for observing <u>and for good shooting</u>! Sighter: <u>optional</u>! I had a lovely position and an observer I could rely upon—also a good rest on sandbags—The first shot kicked up a little spurt of dust—a good 3 o'clock—they didn't move—second shot—no dust—blood. The chap I fired at dropped. I hit him alright—I tell you I can make it mighty uncomfortable for a man at 1,000 yds. I'm in tip top form for strafe-ing 'em—I think a good many lost a few pounds of lard through my endeavours. Of course they reciprocated by trying to make me "fly the track" but I had 5/8" of iron plating where it was of most use—At very close range the Turkish bullets (Mauser pointed)[41] would not have such great penetration as at moderately short range i.e. 300 to 500 yds the latter range for these High Velocity rifles is point blank as you will see by the Turkish Mauser backsight when you get it (I want to register the few curios mementos I'm sending) these are beastly bullets with a bad balance & as soon as they hit, they lose their equilibrium and revolve on their shorter axis & have the same effect as a ricochet bullet caused by the light point and heavy base—the penetration is very great, bulging two 5/16" plates bolted together & going through one 5/8" plate, in the former they leave a hole thus—[42]—but this is not a treatise on ballistics etc.

When using a loophole (size 4" x 3" about) I always kept a sandbag over the aperture so as not to allow the light to show through—when about to fire I'd stand behind the hole & then remove the bag—many a man lost his life through non-observance of this very necessary precaution. If I caught anybody fooling round my favourite position I would most probably give vent to some harsh & bitter expressions—would speak crossly to him. I had a few bullets through my loophole—but—it's better to be born lucky than rich. I was elsewhere. These things give the "sport" an added zest. The Turks were enterprising enough—one night a Turk crept up to one of our machine guns—there was a loophole about 3 ft long for traversing fire and actually had his hands on the gun & tried to pull it through the loophole. The sentry was wide awake however and now he is with his fathers—a member of the celestial choir, or elsewhere! Don't despise the "Unspeakable"—their audacity is astounding and I have the most profound respect for Abdul as a fighter—and he's a

<u>fair</u> fighter, not fair as complexions go—he's a bit discolored, but I'm satisfied there's not a better fighting man in the world than he except perhaps the—er hem! shall I say it—the Australian. I'm also satisfied the "Dinkum" Australian can wallop any other biped on this old mudball.

Whew! its hard work writing like this—its not on the bottom of a bucket (canvas buckets only here) or on a drum as in the old-fashioned pictures—these are things of the past.

After a shell happened to hit wood it was a sight to see the rush the fellows would make for the splinters—like going for soup (or other things) at a railway refreshment buffet. Longing eyes were cast at the crosses made of strips of biscuit boxes marking graves—but they were never touched—its rather curious to see how feeling & sentimental men become under war conditions rough as maybe in some things—and just as diametrically the opposite in other things. Someone strikes up say "The Swanee River" (the old folks at home) others join in and <u>sing</u> it—or keep quiet. Anything sentimental allowed. Comics or anything else cat howled down. A chap off color & his pal "carries on" for him—but they would quarrel over the cigarette & these were more than plentiful mostly—There was never any malice or mighty little—all were striving after the same common good. Anyone who didn't play the game in the spirit and proper acceptance of the term were cursed till they did—and I may say I took my very full share in their disciplining. The cold feet push were terrified of me & I don't mind saying so—we had a pretty fair percentage of these Saturday afternoon near soldiers—they were a long way from being even near soldiers. I'd be sorry to die in their company as Henry V said.

That's a fitting epitaph to the D'Alton boys I saw in the Banner—"For Honour, Not Honours"!

I saw this inscription on a cross near the Turkish lines: I think I wrote it before—

"Mother country, land and sea,
Yield Strong Sons who die for thee,
Grant that through the years that we,
Worthy of <u>thy fallen be</u>."

I don't know that I can attempt to give you any sequence of events through those weeks—how I got jammed in a trench & had a hard job to get out. The bombardments, the delivery of a few letters—the flies—other horrible vermin dirty, creeping, crawling—even Bobby Burns[43] would be hard put to it to express, and elaborate on, this vile theme and he was a past master perhaps through intimate association. Don't let "J.D." see this!, thirst—great 8" greenish black centipedes (so called because they have 1,000,000 legs on each side of their bodies) the—er—effluvia—from No Mans Land—the feeling of exhaustion—the bacon (and bully) salty as Lot's Wife's elbow—the heat & glare exaggerated & aggravated by glaring through periscopes—the lack of real news from the outside world—and so on ad nauseam. And worse than all these horrors was the whine of the—person—who was always parading sick & trying to get away—"It wasn't like this at home"! ugh. I'd rather be lousy & crawled over by centipedes & chance my luck with the bullets than listen to these invertebrates.

<u>Near Ismailia</u>

I started this epistle over 2 months ago & wrote a bit at odd times as exigencies permitted—part on the ferry over the Canal—where we were almost devoured by fleas—one could catch a dozen in one grab—part miles away in the desert. I put in about 3 months on outpost work—far from the maddening crowd. Transport mainly by camel train. Thousands of these quadrupeds are engaged in this work—I've seen perhaps 2,000 in one group. (I'm writing this under slight difficulties—a couple of nasty cuts—one on either thumb & they're bandaged—the flies are troublesome & it's usual for a cut to become septic) it was a hot job & night work especially is tiring. Part was written underground a hole dug in the ground & sandbagged up & a cover of matting & earth on top—quite invisible to aeroplanes.

Some wonderful sand storms (The Khamseen) which would move whole hills some hundreds of yards & water not too plentiful 1 to 1½ bottles a day—so there was not much for washing—however "hope on hope ever"—Hope I'll soon be parlez-vous-ing. Talk of "Somewhere East of Suez ["], where the best is like the worst, where there aint no Ten Commandments, and a man can raise a thirst. In this place of sun, sorrow, sand & sore eyes, and on our mission most of the Commandments are in abeyance—Thou shalt not kill & each one of us itching to do murder to the sinful bodies of our enemies—Remember the Sabbath day, <u>oh</u>! I don't think. Thou shalt not covet. Oh no! its not conducive to covetousness when one is gravel crushing & ploughing his way <u>through</u> (not over) the sand, and the other chap has a horse, oh, dear me, no! one doesn't covet his "ass"—especially when he has about 80 lbs of gear hung all about him—like a glorified Xmas tree, and with the extra Commandment "the baksheesh one" Do unto others as they would do unto you, only <u>do it first.</u>

It's now just June & we have been given High Velocity rifles—point blank 5 or 600 yards. I'm going to write you a bit of an account of the "Lone Pine" affair of last Aug, as soon as I get time. I've been extremely busy these last few months. We have to knock the rough corners off the new chaps—ere this you will know I'm now in a different regiment, about half the old chaps of the 5th—there are not many—volunteered to go to form the nucleus of these new battalions. The motto of the 5th is "Sans Regret"—I left it without much regret—it wasn't the old "Fifth". There's a good deal of sentiment connected with a chaps old regiment & it makes one wild to see chaps wearing the red & black clawing & fumbling with their rifles as though they were slip rails or crowbars.

Whilst out on an outpost (I've just heard that an Enemy aeroplane has bombed this post killing about 8 men) Anzac Day 25th Apl came round again—Certainly a quieter day than last year. The company was fallen in & the O.C. asked those who were present at the landing on 25th Apl to step forward—2 stepped out myself & another—he was there for about 1 day & has been home to Australia <u>not</u> wounded—you know! He doesn't say much to <u>me</u>. I was there 5 months. An Army order was promulgated, allowing[44] those who were at "the Landing" to wear a red ribbon & those who were on the Peninsula at all to wear a blue ribbon—so I got both. I'll send 'em along.

During April we marched from Tel-el-Kebir to across the canal—46 miles in 3 days in full marching order and on one bottle of water per day. The whole brigade started, it was a tough march—doesn't seem much on paper—but we or rather I carried about 80 lbs of gear—hundreds blew out the first day 15 miles. Oh! it's a lovely job, cajoling, urging, damning & ordering men to keep their heads from getting down between their knees and to keep their proper places in the ranks—the while you roll a pebble in your cheek to keep your mouth and tongue from drying out altogether. My feet stand these marches splendidly, no blisters but the very big majority get sore feet. I wipe my toes, at least, every night with a damp cloth—a lot neglect to do this & suffer in consequence.

I must ring down the curtain now & put this in the letter bag—otherwise it won't get home for a couple of months. I'm going to write to mother tonight if I can—just a short note perhaps—as I dont xpect to be able to write for a couple of weeks after this.

My love to all at home from your affectionate Son

June 3

George

Near Ismailia Egypt
<u>June 1916</u>

Dear Mother

I received your letters of 5th & 28th March & 4th Apl at varying intervals (5th March last, of course), and of course was more than pleased to hear from you and especially that you were all well. I read and re-read them: And Peter is by now a soldier!—at 18. I had hopes that it would not be necessary for him to come—not that I think the war is drawing to a close—I don't, but because he's too young. Surely, surely, I <u>know</u>. Don't think that I'm not seized of the necessity for the services of every man—and woman—worthy the name, to render assured the triumph of our cause. I am. Many a night as I lay out in the desert "Somewhere East of Suez", I've thought the matter out, but couldn't come to a definite conclusion. Were he older, say 20, there would have been nothing to think about. But now—the anchor weighed—there's to be no looking back—there <u>will</u> <u>be</u> <u>no</u> looking back, no repining. I have full confidence in him and know he will be a good soldier. And in the years to come people will be unable to point at him the finger of scorn—a coward! And in the years to come he will not curse me for having been instrumental in holding him back. And if he fall—well, it will not be in the garb of a low civilian—a coward, scores of thousands of whom still infest and— no, not disgrace—contaminate Australia. And he will be in good company—a goodly fellowship. "Who dies for England sleeps with God", "For honour, not honours" Words like these & the thoughts they inspire our reward! Though not our only reward, for we <u>will</u> triumph! However several months will probably elapse ere he takes his place in the firing line, a lot may happen before then.

As to those who remain at home—the eligible, I mean, and men <u>must</u> be fit to be of any use—and mince & prance, cough, sneeze, amble, sophisticate, equivocate and lie like troopers (or infantrymen) to save their vile bodies—they are <u>forever</u> fallen. When, if, eventually they are forced to come, as conscripts—with umbrella marks on their sloping shoulders, shoulders that have never felt the caress of a rifle sling, bah! I would not die in their company. Deep thinkers! How long, oh Lord, how long? As to myself I had made up my mind <u>before</u> the outbreak of war, long before any one imagines. Do you remember I could always foresee this war. So I "chucked my job & joined it".

I'm a corporal of grenadiers[45]—"The Suicide Club" we are known as. The greater the risk, the greater the glory. Do you remember what I wrote from the deck of H.M.S. "Novian" in April 1915 at Mudros Harbor. I said I intended to "make the pace a welter" I did. And now I say it again. I have not much time to catch the mail so will stop.

Somewhere in France[46]<br>July 10th 1916

Just a few words in a hurry—glad to say we'll be at the Germans in a few hours now—I just missed a shell case by a few yards—fired at an aeroplane. You will know there's a big "push" going on now—So it's now Adieu again to face the unknown. If my lucky star sets—well I'm ready! Let her go, Gallagher! Fellows here writing adieux to their wives & sweethearts. I've neither—but I've <u>you</u>. All my love to you all—Your affectionate boy

George

Men moving towards the front travel along a sunken road towards the Somme. (AWM EZ0122)

# PART FIVE:
# THE WESTERN FRONT

*'I remember being in the air'.* London, August 1916

*'Shrapnel was driving across no man's land like hailstones in hell.'*
London, August 1916

Before posting the previous letter—which he started in Egypt and finished in France—George sent his family a card to let them know he was in France and keeping well. Only slight references to it, mentioned in other correspondence, reveal the card's one-time existence. Through such means George, like other soldiers, kept his family roughly aware of where he was and whether he was still alive. Undoubtedly the family communicated with friends and family for news of their boys, as well as checking the casualty lists and other reports in the press. During the Gallipoli campaign, for instance, Eddie D'Alton wrote home to his family, and because some of these letters were printed in the *Dimboola Banner*, they became public knowledge.

Like George, Eddie conveyed news of the Dimboola boys whenever he could. In a letter dated 11 May 1915, printed a little over a month later, Eddie described the Gallipoli landing, the entrenchments, artillery exchanges, his brother Henry getting wounded, and himself being wounded.[47] He added, in a passing comment, that 'I saw George Martindale on Tuesday after I was hit, and had a yarn with him.'[48] The day after his letter was printed in Dimboola, Eddie wrote again to his parents, which was subsequently précised in the *Dimboola Banner*. [49] He had apparently 'just been speaking to George Martindale, who had been promoted to lance-corporal.' Poignantly, four days after this was printed, George was writing home that he had just learned of Eddie's death. A few months later, George likely read Eddie's letters when the *Dimboola Banner* was forwarded on to him. He certainly read the paper's coverage of the deaths of both Henry and Eddie D'Alton, making reference to them in his own correspondence.

When George started a letter to his father in the middle of July 1916, he opened with reference to the inward correspondence that he had received, highlighting the problems with getting mail, but also with sending it. The most recent letters he got were a month and a half old. George wanted to know if money he had remitted had been received at home, which he was managing on behalf of two friends as well as himself. By then his father had already got the money, worked out George's probable purpose in sending it, banked it, and written to George about it. But when George was writing, the arrangements Mr Martindale had made and articulated to George were still in the mail.

George's concern about such arrangements was timely. As had been the case before, his letter was commenced prior to going into combat. The letter from '"Somewhere" in France' was written to the north of where one of the largest battles in human history had been underway for over a fortnight. The Somme Offensive was a massive Allied assault on German positions, and George's battalion was part of the Australian forces preparing for a feint against German positions to the north. It was hoped that this attack would draw some of the Germans away from the Somme, thereby weakening their capacity to resist the massive French and British attack.

The day after starting his letter George was sent towards a particular German position, the Sugar Loaf salient. For seven hours the Germans were shelled by Allied guns. Then, at 6.00 pm on 19 July, with his letter still incomplete, George joined the battle of Fromelles. Two Australian Divisions attacked, and were devastated by German machine guns, warned of the attack by the bombardment and still in place despite it. The battle lasted only some fourteen hours, bringing no major strategic advantage, and destroying the effective strength of the attacking battalions. Some of the Australians gained on the German lines but were forced to retreat through lack of support and strength. George's letter was, as he reported to his father, stained that evening in a creek in no man's land, where he was one of the few to make ground against the enemy positions.

It was a few weeks later when George was able to finish the epistle. In the aftermath of the Fromelles debacle he was again promoted to Lance Corporal and then Corporal. But soon afterwards, on 3 August 1916, George was wounded while in a trench and taken out of action. Fortunately, he was able to complete his letter and give an account of the Fromelles action while in the process of being evacuated from France.

"Somewhere" in France
18th July '16

Dear Dad,

I got Dorothy's letter of 27th Mch from East Melbourne, yours of 4th & 18th Apl & 1st May, one from Warrack 2nd May, Mothers of 28th Mch, 4th Apl & 2nd May & one from Billy Moulder of 6th Mch—also a Christmas Card (minus the picture) from Miss Clements a few weeks ago—Lack of opportunity & green envelopes have precluded my writing acknowledgments in detail, please convey to them my acknowledgments & thanks.

I xpect you know that I'm in a different regiment—I sent a card giving the alteration. Had a 2 day & 3 night trip through France—continuous travelling—its a glorious country, specially South & Central Lyons Dijonville & Rouen etc, & we had a great deal of hand waving en route.

We may be right in the thick of it any hour now, on the verge—& somebody is going to get a mauling—we're going to demonstrate the Marne to them over again. It raises anger in a fellow to think of the coarse, gross, brutal German attacking a cultured people such as the French & to see the great numbers of women & children dressed in mourning right through France. By God, there will be some mourning in Germany if we're spared to be with them for a few hours. You can't even begin to realize the amount of munitions & warlike stores everywhere, it's colossal. And even the German language, their Hobengibberish is an insult to the ear & mind.

I wonder if that draft for £200 reached you alright £60 for Joe Bishop £70 for Geo Russell (to be put to their credit at the Savings Bank), and £70 I sent you to use as you like. This sum was sent to you from Tel-el-Kebir on 26th March through the field cashier & I have now a further credit balance, including defferred pay of a little over £80—So, you know!

I haven't got much time now so will have to hurry to a conclusion. I keep a couple of letters from you & from mother & read them often, two I got in Egypt early in 1915—If, when sometimes I get down in the dumps they pick me up—spiritual brandies & sodas so to speak—and I "Keep a going"

[50]In Hospital 5th Aug '16—Well "here we are again". I had to break off this letter in a hurry & stick it in my pocket—the water stains were caused by my falling into a creek in "no mans land" on 19th July—it was in my breast pocket so didn't suffer much, anyhow it's legible.

So, as I expected, it wasn't long before we had a fly at the Huns, and once again my luck was in. As Billy Moulder said in his letter I wasn't <u>always</u> lucky, I didn't <u>always</u> find the Daisy Lobsters. It must be the Law of Compensation, or "Blonnyhossy". I cannot state the losses in my regiment on the 19th but they were <u>12.50 G.M.</u> on the wrong side. "Luck is nine points of the law"—see! How the dickens I got through the Lord only knows—I don't! I'd better start at the beginning however—We had a march of about 20 miles or more to the scene of operations & hung round for a week or so—I'm a grenadier & went up into supports the day before the action—Coming under heavy shell fire en route and after arrival—had some close calls too, one 8.2 dropped 10 ft away from me. I only got the mud.

First night had a gas alarm & suffocated in a medicated helmet & goggles for an hour—but nothing doing our way—morning of 19th July heavy shell fire as an aid to digestion of and accompaniment of breakfast—continuing right on throughout the day, about 4 pm got orders to move to firing line—off we went along communication trench which was <u>not</u> forgotten by Fritz—these trenches were caved in in places by shell fire & were hard to negotiate with our rifles equipment & grenades, food, water & waterproof sheets etc & to make matters worse there was another gas alarm, it was blue murder—hot under the best conditions—but with these suffocating helmets on it was like—er—"going to father" and again no gas transpired.

Got to the firing line & made our way to our positions—the artillery was now going it hammer & tongs—all high explosive & 4.1 universal H.E. shrapnel—the Boches were using from 12" stuff downward we had 9.2" & 6" etc. The air & earth rocked—literally rocked—the concussion would make one lose his balance—both mentally & physically. I'm enclosing a cutting from a London Paper of 4th inst (Yesterday's), you can read it here, and after.

Hundreds of guns were "at it" on both sides, I think both must have been about equal & the Hunnish gunners certainly know their work. Officers stood (as at Lone Pine) with watches in their hands, waiting to give the word "go"—or rather "Come"—10 minutes to go 8, 7, 6, 5, 4, 3 to go, 2, 1, get ready, go! We went over in 4 lines & I'm told there was hardly a man funked "jumping the parapet". Unfortunately for us the enemy machine guns had not been silenced and no sooner did the first man show himself than there broke out a hellish clatter of fire, scores of M. guns mowing over the open ground between the trenches. Scores dropped back dead & wounded in the act of getting out of the trenches but the rest went on, most meeting a similar fate more or less farther out. I fell foul of some barbed wire entanglements that had not been swept away, but got out and through somehow xpecting every second to be laid out. Shrapnel also was now tearing & sweeping across No Man's Land & we felt rather uncomfortable.

I was going well with 15 grenades in a carrier round my neck & bayonet fixed when down she comes & up I go—a huge shell wallops into the ground at my side—I remember being in the air and falling with my bayonet sticking straight for my solar plexus—anyhow I missed it. The flash roar & concussion of the explosion knocked me out & when I came to I tell you I could see Zig-Zags—Forked Lightning etc all in Red. I was lying on one edge of the crater & my

Australians waiting in trenches just prior to the battle of Fromelles, only three of these men survived and all three were wounded. (AWM A03042)

rifle on the other so it must have given me a good toss. I crawled into the hole then, about 8 ft dia & 3 ft deep & had a think. Had a maddening ringing in the ears.

Then I started towards the German trenches, went about 50 yards & came to an old shallow trench about 1 foot deep & 18" wide, I got into this in a hurry there were some other chaps here but not many crawled along this till I could get a good view of the scenery—there were no signs of anybody moving & it was evident the "<u>forlorn hope</u>" had failed. We held a consultation: Some were for trying to regain our lines, but we decided to wait till dark. [51]So we waited—and under the circumstances "wait" is a big word. Shrapnel was driving across no man's land like hailstones in hell. It's what is known as a "barrage" or "curtain fire"—it certainly acts the part of a curtain, it's to all intents & purposes impassable—and the smoke greyish black and white (various types) forms a pall. It was now very evident to me that the attack had been stopped in our sector at least so I strongly was in favour of holding what we had & digging in pending word from either flank—there were a couple of sergeants near & at dusk they decided to retire on our trenches, and so back they went—at dusk the flares started as usual—magnesium flares in appearance not unlike a shot gun cartridge & fired from a pistol, also longer ones 5 to 10 inches long—the latter on reaching its zenith opening out & forming a parachute—of all the world like an electric bulb under a shade & lasting perhaps 11/2 minutes—these two latter are 11/2" diameter & are fired from a small gun from the shoulder. The ground was wet & like pug & I clawed it out with my hands & rolled it into balls like a small football & threw these out. I was wet through (fell in a creek) and it kept me from freezing—by morning I was down 3 feet.

About midnight word was passed out that we were to retire but we weren't satisfied (these same tricks had been tried (and succeeded) on us in Gallipoli.[ )]

It was about this time—perhaps before midnight as I was having a stealthy look round that a chap crawled into the trench we were digging—I asked him who & what he was—he was Harry Richards (son of Jimmy Richards the engine driver) he's a C.S. Major 60th Bn—he had cigarettes and matches—dry ones—also. We smoked—for a match may be struck with impunity in no man's land where it is at night as light as day mostly.

After a long & anxious night dawn came at last, light enough to distinguish colors, for the flares shed a ghostly light—something like a pale green limelight. Our poor little trench was full of a yellowish green haze with a strong smell of sulphur, it only wanted the "Old Lad" himself with his pitchfork to complete the picture. There was also a fog so we decided to investigate in our vicinity. After a lot of crawling we came to the conclusion that we were isolated, but decided to wait till the fog lifted to make sure—also that we didn't go to the wrong trenches. So we lay in a depression in the ground—about 10 o'clock the fog dissipated & we started back (going west).

The first wounded man I came across was my old platoon commander a Mr Anderson, shot through the chest—in just above the right nipple & out between his shoulder blades—he was lying in a shallow gutter on his back & with his gas helmet on his breast, ready to put on (he had had it on during the night he told me). No fewer than 9 huge shells had fallen in a circle round him—probably 8.2" stuff H.E & he was spattered with earth—ears full of it—not one had fallen less than 20 feet away from him, some only 6 ft away, but it's marvellous how one escapes in a bit of a depression in the soft earth.

We got him on a waterproof sheet & tried to take him with us but he couldn't stand the pain of moving him. I don't think he was ever so pleased to see anyone in his life as he was to see me—"How are the boys going" first, then "I can'na breathe but I don't want to go to Berlin this way" (He's a Glasgow chap) I told him I was going for a stretcher & would take him in—he said—All right, Martindale I know you'll not desert me. (We had both been through the Gallipoli mill & were both at the landing there & this begets confidence in one another).

Well I crawled back to our trenches about 400 yards & asked for a stretcher—they looked at me—there were no stretchers and anyhow no stretcher parties were to go out till nightfall. An officer told me that the remnant of my battalion had been relieved that morning & that I was to go out too. It was forbidden for any one to go out again in front. I nodded & walked away & then my eye fell on a scaling ladder about 7 ft long & nice & light.

The officer disappeared, so did I, with the ladder & got out again safely dragging the ladder beside me. I could have howled with rage & mortification when I found there were no stretchers, but soon felt mighty pleased with myself. Got my officer on the stretcher cum ladder & off we sneaked 5 or 10 yards at a time for he was heavy & I was very weak my knees knocking together. We stopped frequently to help the poor beggars who were lying about everywhere, begging for water. We helped & directed about a dozen chaps who were able to crawl, enabling them to regain our lines.

One chap shot through the arm would make no effort to help himself. I tried in vain to get him to move but no, he wanted a stretcher. He might just as well have wanted the moon. Oh, well, I said at last its no use leaving you here to be captured by Fritz or to die of thirst at the same time taking out my persuader—trenching tool handle with cast iron cog attached[52] (these are used in raiding jaunts—they don't take much room to wield & they don't make much noise)—I'll kill you now—He arrived in our lines & had his wound bandaged before I got back—If he hadn't gone I believe I'd have killed him, just for luck!

Another poor fellow I found up to his neck in the creek, one eye knocked out & his elbow smashed to pulp—I got him in too. He was as game as the Great Devil. With his arm off he'd make another Lord Nelson. I believe he would recover.

After an hours hard graft we had only about 100 yards to go. I had now another assistant a Lance Corporal of the 60th & now bad luck overtook us Lieut Anderson getting a bullet through his buttock. The smack & his groan & I went clean Berserker. I grabbed my revolver I know & flourished it in the direction of the swine who fire on the wounded—for such is their custom—damn them. I yelled why the Hell didn't they hit me if anyone was to be hit & so on. This exhibition of rage & disgust was but momentary however.

When I looked round my helper had gone & we had still 40 yards to go. I tried to drag the ladder sledge fashion but it ploughed into the ground & wouldn't free. So I picked him up in my arms & had another go and nearly got to cover when he was hit again through the ankle—anyhow I got him to a covering bank & laid him down (he's about 12 stone) he said then that he thought he could crawl—and crawl he did—about 50 or 60 yards & into our own lines. Just as we got in several stretcher parties came along one chap being a tent mate of mine at Broadmeadows in the old 5th (Bill Houghton is his name). I at once called him & he & his mate took Mr Anderson straight off to the dressing station.

(Later Again) This is a kind of "to be continued". I've just read through the foregoing & have missed a few points I was going to mention, but let them pass. Do you remember my telling you how I discovered & appropriated 7,000 rounds of Small Arm Ammunition in Gallipoli the day after the landing. My Platoon Sergeant was mentioned in dispatches.[53] He is now a Major—I met him again in no man's land—hadn't seen him for several months he has also the Military Cross (Lone Pine). He & I got several poor devils in. About 2 o'clock p.m. 20th I left the trenches, going back—& though there was nothing extraordinary doing I felt mighty nervous. If a shell howled a "Dead March" overhead or landed within 200 yards I'd bob down for a second. I walked or wobbled a mile to the rear & then my knees would hardly hold me up, but I <u>made</u> them. You can do what you <u>must</u> do! I got a lift back (altogether 4 miles) in a limber, though its against orders, the driver stopped & helped me in. I didn't argue.

When I reached the billet where the 59th were, men of other regiments ran out & helped me in, taking my rifle & equipment & dishing me out some tea—I told them to wake me at night as I intended going back to have another go at getting the wounded. Our Regimental Sergeant Major said he would call me—but he didn't. Anyhow there was no need as there were plenty of fresh men. When I woke in the morning I could just stand. I was fully dressed & my clothes were still wet, puttees caked with mud, blood all over me, hands torn by barbed wire & thorns, a patch the size of half a crown off each side of my forehead caused by a piece of shell striking my "tin hat" which had quite a respectable bulge, though not pierced.

I staggered out & there were a couple of A.M.C chaps applying priming coats of iodine to various parts of patients' anatomies, they painted my hands & head. I had a look at myself in a mirror just afterwards & got a bit of a shock, I looked a proper wild man from Borneo, with whiskers blood iodine smoke & grime blended on my visage.

At noon there was a roll-call. We went into action 2 score hours previously a virgin regiment—(90 per cent or more had never seen a shot fired in anger) a regiment at full strength—ninety seven answered their names—not one in ten, 97 out of 1,000 and all practically within half an hour. It's ghastly—shocking, horrible. Our neighbouring regiment the 60th fared even worse less than 80 (eighty) answering their names—out of a thousand—Of the two regiments not one officer escaped being killed or wounded. Our brigade bore the brunt of the action, and paid heavily, gloriously.

Through all this frightful time when every second we knew not which would be our last as sound men or this side of eternity I heard no sound of complaint, the wounded were splendid, the unwounded also, though all suffered. Our Brigadier "Pompey" (Bgr. Gen.l Elliott) is as game as they make 'em. In my Company Commander I mourn the death of a brave soldier and a gentleman (Captain Liddelow). He fell at the head of his Company "C" with his face to the enemy, and his revolver in his hand. He served through the Gallipoli campaign, where he was wounded. I saw him just before the word to "go over" was given, he nodded to me and smiled for we were friends. <u>He knew he was "going west".</u> I read it in his face like an open book but he never flinched or faltered. Whilst the Empire produces men of Captain Liddelow's type, it is safe.

Some men of my section who sheltered in the creek after I implored them to get out were killed. I found them on my way back. They would not listen to my assurance that the front line or row is the safest place in attack. I'll not say anything about the losses to our division, or how they were flooded & shelled out of some trenches they took on our left. I'll say nothing about the whole attack. I might say too much—or not enough. I'll continue this shortly.

Affectionately
George

A photo taken while George was convalescing in England. George is in the overcoat and is now a Corporal.

PART SIX:

# CONVALESCENCE

Mrs Martindale
Dimboola. V.

REGRET REPORTED CORPORAL GEORGE G.
MARTINDALE WOUNDED WILL PROMPTLY ADVISE IF
ANYTHING FURTHER RECEIVED.
BASE RECORDS.
2/9/16[54]

*'Altogether the book is a pitiful & puerile production!'* George's
opinion of Charles Bean's *The Anzac Book*, October 1916

George's evacuation from France to England was detailed in his service record in a series of transfers: 'Wounded in Action France 3/8/16'—'Admit 30th Gen Hosp G.S.W. thigh Calais 6/8/16'—'Embkd for England on H.S. *Newhaven* G.S.W. thigh Calais 11/8/16'—'Admitt Woodcote Park Con. Hosp G.S.W. left thigh 25/8/16'—'Adm Royal Surrey County Hosp Guildford 12/8/16'. Yet, while serious enough to have him removed from the front, the fact that he was writing letters indicates he was probably not in imminent danger of expiration.

It was almost a month after being hit in his thigh when the military authorities sent a cablegram to George's mother—officially next-of-kin—regrettably reporting his having been wounded.[55] Within a week, George had also personally sent a message to his parents. The news, as so often for the Dimboola boys, made the *Dimboola Banner*. Apparently George had 'stated that his wound was in one of his legs, and that he was in hospital in London and was progressing favourably.'[56]

Probably both troubled and relieved to hear from him, the latest letters to George were already en route, the reception of which seems to have prompted George into again writing home. Only some of the letters appear to have survived, a partial letter from his father being a case in point, for which only the last two pages remain. There were also others referred to in the various letters, which have been lost or dispersed.

George's next batch of surviving correspondence, which detailed the circumstances of his wounding, had something of a homecoming theme. By being wounded and evacuated to England, George fell in with a number of old acquaintances and extended family. He had an uncle and aunt in England, with whom he communicated. George was named after his 'uncle George', after all, the Reverent George Gowthorp Martindale, and the families seem to have been regular correspondents even before the war. George's father had migrated to Victoria from Yorkshire and still had close ties to his homeland.

George also fell in with a number of mates, detailed in the letters. Similarly, such mates enjoyed meeting George, including the Dimboola lad Les Hirth, who subsequently recorded meeting with George. Hirth was a fresh recruit who spent time in training in England before heading to France. He described meeting various fellows from Dimboola at Hurdcott Camp in Salisbury Plain on Friday 17 November, which included 'G. Martindale, who had been through the fight at Gallipoli without a scratch, but was wounded in France four months ago.'[57] Apparently that Sunday it snowed, 'and snow-ball fighting was greatly indulged in.'

George was by now in a training brigade, still recuperating from his injuries and being readied for return to the front. But George, like other Australian soldiers, took the opportunity of exploring the country of their ancestors. A week after meeting Hirth, some of the Dimboola boys, including George, took an outing to visit a nearby historic site. Hirth wrote,

Sunday [26 November 1916] was fine, so George Martindale, J. Hooke, and I went to Salisbury. We saw the famous old cathedral, which was built in the year 1052. The structure is glorious, and figures of well-known bishops and kings are carved on the outer wall. The rear portion of the church is a cemetery, where families of high birth are buried, while the remainder of the cathedral is used for services. The choir is composed of boys only; their voices are beautiful. After tea, which cost us 2s for eggs and bacon, we went back. On arrival at camp we had to return our rifles to the armory, and place our kits in a special hut.

George's letters revealed to his family that he saw other famous places as well, but his conversation with his family concerned stories from his real home: Australia. In particular, the question of conscription interested him. A referendum of October 1916 asked Australians whether to support compulsory overseas military service, and some of the arguments put forward about it clearly riled George. During this time he was frequently reminded of the losses Australia had already suffered, especially as he wrote various letters of condolence, only one example of which has serendipitously survived. George's attitude towards the question was, at best, ambivalent.

Meanwhile, Hirth and George parted ways, as the former was sent on to London. There Hirth 'met an old school-chum, Peter Martindale, who seems to be enjoying himself.' George's brother was now in England. As he tried to stay on top of Australian news, and give his family members accounts of his former fighting actions, George also tried to make contact with Peter while his English break from the frontline steadily ebbed away.

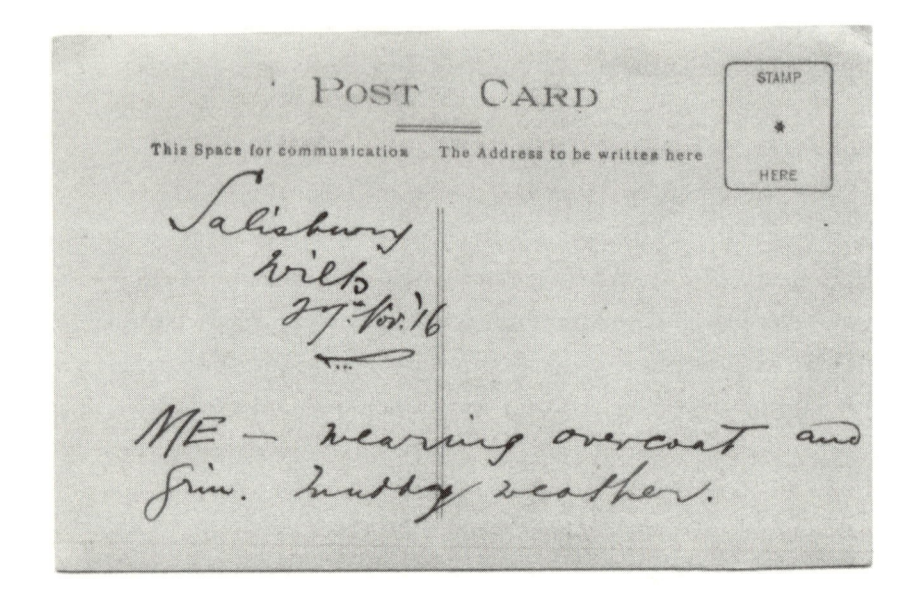

# CONVALESCENCE

Dimboola 16 May 1916 Tuesday

Dear George

Just a few lines to say we are all well at home and to hope that you are well & hearty. Also to say that a remittance of £200 came to hand on Saturday last (13th) £70 from you, £70 from No 892 Pte G. Russell & £60 from No 960 Pte J. Bishop. I placed it in the Savings Bank the same day in my trust a/c. I trust to have the privilege of withdrawing it & handing it back when you have completed your job & return good men & true in full enjoyment of health and a capacity to enjoy the using of it to the advantages of yourselves. I have not had any advice from you so far about sending it. The 1st I knew of it was from the P.O. & then I thought—Russell & Bishop—I can't place them—Next day I thought of the Honor Roll & I noticed that the numbers were not far away from yours, so looked up the names in the old H Coy 5th Battn & there they were. I expect to hear from you & them shortly giving some directions as to its disposal. The claim form which I had to sign described you as Lance Cpl, we have been under the impression that you have been Corporal since last Aug probably it was a clerical error. Peter is now in the Royal Park Camp, he came home on leave on Friday night & went back last night. He looks well & is very well grown, the camp life will do him good, but at the same time I think it is rotten business to be taking boys like him & permitting fully developed men, with large possessions etc to remain undisturbed at home, business or no business.

You are now no doubt somewhere in France but we are not getting any details. We have had two lists of casualties, but as you have all been shuffled up so much we can't tell what Brigades are engaged. Bill Dalitz wrote from Egypt on March 31st & probably you had not left then. I hope & believe your experiences will not be of such an exhausting kind as they were on the G. Penla. I can't discern any appearance of the end approaching but of course I haven't got the real data on which to base an opinion. I think the Germans have plenty of resources yet & it will take a long time to wear them down. The day of winning wars by a day or two's brilliant manoeuvring is over and it is now more of a tug of war. Britain & the Dependencies must mobilise all their resources & get them hanging on to the rope & until that is done there is not much hope of a satisfactory decision.

Ted Gooding & Jack Schneider had a cause celebre in the court of P.S. today. Jack planted one on Ted & laid him out for a qtr hour. Ted may have had over 10 drinks but not 20 on that day. Ike Harkins was the principal witness. Schneider was mulct[58] in the sum of 10/- & costs. The population came from near & far to be on the spot to get the early news. But you will get it all in the Banner. It is just starting to rain, we have had no rain at all up to the present & it is badly needed, but I think it means business now. From press reports climatic conditions etc etc are very agreeable somewhere in France & I hope they will continue so for you & the Army. Time is now up so must close with best wishes for your safety, Father.

I have written to Bishop & Russell acknowledging remittances.

CONVALESCENCE

Codford, Wiltshire
21st October 1916

Dear Maggie

Today is the second anniversary of the sailing of the 5th Bn from Melbourne; Trafalgar Day. I'm afraid I've developed into a poor correspondent, but we are so fooled about that its hard to settle down to anything. I wrote from France & England after I was wounded. Also sent a cable. This place is not far from Stonehenge, Salisbury Plain, about 12 or 14 miles. I had a trip over there on Sunday last & fell in with some New Zealanders. We get on well with them & are great pals—but we don't hit it too well with the Canadians. Likewise we get on well with the Tommies. I had a real good outing and am enclosing some snapshots of Stonehenge. You'll notice me wearing a cap. My felt hat was altogether too disreputable. I wore it several months in Egypt & a couple of months in France & it was always too small so I had to tear the leather lining out. So I discarded it in London and bought this cap. 11/6. I'm still wearing the same uniform I had in Egypt and in the mud & filthy billets (mostly stables) in France. Both tunic & breeches are blood stained—the stains simply wont wash out. The authorities are too beastly parsimonious to issue a decent new rig-out, and will not advance sufficient pay to enable a fellow to buy a decent rig-out. I'm going to remit as soon as possible through the pay office the whole of the money due to me, apart of course from deferred pay, and I have already made an allotment in Mother's favour of 3/- a day. Anyhow to get back to the snapshots I don't think they're too bad & the stains & mends don't show. When at Epsom I met Domeyer & we had our photos taken together near an ambulance he is driving. I've got the film & will post it and some prints.

Beastly bad manners writing both sides of the paper <u>and</u> leaving no margin. But its war time & we must economise!!! I hope you got those photos I sent some time back—taken in hospital. I don't think

I'll be able to write a coherent letter unless I go right back to just before the time I was hit. I've given a bit of an account of the scrap of 19th July in a previous letter. After a few days out (not resting) we got some brand new reinforcements oh! Such loves!!!—I was as much scared of them as I was of Fritz & went back to the trenches—I was now transferred to "D" Coy 59th Bn and was acting coy sergeant-major. On the evening of the 2nd Aug, when we were assembled ready to go into the first line trenches—we were 12 hrs 8 pm to 8 am in these daily—I warned the men (64 of 'em) not to show themselves or their equipment, blankets etc, during the day time & not to rush round the "dixies" like hungry wolves at meal times. I told them what the consequences would be, and that it would not be pleasant, but certainly instructive, and destructive: but of course they knew all about it, oh yes! Took 'em in through the communication trench & was awake all night, for our line was thin & I knew the sort of material I had. In the morning on going back to the supports, 300 yards in rear of 1st line trench, I went as usual hunting up ammunition & grenades etc with a party of pioneers. When I got back there was a Hun aeroplane up & the pack of fools in the supports standing (and moving) about in knots gaping at it. I knew what the result would be. Told the fools to get what cover they could—and it was mighty little, the worst apology for a trench its been my misfortune to see or occupy. Ten minutes later the ball opened. I've been in some tidy brawls but I never saw such a scatter in my whole experience. "Oh, my God! where will I go", some wailed as they ducked this way & that: To H— probably I retorted if you don't lie down and keep down. They had brought the shelling on themselves through knowing too much, or not enough. Fancy watching enemy aircraft as though it was a football match! They gave us about 10 minutes of it altogether I should judge. 5 chaps were lying close together about 2 yards from me, I was sitting close in to the parapet with about 4 feet of earth between me and the 6" stuff they were

TOP RIGHT: The Martindales were builders and carpenters and also did the undertaking in the small town of Dimboola, in the Wimmera region of western Victoria. Photo c.1895

RIGHT: The Martindale family was highly respected in Dimboola, owning a number of businesses including a hardware store. Photo c.1895

BELOW: The box of memorabilia, medals and letters that the family has kept since George Martindale died in 1922.

## THE WAR ALPHABET.

By MICHAEL DWYER.

A for Australia we're leaving behind,
B for Berlin where peace will be signed.
C for the Colonials, the boys who can fight,
D for The Day when our wrongs we shall right.
E for old England, to where we are bound,
F for the Flag we've all rallied round.
G stands for Germany, of honour bereft,
H for His Highness King George V.
I for his Indian troops on the field,
J stands for Justice we'll have e'er we yeild.
K for the Kaiser, who's fighting in vain,
L for the Losses his army sustain.
M for Montenegro that brave little state,
N for our Navy that's doing first rate.
O for "Orvieto," the best troopship of all,
P for the Patriots, who answered Kitchener's call
Q for the Queenslanders, who'll fight by our side,
R for the Russians, who are with us allied.
S for the "Sydney," which made the "Emden" a wreck,
T for the Time, when again we'll come back.
U for the Unity, amongst us you'll find
V for Victorians, all bear in mind.
W for the War, to which we all go.
X is the only one Mic doesn't know.
Y is for You to try and find out,
Z for Zam-Buk, for the Kaiser we'll shout.

T.B.F.   Printed at Sea.

LEFT: The men were full of optimism and patriotism on their way to defend the Empire. At sea, the men would keep their spirits up with poems, songs and music. This was printed on board the *Orvieto* on its way to the Middle East.

BELOW: A postcard from George to his mother sent from Cairo, Egypt dated 20 January 1915.

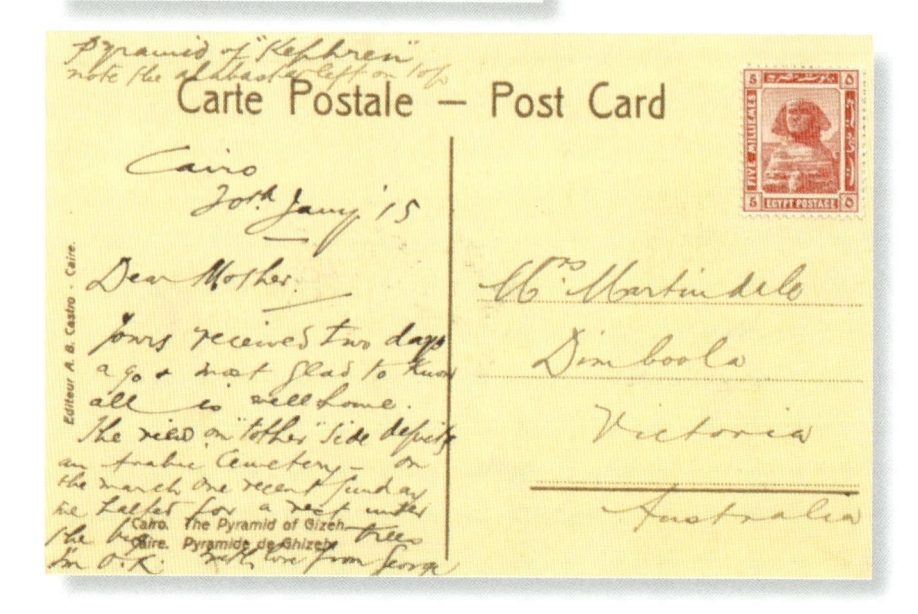

ABOVE: A letter from fellow Dimboola soldier, Henry D'Alton to George's father. In it he discusses Captain Charles Bean's newspaper report of Australian soldiers misbehaving in Egypt. Bean's description of some of the soldiers as 'bad 'uns', and 'wasters' was taken as an affront by the Australians.

ABOVE: One of George's letters to his mother from Mena in Egypt, where he underwent training before being sent to fight in Gallipoli.

RIGHT: A letter to George's dad that had not been completed when George was sent into battle at Fromelles. George and the letter survived the infamous battle, even though the Allies suffered 5533 casualties in one night. The letter got a soaking in the mud of Fromelles.

Somewhere in France
19th July 16

Dear Dad

I got Dorothy's letter of 27th Feb from East Melbourne, yours of 4th & 15th April & 1st May, one from Warrack 2nd May, Mother's of 26th Mch, 15th April & 2nd May, & one from Billy Monede of 6th Mch — also a Christmas Card (missing the picture) from Miss Clements a few weeks ago. — Lack of opportunity & green envelopes have precluded my writing acknowledgments in detail. Please convey to them my acknowledgments & thanks. I expect you know that I'm in a different regiment. I sent a card giving the addresses. Had a 2 day & 3 night trip through France — continuous travelling — it's a glorious country. Specially South & Central. From Dijonville & Rouen &c, & we had a great deal of hand waving en route. We may be right in the thick of it any hour now, on the verge — & somebody is going to get a hammering — we're going to demonstrate the Marne to them over again. It just raises anger in a fellow to think of the Brutal, Cruel, brutal German attacking a cultured people

LEFT: The report of George Martindale's injury written by a fellow soldier who saw him fall. This was the most common way of reporting amd tracking casualties and deaths on the battlefield.

BELOW: Part of the official army documentation regarding George's injuries.

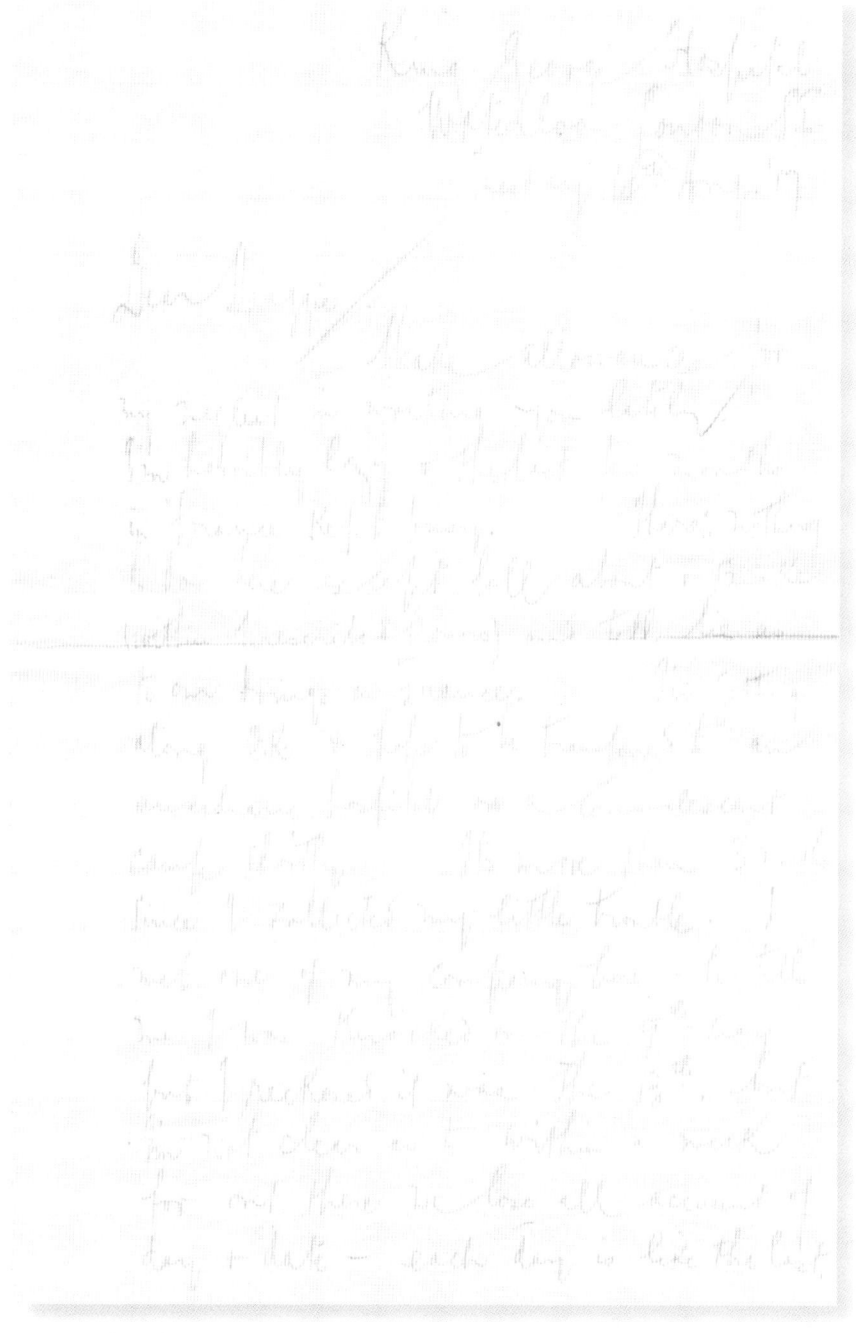

ABOVE: A letter home three months after George's injury in which he hopes to be moved to a convalescent camp. He was returned to Australia as unfit for work of any kind in 1918. George died only four years after the end of the First World War, as a result of his injuries.

LEFT: George after his war service ended, his damaged eye obscured by his hat. He is holding the hands of his nieces, Florence (left) and Marjorie (right). Marjorie kept his letters and memorabilia and handed them down through the family.

BELOW: George's medals and identity disks. George was promoted up the ranks but twice he reverted to private at his own request. He ended his time in uniform as a sergeant.

sending over. One just cut the top off the parapet (which was only 6' high) knocked a barrow load of earth over me & burst 25 feet away. The next fell in front of the parapet perhaps a yard or two away, the ground fairly rocked, the next one I guessed would fairly cap us and I guessed right. Can you imagine what it is to live presumably your last minute on earth? I conclude not! It's an experience believe me which doesn't invite envy in large quantities. I knew a shell was coming, and coming close, but I have made a point of not rushing about, a fellow may run into one. Presently I heard that horrible, express-train-dashing-through-a-tunnel sound, and it arrived a 6" fair through the parapet and among the 5 chaps near me.[59] There was a crash, a perfectly detonated shell, the parapet being enough to explode it. A yell that I could hear for days, one poor devil had shell shock & was slightly wounded, another very badly wounded and three killed outright. I felt as though I'd been hit with a hammer on the left thigh, but took no notice, as it didn't hurt, about 4 or 5 more shells and the bombardment ceased. I told the chaps to keep down, not that they needed much telling & called for stretcher-bearers. These were promptly on the scene and bandaged the two wounded chaps, the fellow with S.S. howling like a fiend when touched. Then they set off to the dressing station. An officer now appeared and said hullo! you're wounded too. Oh! it's nothing only a scratch I said. He turned an A.M.C. man onto me, bandaged it & got another stretcher. I didn't want to leave the trench, but the officer ordered me to go—then I wanted to walk, but No! I had to go on a stretcher.

We overtook the other wounded chaps & got to the dressing station. Here the shell shock chap died, and the other on the following day. Our M.O. here had a look at my leg & re-bandaged it, then my stretcher was lifted onto a carriage with 2 bicycle like wheels (very comfy—thanks!) and off to the motor ambulance on the road. Then off to a field-ambulance and on the operating table, shaved the leg & cut the wound open, on with a pair of rubber gloves

DODGING THE DEVIL

& in with the middle finger, also a probe like a ~~darning~~ knitting needle, nothing doing, back on stretcher after bandaging & had a bowl of tea & bread & margarine—"quais kiteen" (in Arabic "very good") then into another motor ambulance and along to Estaines, and under blankets—also undressed—it's grand to be able to take your clothes off say once a week!

Here there were nurses—the hospital was a school vacated for the purpose—Through the windows I could see the Huns shells bursting round a dozen or so of our aeroplanes, and a couple of fragments fell just outside. There is no doubt as to which side has the mastery in the air. The Huns are like the boy that fell out of the balloon— not in it. Our aircraft do as they like, cross over the German lines, sometimes singly, in pairs and in scores. If the Germans cross our lines they fly very high. Too high for effective observation and they soon sheer off. Our craft fly quite low, low enough to see the pilot.

Here the nurses relieved me of my collar badges—I gave them to them—the Copper Rising Sun. I also lost my revolver here. More tea & bread & margarine and bacon. That night I had a good sleep, and a wash in warm water. It was not hard to take. Breakfast and a smoke and then on the operating table again, more probing & mighty unpleasant. Nothing doing. After a couple of days was put on a convoy (Red + train) and off to Calais—as we passed the sentries (poilus), they presented arms, the old men raised their hats & the women & children waved. These demonstrations of respect and sympathy are more touching than you can imagine, and are quite characteristic of the French.

At Calais we were met by the Scottish Womens Branch of the B.R.C.Scy.[60]—all in khaki uniform, short skirts & strong leather boots with caps which covered all their hair—like a bathing cap or munition workers cap. They were very business like—got us into the ambulances and off to the hospital. It was a treat to hear these girls (some of 'em <u>not</u> flappers) after the everlasting "no compre", when the Flanders ladies didn't want to understand. I was told afterwards that they were all well to do and provided their own cars and upkeep. I know of some ladies (?) in Dimboola who would not stoop (?) to such a task as ministering to a beastly common soldier. He might be no class—not respectable! but then soldiers' blood does not run in their veins, just a thin ungenerous liquid they fondly imagine to be blood! I think the thing that has struck me most forcibly since I was knocked is the splendid way the women of England & France too, generally speaking, have responded to the call of Duty to their Country. I wonder if the women in Australia are doing as much? They have not had the horrors of war thrust on them as have the women of France. There almost every woman & child is dressed in black. Of course one sees the other type, she is merely a well-dressed appetite for pleasure that other people are paid to satisfy, and as much beneath the war worker in any capacity as the mushroom is beneath the moon.

The hospital at Calais consisted of big marquees. On arrival I got clean clothes and had a bath in a bucket of hot water, most enjoyable, and then oh! for the first time in two years I found myself in bed—<u>in bed</u>—and with clean white sheets & pillows and a white counterpane. There were some chaps here I knew and who were wounded on 19th July. I was tired after the train journey, so after more tea I slept—and what a sleep. We could get English papers here.

Did I tell you what part of France I was in when hit? it was near Armentieres near the Belgian frontier and about 8 miles from the big city of Lille. I was X rayed here (Calais) and they decided to send me to "Blighty" (England). So accordingly we found ourselves on stretchers and in the Scotswomen's ambulances and taken off to the pier, alongside the hospital ships—A French officer came up chatted for a couple of minutes (after saluting & shaking hands of course) and handed over some cigarettes, our "Chaffeuress" also gave us some and some chocolate. Taken aboard & sent down a chute & into bunks, I was now nicely out of the nurses view & decided to see if I could walk. Leg was stiff, but I could do very well, and got up on deck. We were aboard for 24 hours before sailing. Then off we went 3 hospital ships in single file and saw the usual mine sweeping going on. Left about 10 o'clock in the morning and were nearly 2 hours crossing the channel, arriving in Dover at 12 noon. Had just tied up when a Hun sea-plane appeared & was fired on by anti-aircraft guns, she dropped a few bombs, doing slight damage and then cleared off. Disembarked and were taken aboard Red + Train and into bunks, and started off, no-one knew where. Ladies brought us flowers, cigarettes & chocolate when on the train. Had a good look at the scenery as we passed through near London & duly arrived at Guildford in Surrey. Into ambulance again and taken to the Red Cross Annexe Royal Surrey County Hospital & upstairs. Whilst on the train we were classified bullet wounds, shell wounds, fractures etc, being placed in separate wards as much as possible—each ward is named after some celebrity as—Jellicoe, Albert, Mary, Nicholas—I was in the "Fisher" ward, 10 beds. As soon as I arrived, I changed again into clean clothes & had a wash, it was about 10 pm, had tea & cake!! This annexe is a girls' school & quite new. On the way from the station I was inundated with cigarettes, fruit, chocolate etc.

We were about the first batch of Australians to arrive in Hospital at Guildford & were quite a curiosity. The patients in each ward are attended by a civilian doctor; these give their time & services without payment, each ward has its own Dr. It was decided to heal the wound in my leg & then operate. I was again x rayed & the lady radiographer a golden haired young woman who had lost her husband in France, introduced me to her mother, a South African, & I had several nice trips in her car, with the eternal cigarettes in. Leg healed nicely—no trouble. So the Dr decided to leave the piece of shell where it was as it didn't trouble me. So I've got a souvenir

CONVALESCENCE

in a nice safe place, where it's not very likely to be lost, unless in the future Fritz knocks the whole leg off. The nurses were extremely kind to us all, also some St John of Jerusalem men. One nurse brought us eggs & cigarettes every morning, she had chucks of her own, another brought apples from her own garden, & we went for "afternoons out" to yet other nurses places.

Guildford is a very old town of 25,000 people & is very interesting. A little girl of 15 years took a great fancy to me er hem! no accounting for taste! and duly carted me off home to hear her play "The Maidens Prayer", of course I enjoyed it very much; at least I said so—and at times it's forgivable to prevaricate. I gave her my hat badge & she was overjoyed. We had invitations from scores of people to visit them & often availed ourselves thereof. On these occasions we would practice "putting" (golf) throw rings on pegs, croquet & bowls. I'm quite an expert at the latter. Prizes were awarded in the shape of socks—woollen & hand knitted, and each of us got a pair. But sitting down to a nicely appointed table for tea!!!!—Bread & butter—<u>brown</u> bread cut thin and <u>real</u> butter. Thin <u>china</u> cups & saucers—comfortable chairs and <u>clean</u> white table linen & silver spoons—great old oak beams black with age in the ceiling, which were generally only about 8'6" high, and oil paintings on the walls. It's almost worth enduring the privations & horrors of this war to experience the pleasure of once more getting back to the comforts of civilization. The people round Guildford are mostly fairly affluent & have nice substantial homes. The river (?) Wey runs through here & I saw an individual in khaki with the gold stripe (a small piece of gold braid 2" long x 1/8" wide sewn on left cuff) tackled by some Tommies just back from France—They discovered he had never been abroad or wounded in his life, so he went into the river (?) (its like a fair sized gutter) The language was prime, I feel that my education in that way had been sadly neglected—It was a shuddering oratoria of blasphemy. The fellow was just having a quiet swank.

When convalescent I went per motor ambulance to Epsom (Woodcote Park) close to the racecourse. I was sorry in a way to leave Guildford, where it was one big "loaf", at Epsom we had to make our own beds and weren't tucked in o'nights. That's the part that tickled me, the sister would come round about 10 pm to each of us & smooth out our pillows & tuck us in like so many babies instead of hard-bitten war-scarred veterans (?) We had to be in bed by 8 o'clock and it would not be dark till 10—long twilight. Then the electric light would be draped in red and the blinds drawn (Zepps). I had been in the Army considerably longer than any of the others in "Fisher" ward, and was the only one who had been in Gallipoli. Whilst there (hospital) an old lady (a nurse) brought me "The Anzac Book", and asked me what I thought of it. You'll notice that most of the contributors are of the Army Service Corps (A.S.C.) better known to us as the "Army Nervous Corps". They had plenty of time for writing (and trashy stuff it is—giving a wrong impression with few exceptions) whilst safely stowed away in shell proof shelters under the hills near the beach—These gentle creatures <u>sold</u> Maconochies Army Ration at 1/- a tin to those who were fortunate enough to have a "bob", and with the money thus obtained got stores from the ships and retailed these in turn at these immoral prices—salmon 3/6 tin, small pineapple 2/9, condensed milk 2/6 & 3/-, small sardines 1/- tin, small box matches c/p[61] 2d dozen—3d <u>per</u> <u>box</u>!—"Army Nervous Corps"—what a name & how well earned! Some of these budding authors would turn Ananias green with envy. The best I think are the drawings "Apricot again!" with its chagrin satiety & disgust, "Kitch"—Kitcheners Army & somewhat characteristic of the troops at Suvla Bay, and an advertisement near the back page re converted shells etc. Altogether the book is a pitiful & puerile production! But I'm digressing.

At Epsom I got a towel & piece of soap and a shirt—second hand, or second back, but could have the pleasure of a hot and cold shower bath every morning of which you may be sure I was not slow to avail myself. About a week after arriving at Epsom I was advanced the princely sum of five shillings. I'd received 40 Francs = £1·8·8 about 6 weeks previously in France—I felt a bit of a Croesus and immediately squandered 5d of it in the way of a hair-cut. I felt tempted to buy motor cars & jewellery with the rest—but restrained myself! I met here young Elliott of Antwerp & Dimboola. He has lost the right eye but otherwise looks very well. He will probably be home by New Year & I asked him to call & let you know he saw me.

Also met Domeyer—as I said before he is driving a motor ambulance of which I will send a photo. This was the first time I had seen him since the Battle of Lone Pine started 6th Aug 1915. He is looking same as ever. I was mighty glad to see him & he me & didn't the old tongues wag: we had an orgy of talking for a week, we joked & laughed & spoke seriously, discussed things ancient & modern. Talked of home & home people, the "good old times" out shooting & sparrow catching, fishing etc—I think one of the best outings in my life was one Saturday night duck shooting with poor old Henry D'Alton (we had Ob. Mac as side kicker and Don the bulldog who snored horribly in the wee small hours—Henry & I were in some straw & cursed him roundly) & the following day we had a splendid time among the hares rabbits and—tell it not in faith—pigeons (<u>not</u> bronzewings). That's the day we got Paddy Nicky? the terrier and the long, short legged, curly black mutton hound. Didn't he lead us a dance? I smile now as I think of it & how Rankin said "Bumper" will get him! but "Bumper" was a failure. We laughed over the way when, one Sunday morning we chased the aforementioned mutt and he swam the river near the Chinese Camp, and "Barney" alias "White Wings" fell with me & I sprawled into a muddy pool. He told me he sold him to Gebert for £3, and that he would owe me 30/- Ha Ha! We retold & laughed over the Antwerp trip when Barney kicked Gersch's gig to bits, also the disastrous consequences to Barney. We

DODGING THE DEVIL

agreed it was a pity he hadn't kicked the gig's owner. However that will keep. If I get home I'll disarrange his features—demonstrate the Marne to him over again—with others if necessary. Also the fishing trip to Antwerp with Sam Wilson—I'd just heard that poor old Sam has "Gone West". He was killed at Messines in Belgium by a shell outright. No suffering. They're getting us (the boys of the 1st Division) one by one. Who's next? At least Sam & I between us have cost the enemy very dear. "Sans regret" is the motto of the old 5th.

The ambulance came in very handy—we often went over to a club in a village called Ashstead about 1 1/2 miles from camp through some beautiful park land, where deer, rabbits, pheasants etc abound. It goes without saying that we had no designs on these—oh, dear no. We discussed mothers chickens in Domeyer's garden—he assures me he found them very plump (there was good picking in his garden, seeds etc) and tender. We didn't forget to live again our shooting excursions on the heath (beg pardon Dimboola Downs) when we cut a passage through a wire fence on the river frontage near Gambels and Walter called and started to gently chide us—we quoted him the first law of the Medes and Persians—"He who contraveneth the law etc."—he retired crestfallen—possibly to pray for us—or swear at us. Since that I've had some most exciting—or to be more precise—terrifying times cutting, not no. 8 wire, but barbed wire with the barbs as close and plentiful as devils in H—. In many cases the barbs are so close together as to preclude any possibility of getting the nippers between. I got to know quite a lot about barbed wire and invented a good scheme for "getting" the Hun patrols. I had charge for a few hours each night of about 350 yards of front line trench and carried the star shell and parachute gun. I'd go along to the Lewis guns and to the Maxims (machine guns), and after quite a pause fire a flare. They would be on the qui vive and let fly on the Huns barbed wire—I remember the first night I worked this. We killed two of the enemy patrol. I went over the lid later and had a look for myself, one big Hun was lying right across his own wire, he had evidently been standing up when—Domino! His pal was lying a yard away. It does one a lot of good to know he has sent a couple of these—er—well—potential <u>murderers</u> (they fire on the wounded) to plead their cause with the Great Judge. When I think (and that's often) of how my platoon commander was shot twice whilst I was carrying him back to our lines I ask nothing better than getting to <u>close</u> grips with these unspeakables. They'll get no mercy from me but there will be some strange faces in Hell. Mercy Kamerad! Bah! I'm drifting from England to France—I'll get back.

In Ashstead we got to know some very nice people who were down from London on account of Zeppelin risks (I think it ridiculous as one has about just as much chance of being struck by lightning as by a Zepp bomb). There were in the family father mother 7 girls and 1 boy (poor devil!) also an aunt, nurse, governess and servants. There was croquet playing galore but I preferred to loll back in an easy chair on the lawn and yarn and smoke my hosts most excellent cigars—close my eyes and think I was back in France or Egypt and then open 'em and find I wasn't. Then we'd go in and have tea and could never escape without a nice chocolate or iced cake each and pockets full of apples. I think auntie was a bit "shook" on Domeyer—she was about 40 not out. I asked him about it but he assured me he didn't love her—and I believe him—so would you if—! He would take a car load along with us for half a mile or so and then after a lot of oh!ing and squealing during the alighting process we would go on without them. They were jolly good sports. We heard Walter and Mary had made a match of it—affair of the heart and all that, and only agreed that it was a most romantic occurrence; he was ungentlemanly enough to suggest that it served 'em both right! Aint he a nasty man? And Walter has got 'em off! It's an ill wind that blows no one any good. Oh! while I think of it I met Rob Ross and Charlie McDonald (of State Forest Dept) and we had a great old chat and many a laugh. They both look very well. Also met Randolph Wall of Jeparit—hadn't seen him for many years and he's not too well and I'm told that Charlie Wall was killed at Fromelles near Armentieres on the 19th July—only a few hundred yards from where I was at the time. People in Australia often get news of what is transpiring here before we, half a mile away, know of it. I also met Sil Eddy the tailor, at Andover, Hants.

There's a lot of talk re conscription at home and I'm afraid the men here will mostly be against it. It's a cowardly way to look at the matter and in almost every case a matter of expediency—they have brothers or something of the sort. As I have pointed out to scores of fellows here—and who have never been under fire—if by <u>forcing</u> ten of the likes of X or other tribes, the life of one <u>man</u> at the front could be saved—even at the expense of the tens existence—Australia would be well served. She can well afford their loss (if loss I may call it). If the State is not worth fighting for it's not worth living in—indeed the individual should not have the privelege of living in it. And these less than men are to perpetuate the race! Heaven help the race. One has only to look back for examples Assyria, Greece, Rome, Carthage. These all point the moral. But I'm wandering from the track.

From Epsom I went to Salisbury Plain—to Derham Down near Andover in Hampshire—Derham Down is in Wiltshire and is a most desolate spot—it's more dreary even than the desert in Egypy and it gets on ones nerves. I went to Andover (21,000 people they say but I don't think there can be more than 10,000) on several occasions and picked blackberries in the hedges on the way. I also picked some holly—red berries and all—and was going to send a sprig home, I kept it for a few days and it withered and the berries dried up so that it was not worth while sending. In imagination I could see the pudding on Christmas day at home and this sprig of holly stuck in it—and I was going to reckon out the time and be with you all at the table in spirit. Anyhow I'll be there anyhow, holly or no holly. So—keep at the coil.

No doubt I'll have my Xmas dinner D.V. in France amidst snow (and perhaps hail made in Germany) last year it was as Lemnos—the year before it was in Mena Egypt—that's about twenty years ago. And as for Xmas 1917—I'll be more than lucky if I see that. There's a lot of work to be done before then. However, sufficient unto the day is the evil thereof—Do you know Maggie that I've developed into an out and out philosopher. I've been all my life a bit impatient and still am a bit— But now I have the faculty of looking on the bright side and saying— nothing is so bad that it couldn't be worse and all these things are sent to try us etc—it's a great asset and helps a lot. Keep a'going!!

Did I say I got a budget of letters from home (8 in one envelope from headqrs) in one of them from yourself 16/5/16 you say Peter "is a big fellow for his age, bigger than Father or you and looks very well 9'10" is his height and he weighs about 10 stone"—Yes! I agree, he must be a big fellow, but I should say rather thin if only 10 stone! Never mind Maggie it's only a slip of the pen. It would be rather awkward for him in the trenches if he were that tall. I got the photo of him sent by Joe Wilson and think it very good. On the 13/6/16 you say you got both the hat bands. Good shot. So old Coffey's wish will not take effect this time after all—I've often wondered on whose sinful body the wish would take effect.

Now I think I'd better stop for the time being—I want to write to Bob and Dorothy—(I've neglected them shamefully) and mother and father. Though I know you all read the letters I write—I also want to write to a few friends (for I have some very good friends you know) I've had 4 letters from little Edna Gray of Stawell—though she's a young woman now. I also have a couple of letters of condolence to write also—I heard from Charlie McDonald that you were all well at home and that matters to me most of all. I've seen the Taylors Col was wounded and saw Charlie Collard.

My love to you all at home<br>
Your loving brother George

DODGING THE DEVIL

[The following is a condolence letter written by George to the father of Charlie Wall, presumably written about this time. The text survives because it was subsequently published in the *Dimboola Banner*.][62]

Codford, Wiltshire

Dear Mr Wall,
This is to convey to you all my heartfelt sympathy with you in losing Charlie. I only heard a few days ago that he was killed in action near Armentieres, on the 15th July, and within a few hundred yards of the sector I was in. It's scant comfort to say that these things are the penalties of greatness and the price of Empire; but had Charlie known what was in store for him, and had the chance to withdraw, I know he would have shouted a thousand Noes! "Who dies for England sleeps with God."

## CONVALESCENCE

[This is a partial letter to George from his father, most likely written on 22 August 1916. The first two pages are missing. From internal comments on recent events, its composition can be confidently placed between 20 and 23 Aug 1916, neatly aligning with George's subsequent reference to a letter from Mr Martindale dated 22 August.]

By this time you will have had the full benefit of all the achievements of the dirty Hun in making himself offensive. I gather from the papers that the Australians have sampled him, and are persistently proceeding with the task of teaching him that he is <u>not</u> "top dog" as he has been in his ignorance & blindness assuming. In the process we sincerely mourn the loss of good old Sam Wilson and many others equally worthy. We feel almost sure that you & Bert arrived in France too late to have had had an opportunity of seeing him over there.

    We got the card on Sunday last which you wrote on 4th July saying you were well, we feel sure it was from France but there was nothing to indicate it. A man named Harrison calls on us representing Geo Russell's hardware house, he has a couple of sons there, one of them is Corporal in your Battn & Company, no doubt you know him, his father is <u>allright</u>. Mr Gibbons' three sons are there also. No doubt you have met many men from Dimboola. I believe Sam Barmby & Charlie Chidzey are there about now. You will regret to know that J D Scott died & was buried last week. He was buried in Geelong & a party of 10 of us went from D'la to see that last of him.

    The Prime Minister Mr Hughes has just returned home after a triumphal passage through the Empire and a brilliant season in London. Everything points to him proposing compulsory military service as soon as Parliament meets & I think it will be adopted. There will then be a certainty that your forces will be kept at the full strength and a final victory will avenge the fallen.

We are kept busy in the yard with work having enough in sight to keep us employed till Christmas. We are doing quite a lot of work at Dr Ingham's Hospital, the Grandstand in the reserve, the National Bank &c &c so can't complain on that score.

Probably ere this you have had leave & paid a visit to Old England & I'm expecting shortly to hear news to that effect. Your uncle Geo will probably have notified you of his change of address from Rothersham to 29 Rossington Road, Endcliffe, Sheffield.

Wednesday night

Mother just got your note written at sea on 28th June—pleased of course. Mr Harrison was here today said he had news on Satdy last that his son Cpl Harrison is wounded in France. I am enclosing a photo of the Dimboola Band from which you will realise that the eligibles have not stayed behind here but are with the other good men at the Battle front. This is the eve of the election and I am leg weary.

It is nearly closing time I am enclosing a print of Bobs baby girl she moved but you will not mind that they will send a proper one when they get one. She is a dear little thing & is very proud of me, also of Bob & George & Peter. Dorothy is here for a week. Warrick & she are going to live in Shepparton then. They have left Beaufort. Bob Suhr wishes to be remembered to you. He has been in the Horsham Hospital for 3 weeks but is now home again & fairly well. He is getting very frail. Your old friend Herrmann Melke always makes solicitous enquiries after your welfare and hopes to see you safely back. Time is up so I must close with hopes for your continued safety.

<u>Your affectionate Father</u>

CONVALESCENCE

Hurdcott
Wilts. 23/11/16

Dear Dad

Your <u>very</u> <u>interesting</u> letter of 22nd Aug duly received & I'm glad to know all at home are well. Also a couple from Maggie & Dorothy and one of 27th Sept from Mother—a Balaclava Cap & cigarettes from Dorothy and a nice muffler from Bella Brewer: This makes 3 parcels this year. I'd much like to have a "Banner" giving details of the proceedings on the night you administered the <u>well deserved</u> strafing to Henry Walsgott. Though not there in the body I bask in the reflected glory. In times such as these & when dealing with murderers and <u>Traitors</u>—for who is not <u>for</u> us is <u>against</u> us—there must be no spineless equivocating. Damn their feelings—they have no conscience. Today we hear of the sinking of the Rest liner "Britannic"—and also of the death of The Austrian Emperor. I was aboard the Britannic in Mudros Harbor about last Xmas. She was a fine new ship of 46,000 odd tons.

 Yes, Corporal Harrison was in my company, I know him very well. He is a very fine chap. I think I remember his father too. Glad to know you appreciate those twenty page letters. What you say about them nearly makes me blush!!! Mother wrote some time back saying she pictured me growing a beard and with rough hands. Oh, dear no! For awhile I wore a hirsute adornment on my upper lip. I don't think that it suited my particular sort of beauty so the scythe went in, but the greatest objection was that it was in the way. But as for chinchilla on the larynx, no! perhaps in France this winter to dispense with a muffler. Soldiers are not beastly common tradesmen, they're members of a profession and mostly keep their hands in good form. Mine are.

 Military training for <u>all</u> would be a blessing (in disguise some would say). One can see the result here—pick a soldier with even 12 months training. To gaze on drafts from home, reinforcements etc would fairly make the angels moult. Nine tenths seem gone in the knees & lean forward from the hips & most seem to have a pillow stuffed up between their shoulders. They slouch along, hands in pockets, clothes thrown on any old how, and in camp & everywhere make more noise (including those <u>awful</u> things "Australia will be there" and "Heroes of the Dardanelles", the perpetrators of which should be tarred & feathered) than 50 times their number of old chaps would. It's strange how a hop over the parapet quietens 'em down, and now I know why so many Sergts Major turn grey so young. I smiled over that episode of the carbon copy that wasn't a carbon copy. Better luck next time.

Sorry indeed to hear of J. D.'s decease. He was a good old sticker. On Sunday last I met Edwin Lehmann & on Monday Les & Alf Hirth. They all look very well and I was most pleased to hear from them that all at home were very well. Jim Hook is here close handy, I'm looking him up tonight, likewise two of the Arthurs of Wail and a brother of A. W. Ward of Murra Warra. I can hardly get a word in edgeways with Les: and that's something. I pointed out to them the constellation of "The Great Bear", analogous to our Southern Cross—and the North Star.

24th / Saw Jim Hook last night—he was very pleased to see me. He looks very well and tells me I am looking younger. I certainly feel well. We had a couple of hours good solid "jawing"—it does one well to see old faces. I've found that Peter has arrived in England per troopship "Nestor" and I'm making every endeavour to locate him— so far however, without success. I don't know his Regt no. Battn or even to what division he is drafted. I'm hoping he'll write to me—He should have no trouble in finding me and I want to have a talk to him, giving him the benefit of my past experiences, and good advice against the time he is "up against it". I expect he will be in England for 3 months or so, but I'll eat my Xmas Bully beef & biscuits in

France, and try to imagine I'm home & helping to polish off those nice young roast ducks & green peas. I'll be yearning for a good old hot north wind—dust & all included & something nice & hot, whilst you at home will be saying—Isn't George a lucky dog—up to his eyes in snow & none of this beastly dust. We'll both have the laugh of one another. I picked a sprig of holly, berries & all, and proposed sending it home in time for Xmas. I kept it a few days & it withered and was hopeless—However you must take the thought for the deed.

I've had a letter from Aunt Nellie at Sherfield Manor near Basingstoke Hants. It was enclosed in one from Uncle George & took over a month to reach me. She lives only about 48–50 miles from here as the crow flies, but it's much longer by rail and we are 6 miles from the nearest station. I am most anxious to get over to see her—I could go per bicycle in a day but leave is next door to unobtainable. I'm going to see the Colonel about leave & if he will not grant it, well I'm afraid it will be another case of disobedience of orders—<u>if</u> I'm caught. The new arrivals are treated much better in every way than we old hands. If things are not to their liking there's a huge roar like the day of judgement—and it works. If a fellow has had a couple of years service (and they are mighty few) he is expected to work on like a machine & have no relaxation. All work & no play etc etc—

I wonder if the figures giving the results of the polling on conscription amongst the overseas men of the A.I.F. will be made public. I guess not. It would let the cat out of the bag & would cause a pretty tidy sensation. It surprised me—that is, the talk & feeling here—I have not heard the results. But I'll not get on to this topic or to the scandalous and off hand manner in which we are treated. I think I've chewed it to a rag before and really to do it justice I'd need to have some vitriol mixed with the ink and my pen would need to drip corrosive sublimate.

Did I tell you that Harry Richards was awarded the D.C.M for work on the 19th July. We were together in no man's land all night & morning. I enclose a cutting which also includes the name of a pal of mine from the old 5th, C.S.M. Jack Thorburn D.C.M. He served right through the 5th's sojourn in Gallipoli—nearly 6 months. Talking of medals I expect to get a few. There will probably be one for Gallipoli with perhaps a couple of clasps, one for Egypt—I was E of Suez during minor engagements this year, and its said that all who were in Egypt at the time of the proclamation of a protectorate 18th Dec 1914 will receive the Egyptian Star. There may be a separate medal for France & Belgium. These, taken with a potential V.C. D.C.M. etc etc would make a decent string of colors. As soon as Peter sets foot on French soil he too will be entitled to the General Service Medal. If I "go west" you will be entitled to wear these decorations—but on your right breast, so I understand. Trot 'em out on the occasion of the annual Rifle Club Dinner. And talking of Rifle Clubs—a good scheme would be to initiate a "Machine Gun Club", in conjunction with the Rifle Club—a machine gunner, like a marksman cannot be turned out in a day or a week. The machine gun is credited with causing 57% of total battle casualties, and I should say that is just about the proportion. They're devilish engines of destruction altogether. I've seen men mown down in swathes by the stream of bullets they pour forth. They cackle to the tune of about 600 rounds a <u>minute</u>. There should be no dearth of returned <u>disabled</u> machine gunners, who could be engaged on instructional work and who could visit the various centres. I daresay there are plenty not yet discharged from the Army who would be good to take it on. They are getting their pay from the government and would doubtless welcome the opportunity of taking this on. It should be easily worked out. When I get back I'll be chief Anarchist to the Club. <u>Jobs</u> executed with dispatch. I'm a grenadier commonly known as a "bomb thrower" and a member of the "Suicide Club". This also is a bit of an art & requires practice.

## CONVALESCENCE

Now this is the last sheet of the pad and I've just got the price of a stamp, so will knock off for the time being. The Huns have sunk another hospital ship in the Aegean—the Braemar Castle! In your letter you said something re British v German or Neutral, on the half sheet of paper left I'll write a couple of verses that I consider very good and need no elaboration. With love to all & every wish for your continued welfare, your affectionate son, George

Potters' Clay[63]
"Nec propter vitam Vivendi perdere causus"[64]
Though the pitcher that goes to the sparkling rill
Too oft gets broken at last
There are scores of others its place to fill
When the earth to the earth is cast;
Keep that pitcher at home, let it never roam,
But lie like a useless clod,
Yet sooner or later the hour will come
When its chips are thrown to the sod.

Is it wise, then, say, in the waning day,
When the vessel is crackt and old,
To cherish the battered potter's clay,
As though it were virgin gold?
Take care of yourself, dull boorish elf,
Though prudent and safe you seem,
Your pitcher will break on the musty shelf
And mine by the dazzling stream.
Adam Lindsay Gordon

Neutral
That pale word "Neutral", sits becomingly
On lips of weaklings. But the men whose brains

Find fuel in their blood, the men whose minds
Hold sympathetic converse with their hearts,
Such men are never neutral. That word stands
Unsexed and impotent in Realms of speech.
When mighty problems face a startled world
No virile man is neutral. Right or wrong,
His thoughts go forth, assertive, unafraid
To stand by his convictions, and to do
Their part in shaping issues to an end.
Silence may guard the door of useless words,
At dictate of Discretion; but to stand
Without opinions in a world which needs
Constructive thinking, is a coward's part.
<u>Ella Wheeler Wilcox</u>

24/11/16

I discovered that I had another <u>full</u> sheet—and have just received 3 letters—one from Dorothy 31st July, one from Warrack & Dorothy 8th Aug, and one from yourself 21st March, & enclosing cuttings from "The Age" giving particulars of a council meeting at Northcote. The voting tickled my fancy, 12 <u>for</u> Cr Plant's motion, 1 <u>against:</u> Cr Schwaebach. Hasn't this name a decided German smack about it? There was also 1 "neutral" Cr Cain—he didn't vote. He richly deserves the things said of him—personally I'd be inclined to argue the point with him with a meat chopper. Warrack said they were expecting snow in Beaufort & that he & Dorothy were looking forward to see it for the first time. He prophesised that someone was going to get a whack under the ear or somewhere—presumably with a snowball. We had a fairish fall here this week & some would-be sport hit me fair in the eye with a piece of ice about the size of a goose's egg. The lad pounded & rolled it as hard as a stone & it caught me fair on the ball of the eye—we were not snowballing at the time. I had a sore eye for some days, of course as soon as I collected it I was looking for gore, but nobody threw it, oh no! To put it mildly there were some cross words used!! We've had some bitterly cold days here, I've been frozen that stiff that I could hardly speak or smoke. Everybody was shivering—like so many cheap jellies. Just about the end of my tether. My kindest regards to all old friends Bob Suhr, Hermann Meeke etc—How's Campbell Hill? Glad to know Tilley's are well & hope you see them occasionally. They were exceedingly good to me. I well remember the Sunday morning we heard Germany had declared war with Russia & Geo Tilley & I lopped a pepper tree & hoisted our flag. I knew then that it was but a matter of hours before we were at it. Finish!

George

Salisbury Plain
Wiltshire
30th Novr '16

Dear Dad

I only received your letter in which you said you'd be interested to hear an account of the battle of Lone Pine. I've promised myself I'd write from time to time but have put it off for one reason or another—This "unpleasantness" took place fifteen months ago & one becomes a bit hazy over details, though incidents were noted vividly at the time. The last time I wrote re Gallipoli was I think May and the place Egypt—during hot weather—today it is the reverse—cold as charity, ice lying all over the place & thick enough to bear a man's weight in places—the old inhabitants prophesy a very severe winter.

 I think I got up to the time we left Cape Helles—and it was freezing there—and entered on a period of hardship. We were back at Anzac just before Liman von Sanders & Enver Pasha arrived & gave orders that we were to be driven into the sea at all costs. The guns I remember were rather active & we in support suffered accordingly—a couple of days ago I posted Maggie a part of the front of my slouch hat, through which a shrapnel bullet had passed, at about this time. They (The Turks) attacked in a determined manner on the night of the 18th–19th May. We (the 2nd brigade or rather the remnants) were "standing to" all night—that is we were taking what little shelter was possible. There was some particularly savage shrapnel fire during this time & we had a rather rough time.

 During the early hours of the 19th the Turks made their most determined attempt to break through. Some got into our trenches—but they never got out alive. Our chaps were quarrelling as to who should be on the fire steps—come on, it's my turn, you've been there 5 minutes! Our casualties were 500 killed & wounded, Abdul lost about 4,000 killed & 9,000 wounded in front of our lines. The day of the armistice (24th May) we counted in one space of 100 yards x 80 yards 400 dead Turks. I can give you my assurance they <u>were</u> dead & when they were moved, oh! I needn't go into further details but our burial parties quarrelled a bit, Here! take 'em as they come! no picking out the small ones & leaving the big fat—s for me. The Turkish officers were dolled up as though on parade, to impress, no doubt. They were a fine, smart looking lot—one must defer to a brave and chivalrous enemy—The only trouble was they had met Australians: that was their bad luck. This was their last serious attempt during the campaign to break our lines & was a nasty set back for them.

[65]On the 25th May I saw the last of H.M.S. Triumph, torpedoed off Gaba Tepe—By her gallant work she had won the hearts of the A.N.Z.A.C. She fully upheld the glorious traditions of the British Navy—she was not misnamed—even as she disappeared, she triumphed! I must also record our pride in & admiration of the Destroyer Flotilla—like so many sheep dogs round a flock—lean, grey & sinister—poking their inquisitive snouts everywhere. I could perhaps elaborate, but I want to get on to Lone Pine—<u>Not</u> Lonesome Pine; and I think I described a bombardment of Maidos on a previous occasion—so much is crammed into such a short period that one is apt to forget—or reiterate.

Now, after this fruitless effort by the Turks, a time of real hardship and privation is on the Tapis. One could only describe isolated incidents: I have a small note book with a few notes & impressions set down as they appealed to me at the time. I'll send along a copy of some in the near future I hope. On the 19th May I received my lance stripe & on the 18th Aug, the second & of course felt mighty proud. I will write also re "promotion & all about it"—but for that purpose I'll need <u>red ink</u>, perhaps I'll find in the process that the English language has its limitations. To give full vent to my feelings of more than disgust I would need to employ a mixture of

## DODGING THE DEVIL

Dago and Arabic. But I'm digressing. From the time we returned from Cape Helles (16th May) till the 4th Aug, I was stationed at a place in our line overlooking the "German Officers Trench" 120 yds distant and the "Snipers trench" 80 yds distant—I was for <u>all</u> the intervening time <u>on</u> duty, 3 hours <u>on</u> and 6 hours <u>off</u>, <u>on paper</u>. But nearly every night there was something doing or somebody thought something would be doing. Some nights I would feel that an attack was coming & stay on in charge of a section all night. The flies saw to it that we didn't get much sleep during the day.

We arrived at Lone Pine at midday, I think, on the 5th Aug, & during the afternoon the enemy put up a placard announcing the Fall of Warsaw. We replied by sending a score of bullets through the notice—"Varsaw est tombe, Russie sont perdu"[66]. A day later the trench from which this notice had been flaunted, fell. Amusing! On the morning of the 6th Aug I was on duty in the front trench when the howitzers were "registering"—the Turkish front line was only 40 yds distant & we had some narrow squeaks from our own shells—"Yankee muck" the N.Z. officer on observation told me. One of our own howitzers (5") dropped several shots very close to us (5 or 6 yards); there was some rather warm language over the telephone & the observer ordered the particular gun out of action—I heard afterward that there was treachery, but cannot vouch for the accuracy of the allegation. I think it was faulty ammunition combined with faulty gunnery.

I had a job burning sulphur flares giving off a dense smoke on the morning of the 6th. Aeroplanes were up & duly made observations & photographs of the trenches. Had our midday bully beef as usual & sewed on the white patch, like a mustard plaster between the shoulders & a white band on either (each) arm. It's now afternoon & we don't know who's going over the top—The boys are giving messages to be delivered in case of accident—now! don't forget if I go out, you'll write & tell them so & so! Yes old boy & you'll—

A trench at Lone Pine after the battle. The parapet is draped with Australian and Turkish dead. (AWM A02025)

and so on. The whole place was like a honeycomb, galleries being pushed well forward and new trenches formed & cut to within a few inches of the surface of the ground—until the roots of the grass were visible—lighted by vents & with telephones all O.K. And then we knew who were to go over—to the 1st Infantry Brigade was allotted the honor of kicking off at Lone Pine—two battalion of the 2nd Bde in support (5th & 7th Battns). Each man was given an issue of rum—carried 2 empty sand bags & fighting order—

All was ready—to the second 70 guns opened on the enemy trenches wooff! wooff! wooff! Bang! Rough House front of 400 yards! Abdul's domicile seems like everything, to be soaring heavenward. Too much din to think. 15 minutes and—silence! profound & ominous—there had been the usual wrist watch business going on but as soon as the guns ceased speaking the boys "went over", losing comparatively few men in the process. As soon as they hopped over we took their places & came in for the reciprocal "hand out". In the particular bay I was occupying there were 6 all told—a H.E. came our way killing 3 outright & wounding 2 others—I missed everything, though I was the central figure. In a very few minutes we heard that 4 lines of trenches had been taken—I looked out and could see where our right flank had advanced about 400 yards—the appointed signal, a Red & Yellow flag was planted there alright. And now is where the ugly part comes in—the wounded crawling back through the tunnels.

[67]Somebody's "pinched" my pad & there's trouble! It was decent paper and cost 1/3!

When the first crowd "went over the lid" we fully expected to follow but the deed was done—see Ian Hamiltons despatches—a sick, dejected, and hard tried Brigade but—"They'll do me" The New South Wales Battalions. I was with the party holding a section between "Saps" B4 and B5 (The Pimple) The Pimple as its name implies, was a salient pushing forward from our lines. I had B4 to look after & had a rotten time. I can face the ironmongery & hardware "MADE IN GERMANY" alright, but the wounded are not a very pleasant sight. That night the 6th I held many a man in my arms as he gasped or whispered his last words or requests. I've respected them and done my best. By Heaven, The Boys were game!

At 10 o'clock or thereabouts I couldn't stick where I was any longer & I got "over the top" & helped some of the wounded (Thus was in contravention of orders—but Nelson put the telescope to his blind socket—and Napoleon was twice—as a non-com—(re) arrested) Here and now I must chronicle the actions of the A.M.C. and the Stretcher Bearers. I cannot say enough in appreciation of their services. Though they don't hop over with the first line they do (with exceptions) most patient heroic work. They, too, "will do me"! I got back to my lines at something A.M. & had a long drink of rum—water—finish! It was a bit warm but cheering. <u>Water</u> was more precious than rum! At daylight I lost a couple of good pals, a shell insinuating its way into a small dugout & taking off a couple of heads. 960 Joe Bishop missed Heaven by a matter of inches—Pro Tem!!![68] "We'll all go the same way home"

On the 7th an officer came along calling for volunteers as "Bomb Throwers"—I said I'd have a fly—but they wanted <u>men</u> (not N.C.O's). I committed the heinous offence of leaving my post & going forward—I think in the hereafter I'll be forgiven, for I wasn't out in the front line half an hour before I sent one of our discolored acquaintances to join Allah, The Great Judge. He made a mis-cue—his foot slipped—I beat him to it—Finish!

Can I describe Lone Pine—? I don't think The Great Devil himself could! I don't think that anybody can. It wasn't warfare, it was slaughter. We stood up to it in a hail of "bombs" (grenades) and once again Abdul <u>had</u> to ring off—he had met a better man! It took us 3 days & nights to convince him. Shell fire by day—grenades by night—There was a flicker from bursting grenades so constant as to furnish almost a good enough light to read by! Here also were some awul sights to be seen. What with removing the wounded and dead. ~~The latter,~~ no! I won't write about it. I saw about 200 of <u>our</u> chaps put in <u>one</u> grave at Lone Pine. Abdul fared much worse I saw 500 or more planted in one hole. But of course these figures don't indicate what really happened.

No sooner had I got over to the Turkish trenches than I was covered with big black fleas—The Turks had dogs ad libitum[69]—one of which I tied to an unexploded 8.2" and he pulled it along the trench. With all speed I cut the artificial ligament. It's of no use taking unnecessary risks. We have good reason to think that the Turk had the comfort & consolation of ladies company. I've dug up several articles of—I'm sure—ladies attire, frills lace & all. Some of our chaps turned a real nice green!!!

The whole thing generally was rather well planned & executed—carried out with irresistible "Dash". Then of course the landing at Suvla Bay was effected—let that be a closed book, please—I saw quite a lot of it using glasses & with the naked eye: I'm not going into details regarding what happened at L.P.—too disgusting. Only, the better men won. 7 V.C.'s were awarded "for valor" at Lone Pine, 700 and more were <u>earned</u>. I'm with Peter tonight and I'm blest if I can concentrate on what I'm writing. From early in August 1915 to Sept when I left Gallipoli was rather quiet. By "quiet" I don't mean a nice peaceful uneventful time, but comparatively. It's no use, I must ring off. My next will be about Lemnos, and then Egypt.

Your affectionate Boy<br>George

2

The whole thing generally was rather well planned & executed — carried out with irresistible "Dash". Then of course the landing at Suvla Bay was effected — let that be a closed book, please — I saw quite a lot of it. Using glasses & with the naked eye.
I'm not going into details regarding what happened at S.P. — too disgusting. Only the better men won. 7 V.C's were awarded "for valor" at Lone Pine. 700 and more were earned. I'm with Peter tonight and I'm blest if I can concentrate on what I'm writing. From Early in August 1915 to Sept when I left Gallipoli was rather quiet. By "quiet" I don't mean a nice peaceful uneventful time, but comparatively. It's no use, I must ring off. My next will be about Lemnos. and then Egypt

Your affectionate Boy
George.

23rd Dec '16

Dear Dad

"An Australia stripped of its <u>fighting</u> males—note the "fighting"—falling an easy prey to any covetous Asiatic nation"!!! I was under the impression that all the "fighting" males had enlisted & were here. Of course we know that there are scores of thousands of "neutrals"—but we regard them as unsexed—neither one thing nor the other. We know also that there are men who are <u>physically</u> unfit for service overseas, for war demands the finest & fittest of men and weaklings are a hindrance & a positive source of danger to an army—to their own comrades & not to the enemy. This bogey—this Yellow Peril, is a wishy-washy, puerile <u>excuse</u>—not reason—for the stay-at-homes. The <u>real</u> and <u>only</u> <u>reason</u> is that they're afraid of injury to their damned carcasses—Business! higher duty! the Nunc Dimittis attitude of mind! bah! Hollow, transparent excuses! And these are the—things who profess that they are staying behind to defend Australia from the discolored men. In my mind's eye I can just see these beauties, in the face of invasion, rushing to arms—oh! yes!! If such a thing should happen it would be left to the schoolboys and old men—to the unfit in body but <u>not</u> in spirit—and to the women folk to resist. <u>They</u> would not be of any use—they would take to the bush and invent still another excuse alias reason. And as to business, it's a case of somebody fighting for all businesses, or no businesses at all—or at best under German Government.

 Anyhow—tired as we are—we chaps here are not hankering for their assistance (?) They would allow The Khaki Line to be broken. They're better where they are—but it's a rather rotten outlook for Australia if they're to be the fathers of the future generation. Higher Duty! A man's first duty is to the state—to the Nation &

Empire. I've met during the past few weeks chaps not long from home & have had speech with them. I want to say how proud I am of the way in which they speak of you—You don't hide your light under a bushel—and how proud I am of you.

Your affectionate boy George<br>I've heard of some nice little episodes & chuckle

The soldiers received sheep skin jackets, shipped from Australia, to ward off the cold.
(AWM EZ0123)

PART SEVEN:

# FRANCE, AGAIN

*'I keep meeting chaps I knew at home, but am sorry to say that I've heard of the deaths of nearly all my old comrades.'* December, 1916

With his return to France, George's correspondence slowed. He was shipped across the English Channel on the S.S. *Princess Henrietta* in early December 1916. During the journey he got sick, and back in France he was sent to hospital with laryngitis, only rejoining his battalion two weeks later.

George's 1917 New Year did not start with another drinking-induced punishment. Rather, he was still recovering from another brush with the military authorities. The reason lay back in the middle of the last September, while he was in England. He had been found lying drunk on a pavement in Piccadilly in London about 9.45 pm on 15 September. Unable to even stand, George was taken and confined in a Guard Detention Room at Horseferry Road. The following afternoon, he escaped.

Apparently a few of the prisoners had broken free, but George was soon taken back into custody. Subsequently written up as two charges—being drunk and escaping custody—George was tried at a Courts

Martial on 3 October 1916.[70] He pled guilty to both charges, did not cross examine the prosecution witnesses, and brought no witnesses of his own. The result was that he was punished relatively lightly by being reduced back to private. The time served while waiting the trial also seems to have been considered a factor. The veteran was too valuable to the military for any more serious outcome to have been likely, especially when George explained the mitigating circumstances that explained his anomalous actions:

I was on furlough in London on the 15th September. I went to a dentist and had cocaine injected. After leaving the dentist I had some whisky. I think that that with the cocaine helped to make me drunk. I had just been discharged from hospital and was feeling weak and run down.

He had, after all, returned to the detention room when confronted.

George's cocaine-induced misadventure proved no obstacle to his military advancement. Only two brief letters survive, which George wrote two days before formally rejoining his battalion, probably while en route. These, like three letters from home which he probably received in the subsequent months, tell little of his duties and trials at this time, but reveal that a regular correspondence was kept up from Dimboola. But George's promotions chart something of the continued fighting. In early January George was once again promoted to Lance Corporal, this for the third time. George was made Corporal on 17 February 1917 because Corporal Stephens was evacuated sick, and his next promotion to Sergeant in early March came because Sergeant Hayes was missing. George's war, therefore, showed little sign of ending.

# FRANCE, AGAIN

France[71]<br>Decr 27th '16

Dear Dad

Just a word to say I'm off back up the line for a little more unpleasantness with the Huns & hope to do quite a considerable amount of damage, putting a few out of circulation. We are feeling confident that ere long he is going to be forced to realize that he is not of such high candle power as he imagined himself to be— we feel like the winning side. People say I've done my whack but that time will only come when we leave him beaten flat & without question. I may not live to see it but the time will come as surely as the track follows the wheelbarrow. I'm sorry to have to record that I heard a few days ago that my pal George Russell was killed in action (during November I think). I don't know who is his next of kin or their whereabouts. By enquiry you would be able to find out (at Victoria Barracks, Melbourne) and I'd be glad if you would write to them, conveying my deep sympathy & saying that he died as he lived—a fine soldier and a man—he was killed whilst in charge of a patrol in no man's land and was I believe buried in a cemetery some miles behind the lines—His No was 892 L/Cpl George Russell D Coy 57th Battn 15th Bde A.I.F. You could ask them for instructions regarding that £70—placed to his credit in the Savings Bank.

By even mail I'm writing to 960 Pte Joe Bishop who I'm told is now in England & classified as P.B. (permanent base) He is about 57 years old—but on enlistment gave his age as 37—He's a veteran old warrior having served in N.W. India in several punitive expeditions, in the Burmese War, China, and right through the S'African War—He played the game in Gallipoli and France & has never been wounded. It seems quite remarkable. A week ago I got letters from yourself, Mother, Maggie & Dorothy—Bella & Bertha—also the scarf they all had a hand in—it's very nice & useful & I'm very proud of it & the thought that inspired its production.

I keep meeting chaps I knew at home, but am sorry to say that I've heard of the deaths of nearly all my old comrades. Please express to Cambridges when you see them my sympathy with them in the death of Dave Cambridge and to Mrs Fortington in her sorrow at Harry's injuries. Col Taylor I'm told is pretty right again though I can't say if he will return to the firing line—Sam Barmby is engaged I believe on salvage work behind the lines & is well. Norman Haines is here in the same camp & looks well. I had a very quiet Xmas as indeed all had & of course all were thinking & talking of what their folk were doing at home, reckoning up the difference in time (10 hrs) etc. I'll ring off for the present & get this censored. With love to all at home & all good wishes for a prosperous & peaceful New Year & your continued good health.

Your loving son George

Australian soldiers making their way through a ruined town. (AWM E00371)

# FRANCE, AGAIN

France[72]\
27th Decr '16

Dear Peter

Just a word to let you know where I am at present. I'm going up the line in the course of a day or two & would be glad of a line saying how you are keeping and giving your present whereabouts. I suppose you've written to Uncle George at Sheffield and Aunt Nellie near Basingstoke. I would be glad if you could get along to see one or both of them. You can write to me "D" Coy—you know the regiment (59th). Had a rather tame Xmas—Hope you had a good time. I'm thinking of transferring to the old 5th & will advise you of any change of address. I have had a week in hospital—'laryngitis' don't feel particularly fit but hope to be better when I get along near Fritz. I've had a couple of letters from Dorothy, Bella & Bertha Brewer, Maggie Mother & Father & am glad to say all are very well.

Your loving brother George

Dimboola 28th Novr 1916

Dear George

A couple of days ago (last Sunday) we got a batch of correspondence from you and were pleased to get the news. Bob brought the letters along on Sunday afternoon when Maggie had a party of 4 girls there getting themselves snapshotted to send their little selves to their boys at the front. While they were all looking at the snapshots of you and party at the Hospital I snapped them. Maggie is going to send you some copies.

Of course the interesting part of your letters—oh pardon—they are interesting in all parts—I should say the thrilling parts were those describing your experiences on & after climbing over the parapet on 19th July & thereafter. It seems cruel, when realising as far as we possibly can what the job is and what it means, to continue to think along the lines of wishing to know or thinking that you are still braving the Grim Reaper. It is hard for us. But what would you have. The choice is a very crisp one and covers very little ground. You have either to fight, or submit. I do feel that you would choke rather than swallow the latter alternative. Hence I think of you & picture you as disciplining your mind as to convince yourself that no other place would be honorable or possible to a man of metal and so you have the clear consciousness of doing your duty—nothing less than that could possible enable a man to retain his self respect and if he is minus that then indeed he is fatally lost. I would like to have the opportunity to myself accompany you & the many clear minded & brave men who are in the <u>act</u> of defying the ~~Hun~~ hun to his teeth. Your experiences must be unique, having <u>landed</u> on Gallipoli, charged at Cape Hellas, fought at Lone Pine & charged the guns at Fromelles. Surely a record to make a man hold his head high—"He that shall live this day & come safe home shall stand a tip-toe when those days are named & rouse him at the word, Gallipoli" Fromelles

&c &c. I have to thank you for so bearing yourself that your comrade Lieut, what his name, <u>knew</u> you would go back for him when you procured the means of assisting him into safety. I only looked your letter over once & the others also, and sent them on to Dorothy at Kaniva. You only touched on your adventures to 20 or 21 July & said nothing of how you got disabled & had to go to hospital on 3 Aug. That will come later & we are being trained in patience the same as you are. I am trying to carry myself here as an Englishman should. I'm sorry to say that there are many who can be bluffed from saying out in the open what are supposed to think in such a mixed community as this. I try to bear myself so that <u>you</u> would not be ashamed of me should you be permitted to return, all the more so should you not return but be called on higher—

Time flies & I think Mother & Maggie are writing you. We had a <u>communication</u> from Peter today he cabled for £11 so we <u>know</u> he is allright. Apparently he is in London. I certainly feel much more concerned about him than I do about you, he is so young you know. I hope he will live to return & have a happy & honorable life, but there are worse things than being an honorable corpse. Must close this ramble as its 10 to 9 so wishing you the protection of Heaven remain.

<u>Your Father</u>

Dimboola 5th Feby 1917

Dear George

Yours of 30th Novr &c came to hand and we were pleased to have it. It detailed the events of 6th Aug 1915 & succeeding days at Lone Pine with some of the <u>varied</u> impressions you gathered there. A great pity that so much gallantry should have been expended on such an imperfectly conceived & insufficiently provided a scheme. The only result seems to be that it further demonstrated to the World at large that Australians are to be reckoned with. When they determine anything, they are not to be denied.

We also got the registered pkg & mother is wearing the Victim's ring for luck. In todays paper we get the news of the break between America & germany on the submarine issue. Wilson having told bernstoff to "get out". I think the new development will put increased confidence & determination into the Allied Armies & that both you & Peter will gain in strength to perform your duties, from the fact that your enemy has finally after a long trial extending over 30 months, been found guilty before the court of public opinion in America of being unfit to associate with reputable people. The next step will probably be open <u>war</u>.

I've got the idea that the hun has been riding for this fall and has got to find a way out of his difficulties (created by the British Navy's blockade) at any cost, and that he counts on America sitting at the table to draw up peace terms acting as a restraining influence on the outraged Allies.

We were very pleased to know that you had linked up with Peter. By the time you get this no doubt he will be in France & will join with the rest of you in beating down the arrogance of the bully of Europe. I expect you will all have a desperate time during the coming spring & summer & hope you will be able to make yourselves so <u>offensive</u> that the enemy will be reduced to something approaching reasonableness.

Mr Wall got your letter of condolence re Charlie's death, he was very much moved over it & sent a copy to the "Argus". I showed it to almost everybody. Harvest is just being carted in. It is very late this year but fairly plentiful. There is not much prospect of any building as materials are too dear. G.C. Iron & timber has doubled in price since the war started. I don't mind if people have to roof their shelters with bark as long as all available resources are concentrated on the war.

13/2/17 Have omitted completing & posting this for some days, from various causes. A few days ago news came that Murdoch McRae a cousin of Harry Armstrong had been killed in action. For about 7 years he worked for Jack McKenzie. Today news comes through that young Rod McKenzie[73] has been killed in action[74] on 1st Feby and a party of D'la men rang up Rod McKenzie & conveyed our condolences to the family. Arthur Wilson volunteered last week & passed Dr Ingham he expects to go to Melbn for final medical exam tomorrow. Last night Dolph Luidner came & got an enlistment form & I think he will pass the medical man alright. I heard that some very good reports came through on the conduct of Harry Armstrong in rendering aid to wounded in face of the enemy.

[The letter ends here. Presumably some more pages are missing.]

## DODGING THE DEVIL

[The following is from an undated, fragment of a letter from Mr Martindale to George. It has a 'Martindale & Sons' banner, and is in Father's handwriting. Internal information means it can be dated to c. 12–18 February 1917.]

[...] and am pleased to think it more than likely it is true if you should meet him give him my compliments and salute him for me. Last Sunday was Hospital Sunday & Dimboola put up a record collection of £51- notwithstanding the varied calls we have to respond to. Maggie put £50 with the War loan last week I am helping her to do it by instalment and just here Florence has come in to help me finish this letter so it wont take me us long. It is a hot day & Ivy has got her hands full with two of them, so I have to help bring a nurse and have Florence in here (office) very hot day & the electric fan going to give us a breeze. Of course this is all very domestic & will be interesting to you only when you get your present job completed. We have a fair amount of jobbing work & Bob is a tower of strength, as I'm afraid I don't do much now to push things along. However to close I can only wish you strength and ability to continue faithful to the end however & whenever that may come.

Your affectionate<br>
<u>Father</u>

I had a letter from your uncle Geo saying you had allotted some of your pay for him to collect, but giving no further particulars.

PART EIGHT:
# HOLDING THE LINE

*'Family and men join in wishing you many happy returns and congratulations Martindale'.*
Cable message received in London at 12.15 pm, from Dimboola to George, 24 Mar 1917.

*'Saw George Friday Doing Well Writing Martindale'.*
Cable message received in Dimboola at 19.55 am, from London, 18 June 1917.

Blips of electrical current carried the messages from Europe to Australia. Received in Melbourne, they were conveyed to the next of kin. Mrs Martindale learned only the bare essentials of her son's situation, captured in snippets of information like:

SERGEANT GEORGE MARTINDALE ADMITTED HOSPITAL FOURTEENTH MAY GUNSHOT WOUND HEAD DANGEROUS WILL FURNISH PROGRESS REPORT [30/5/17]
    CONDITION SERGEANT GEORGE MARTINDALE STATIONARY [5/6/17]

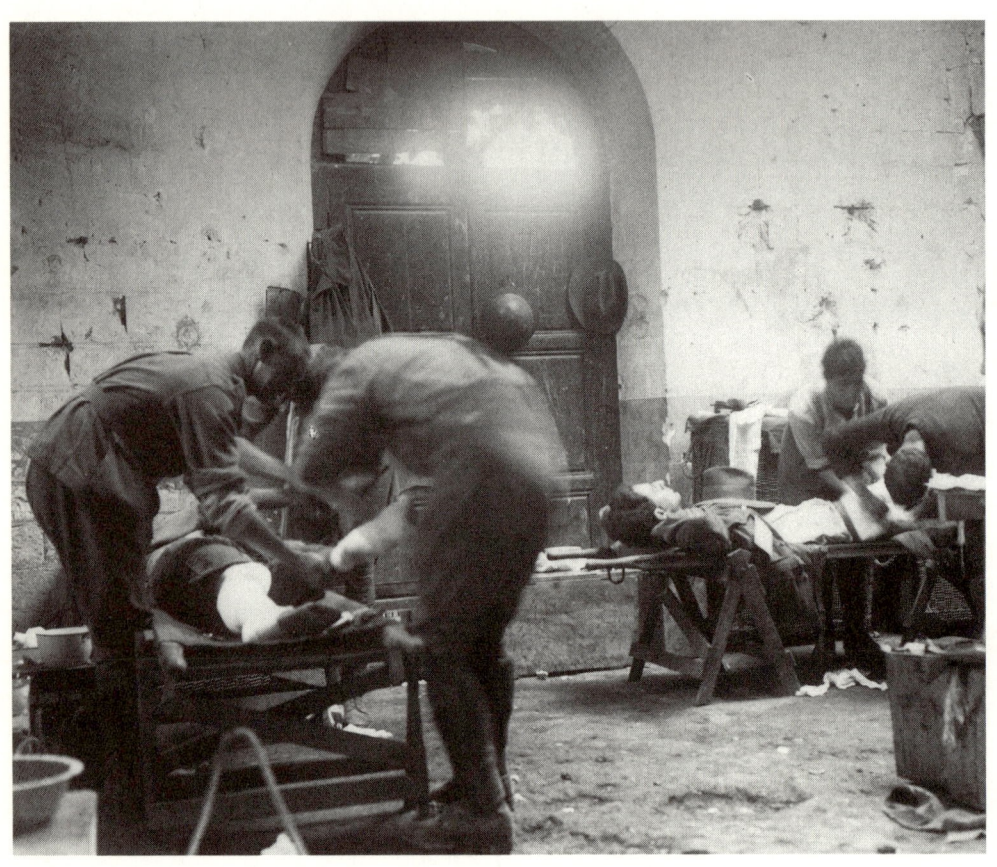

Field ambulance members dress the wounds of Australians at an advanced dressing station.
(AWM EZ0066)

SERGEANT GEORGE MARTINDALE PRONOUNCED OUT OF DANGER FIRST JUNE RIGHT EYE DESTROYED [12/6/17]

SERGEANT GEORGE MARTINDALE PROGRESSING FAVOURABLY [27/6/17]

SERGEANT GEORGE MARTINDALE REMOVED FROM SERIOUSLY ILL LIST [25/7/17]

George had been seriously wounded in action on 10 May 1917, during the battle of Bullecourt. Like Fromelles, this was a supporting attack, designed to aid a nearby British offensive against Aras. Australian forces sustained heavy losses, including George. An exploding shell knocked him unconscious, its shrapnel penetrating his helmet and seriously damaging his head and face. A brief account of the event somehow later made its way into the Martindale's collection, written by Tom Kent:

Sgt Martindale

Hit in right temple by piece from whizz-bang shell which exploded in parapet of support trench at Bullecourt.

Capt. was standing on one side of Sgt Martindale & I on the other. When the shell exploded Mart fell to the ground bleeding profusely from head. He was put on stretcher & carried to rear where he was attended to. The officer was badly shell shocked.

That about 11 May 1917

Tom Kent

After surviving Gallipoli unharmed, overcoming his Fromelles injury and returning to combat, George's slack and bleeding form was quickly conveyed away from the action and rushed to England. His active role in the war was over, but another battle was beginning.

The medical reports in George's file capture the terrific damage done to his body by the blast. In the King George Hospital in London the medical officer jotted down clinical notes taken in France. George had 'Shell wound entering Rt frontal region' and there was a 'Large opening into skull'. Apparently there was also 'Brain tissue exuding'. An initial operation removed debris from George's 'orbit & Rt Antrum', meaning his eye and sinuses. The damaged bone and tissue was also tidied as best as possible, and various rubber drains inserted. Apparently George attempted to pull one of these out, perhaps indicating his discomfort. When he arrived in London he was suffering from a 'Large septic cerebral hernia'. George, who experienced 'several epileptic fits' and an 'exceedingly weak' pulse, was put under 'Careful watching'.

George's battle with infection lasted a long time. On 28 May the septic hernia was still large, 'Pulsating & hanging over Rt eye'. Moreover, 'The Rt orbital bridge is destroyed', the 'Rt eye-socket is very dirty', and 'Separation of eyelid causes pain'. Only on 12 July were there positive developments recorded, when George's eye was 'quite clean', the hernia was gone, and there was 'return of power in upper eyelid'. On 24 August George managed 'Sitting up all day'.

In the meantime, George's uncle had visited, and telegraphed news of George home to Dimboola. [75] Received at 9.55 am on 18 June 1917, it said simply 'Saw George Friday Doing Well Writing Martindale'.[76]

With another operation in September, George appeared to be progressing as well as could be hoped. Yet on 8 October he suffered a sudden relapse, collapsing in the lavatory, where he was found suffering from fits, twitching eyelids and a dilated pupil. Motor function was of considerable concern to George's doctors. They knew, as it had been recorded, that cerebral tissue had escaped from George's wound. He suffered some memory impairment, some deafness, and the fits were obviously a continuing problem. Remarkably, however, he reported feeling much better the following day. More remarkably, even in the early stages of this recovery process, he had been writing letters.

**E.T. No. 7.**  COMMONWEALTH OF AUSTRALIA.  No.
POSTMASTER-GENERAL'S DEPARTMENT, VICTORIA.

Office Date Stamp.

# CABLEGRAM.

This message has been received subject to the Post and Telegraph Act and Regulations.
All Complaints to be addressed, in writing, to the Deputy Postmaster-General.

| Number and Route. | Station from, Date and Time Lodged. | Number of Words and Official Instructions. |
|---|---|---|
| Eastern / 14 | London Sub 18th 9.55am | 10   LCO  9 50 |

Martindale
Dimboola

Saw George Friday
Doug well writing

Martindale

DODGING THE DEVIL

> E2 Ward
> King George Hospital
> London S.E.
> 23rd July '17

Dear Peter

Just a word or two to say I'm still dodging the devil and going on alright. The hole in the forehead is healing up rapidly. There will be a scar (or hole) about 5 x 3 inches & 1 1/2" deep extending from the right temple to the centre of forehead at the edge of the hair. It will rather spoil my er hem! beauty—but it's an honourable scar and not in the rear this time. The piece I got in the leg last year came from behind and is still there, so I have possession of both fragments of missile. The piece of HE that connected with my nut is 2 1/4" x 5/8"—it penetrated my steel helmet! I am sending your address to Aunt Nellie, she will write to you. Have you heard from home lately? I am now allowed to get up & walk about the ward and go on the roof from where a good view can be obtained. The hospital is not far from St Pauls Cathedral & the Tower Bridge & only a few hundred yards from the Thames. We have chaps here from all over the Empire, U.K. Canada Newfoundland N.Z. and little old Australia. Lots of visitors & the nurses & sisters are very kind and good sports. I've nothing to do but sleep & I'm making up for lost time. I wrote to you about a fortnight ago, hope you got my letter. I enclosed a couple of snapshots from home. Now there is nothing I can think of of interest to you except that I think we have the Huns thinking hard. It's quite on the boards that this war will peter out this year and in the way we want it. I hope it does and that you will safely weather the storm and return home after duty well done to enjoy a long, happy and honorable life and by James wont the old Dad be a proud man.

E 2 Ward
King George Hospital
London S.E.
23rd July '17

Dear Peter,

Just a word or two to say I'm still bodging the bowls and going on alright. The hole in the forehead is healing up rapidly. There will be a scar (a hole) about 5 x 3 inches & 1½" deep extending from the right temple to the centre of forehead at the edge of the hair. It will rather spoil my er hem! beauty — but it's an honorable scar and not in the rear this time. The piece I got in the leg last year came from behind and is still there. So I have possession of both fragments of missile. The

Supper time so bon soir, look after yourself & don't forget to write home.

Your loving brother<br>George

My kind regards to the Dim boys who are with you.

HOLDING THE LINE

King George Hospital
Waterloo London S.E.
Tuesday 14th Aug '17

Dear Maggie

Make allowance for my neglect in writing you lately. I'm horribly lazy & the last few months in France kept busy. There's nothing to do here except loll about & smoke (within prescribed hours) and tell lies as to our doings in France. I'm getting along O.K. & hope to be transferred to an auxiliary hospital or a convalescent camp shortly. It's more than 3 months since I collected my little trouble. I met one of my company here—he tells me I was knocked on the 9th May but I reckon it was the 13th, but I'm not clear as to within a week for out there we lose all account of day & date—each day is like the last <u>or worse</u>! A piece of high explosive shell penetrated my steel helmet & forehead (right frontal) & knocked my right eye out. I have the piece (of shell) it's about 2 1/4" x 5/8". Here it is[77] it will make a good paper weight.

<u>Friday 17 Aug</u>

Was out on Wednesday afternoon & visited the house of Parliament also saw the procession of United States troops.

**B.R. Form No. 9.**

## AUSTRALIAN IMPERIAL FORCE.

JW.

BASE RECORDS OFFICE,
VICTORIA BARRACKS,
MELBOURNE, 10th Dec., 1917.

Dear Madam,

I now beg to advise you that Sergeant G.G.Martindale, has been reported convalescent and returning to Australia.

~~His postal address will be:-~~

~~Australian Imperial Force,~~
~~Abroad.~~

In the absence of further reports it is to be assumed that satisfactory progress is being maintained, but anything later received will be promptly transmitted, it being clearly understood that if no further advice is forwarded this department has no more information to supply.

Yours faithfully,

**J. M. LEAN,** Major,
*Officer in Charge, Base Records.*

D.194/3.17.—C.8416.

First came some mounted police then the Guards Band, then a bagpipe band (kilted of course) and then the 'murkhans who had a great reception. They cannot march for sour apples. They just slouched along any old how, some with their rifles at the slope, some with the muzzle forward, some carrying the rifle by the sling on the arm like a basket & some looked as though they were going rabbit shooting. Some were smoking & others chewing & others cat howling etc. They are in Khaki uniform not unlike the British but instead of puttees wear a kind of short canvas legging. Slouch hats with red & white cord instead of a band. They are a likely looking lot, not particularly big in stature, but tough looking & they'll need all their toughness. It may be skite but none of 'em can hold a candle to the Australians in appearance and as for marching, oh!—At least that's the considered opinion of yours truly.

After this rag time cohort had cake walked past we repaired to the House of Commons. There were 10 of us all overseas fellows 6 Australians & 4 Canadians & after signing an agreement not to create any disturbance we passed into the strangers gallery for an hour or two & listened to the debate. Then under the guidance of a member we were taken all over the place and places of historic interest pointed out to us. We had a look round the crypt (a small chapel) it has a most wonderful carved roof and stained glass windows, inlaid marble, brass work etc. Saw the place where the gunpowder was placed ready to be fired by Guy Fawkes. Even to this day on a certain night once a year the party of beefeaters investigate the place—Quite a lot of old customs still survive here. We saw many celebrities of the political world—Ramsay McDonald, Commander Wedgwood etc. aldo Admiral Lord Charles Beresford, who raised his belltopper to us. By the way a great many men raise their hats to us hospital blue clad chaps—the blue is more popular than khaki.

Yesterday—Thursday a party of us went up the river for an afternoon's outing and had a pleasant time. We were the guests of the Exmouth Street Traders. All sorts of nice things were said about us and our sacrifices—I'm feeling for the wings sprouting. This is the lighter & brighter side of war. I wish Peter & I could change places on these jaunts often if only for a few hours. Though I don't mind owning I've had enough of war to last me a lifetime. I'll ring off now or I'll not get this letter into an envelope. Hoping this will find you all in the best of health & hoping to see you all in the near future. With much love from George

## PART NINE:
# DISMISSED

*'I don't mind owning I've had enough of war to last me a lifetime.'*
August, 1917

The documentary trail of George's war started with forms and their standard questions. George's age, height, eyesight, and so on, all helped officialdom assess his fighting potential. Similarly recorded on standard military forms is the story of George's inability for continued fighting, and his transition from soldier to permanent invalid. A medical board looked at his case and filled out the answers on George's behalf. The process told its own grim story. Question 22 asked 'Is the disability permanent?' The medical board answered in the affirmative. 'To what extent is his capacity for earning a full livelihood in the general labour market lessened at present?', asked question 24. 'Total', they wrote, and recommended that Sergeant George Gowthorp Martindale be discharged as 'Permanently unfit all services'. George was shipped back to Australia in late November 1917 on the hospital ship *Karoola*, arriving in Melbourne on 10 January 1918.

The war in Europe continued to grind on for the better part of the year, with George now on the sidelines, watching its progress from afar, much as his family had done for the past three years. Officially, he was discharged from the AIF on 19 March 1918, but the Martindale's story was not yet finished. Peter was still in the fight.

George's return home to Dimboola was, quite naturally, met with some fanfare. He caught the Melbourne to Adelaide train on Friday, stepping onto the familiar platform at Dimboola a little before 7.00 pm. There he was 'welcomed home by a large crowd of his fellow citizens, including the town band ... and by them escorted to the home of his parents'.[78] With that, he slipped into relative documentary obscurity, much like before the war. A letter from his father held by the family puts him in hospital in Melbourne in late 1919, indicating continued poor health, but beyond that there is little to trace George beyond those first few days home.

A few days after returning to Dimboola, on Wednesday afternoon, the Martindale family hosted a small gathering. The Dimboola Recruitment Committee came to welcome home and congratulate George. Mr Martindale was the Committee Chairman, and had similarly led such welcome parties to the homes of other returned soldiers. So George was thanked for his service, and offered wishes for continued improvements to his health. He was told that 'Australia's soldiers had conducted and immortalised themselves ... when the history of the war came to be written they would be classed in the same category of those heroes of Waterloo and elsewhere who had won never-dying fame for their bravery'.[79]

To all this, George said little. Reportedly, 'he thanked the recruiting committee for their kind words, and added that he was extremely pleased to be back again.'

But Mr Martindale stepped in to offer more lengthy remarks on George's behalf, subsequently printed in the *Dimboola Banner*:

He said that George had made the speech of a soldier, who had very little to say; but that little was to the point. George was proud and

**Statement of Service of No.** 901  **Name** Martindale

| Unit in which served. | Promotions, Reductions, Casualties, &c. | From— | To— | Remarks. |
|---|---|---|---|---|
| 5th Btn | Corp | | | BRL 89/as stated muster 28.9.15 |
| | Reverts to ranks at own request | 30/9/15 | 16/1/16 | BRL 89, 28 & 98, BRL 30/16 |
| 57th Batt | Trnsfd to 51st BATT — transferred from 5th Bn | 17/2/16 | 14.3.16 | BR 38, BRL 38 |
| 59th Btn | Trans. from 57th Btn | 15.3.16 | | BR 49 BR list 51/16 |
| 59th Bn | Corporal | 17.4.16 | 11.6.16 | Promotion BR 51/31 |
| 59th Bn | Private (Reverts) | 12/6/16 | | BR 65/105 |
| 59 Btn | L.Corpl | 23.7.16 | | Pro. BR.L 67 p.59 |
| 59 Btn | Corp | 30.7.16 | 2.10.16 | do do |
| 59 Btn | Pte | 3.10.16 | 4.1.17 | |
| 59 Btn | L/Cpl | 5.1.17 | 16.2.17 | |
| 59 Btn | Corporal | 17.2.17 | 4.3.17 | |
| 59 Btn | Sergeant | 5.3.17 | | |
| 59th Btn | (Sgt) Discharged | | 19.3.19 | |

I have examined the above details, and find them correct in every respect.

pleased to be at home because he was there with the sense of duty done. Had that not been the case, he (Mr Martindale) was sure that neither he nor his mother would care to see him there. It was almost impossible, after having been brought up in that home, that he should have remained there when duty called him elsewhere.

By Saturday, Mr Martindale had turned his attention back to active recruitment.[80]

Returning to Dimboola, George could not have entirely left the war behind. Through the pages of the *Dimboola Banner* alone, he could learn of a steady trickle of returning soldiers, some of whom he had met overseas, most of whom his father visited with the Recruiting Committee. George may have read the letters of men still overseas, many of which were responses to the delivery of soldier's comforts, a phenomenon that actively connected Dimboola residents with Australia's boys on active service. Undoubtedly, he also heard of the deaths of lads from his region. He would have sometimes learned of where and how they were buried—which was of great concern to grieving families—as strangers might write to Australia trying to give some solace by providing information. Some soldiers or strangers even offered to photograph the graves of loved ones that could never realistically be visited.

Eventually the war ended, but George's wound never fully healed. He was photographed a couple of times after returning to Dimboola. One image caught him in civilian clothing, holding hands with a pair of nieces, the shadow of a hat discretely covering his lost eye. In another, standing in uniform, he is turned to present in semi-profile, again deliberately hiding his scars. He never worked again and died in April 1922 from complications arising from his injuries.

During the years immediately after the war, the residents of the Dimboola district decided to establish a memorial school. It was built on a prominent rise in town, and became the focus of commemoration services as Anzac Day gradually turned from a government-orchestrated recruitment drive to a day of mourning and solemn remembrance. George's name, with fifty-four others, is inscribed on the 'Roll of Honor' to the dead. Another 209 names are inscribed on the 'Roll of Honor' to those who 'Returned from Service', among which was that of Peter Martindale.

More names were added to the memorials during the twentieth century, and an avenue of trees was also planted to further remember the fallen. Beautifying the present and educating future generations were the last gifts from relatives and friends to the memories of the Dimboola boys.

George's letters were his gift to his family and posterity. They retained something of the scent of the trenches about them, even as the paper and ink faded over the years. Some continued to bear the physical stain of no man's land, making contested France real for a small part of country Victoria. By his writing he honoured his mates, reflected often on his ideals, cherished his heritage and condemned falsities. George certainly often wrote in an idiom of his time, but he also looked well beyond it.

# APPENDIX ONE:
# EXPLANATORY NOTES

The following is intended to provide modern readers with an aid to interpretation. Where possible or helpful, specific people or incidents mentioned by George and his correspondents have been briefly described or identified. Additionally, because George frequently quoted from, or made allusions to, material that is unfamiliar in the twenty-first century, contextual explanations or fuller quotations are given to help illuminate George's meaning.

### From Father, 30 Sept 1914
'Mr Menzies' would be James Menzies, Member of the Victorian Legislative Assembly at the time, and a former Dimboola Shire Councillor.[1] He was the father of Sir Robert Menzies, later Prime Minister. Mr Martindale's passing comment of a conversation with Menzies on Tuesday, presumably in Melbourne, highlights Martindale's place as a regional figure of note with prominent social connections extending throughout the state. Menzies visited Dimboola during September 1914 to investigate conditions in the Dimboola 'Aborigines Camp', where the two worked closely together.[2]

## To Bob and all at home, 24 Oct 1914

The only surviving letter in the collection written by George to his brother Robert, it describes the departure from Melbourne of the 5th Battalion on the *Orvieto*. This occurred on 21 October 1914. George also dwells on his experiences of accommodation and rations while at sea in terms quite similar to those given by Keown in the battalion history *Forward with the Fifth*.[3]

Their father, Mr Martindale, was steward in the dog trials at the Dimboola Show in October 1914, hence George's query about the 'mutton hounds'.[4]

The 'ditty' was widely reported in the Australian press, with slight variations, although the punchline was always the same. Another version runs:

> "I'll go one," said Russia,
> "And I'll go two," said France;
> "I'll go three," cried Austria
> (But she never had a chance).
> "Then I'll go four," said Germany,
> "And change the blessed map"
> But she dropped down dead when John Bull said: "I'll go NAP!"[5]

Reportedly this song, of which George's version was the original, was actually composed by one of the Dimboola boys while in the Broadmeadows camp.[6] The ditty's logic and punchline was derived from the card-game Napoleon (abbreviated to 'Nap'), where making a bid to take five tricks (the maximum) was to 'go Nap'. Essentially it was ranking the protagonists by capacity, and claiming top spot for England (proverbially known as 'John Bull').

EXPLANATORY NOTES

**To Mother, 24 Nov 1914**

Written near the end of George's journey across the Indian Ocean, this letter reflects on the voyage, particularly the encounter between HMAS *Sydney* and the German SMS *Emden*. By attacking a British transmission station in the Cocos Islands, the *Emden* had revealed its position. Distress calls were received from the threatened station, and the *Sydney* was ordered to hunt down the German ship. Faster, and better-armed, the *Sydney* fired on the *Emden* while remaining beyond the German guns' range. Badly damaged by the attack, the *Emden*'s captain ran the ship aground and surrendered. One hundred and thirty-four men were killed in the action and, as George's letters relate, German prisoners of war from the *Emden* were transferred to the *Orvieto* while it was en route to the Middle East.

George enclosed two poems with this letter, which had been printed on board the *Orvieto*:

The Fifth Embarks
The Fifth Battalion, Australian Infantry, under the command of Col. Wanliss, embarked on board H.M.A.T. "Orvieto," A3, on October 21st, 1914, for Active Service Abroad.
By Michael Dwyer

> The month was October—Nineteen Fourteen;
> The sun it shone brightly o'er that martial scene,
> For one thousand young heroes, Australia's pride,
> Were embarking that day for a land o'er the tide.
>
> "Orvieto, A3" was the name of the ship,
> That was taking so many on their maiden trip,
> And while some said "Good bye," and others shed tears,
> The bold Fifth embarked amid loud ringing cheers.

201

Just picture the trooper, so stately and grand,
And the brave lads embarking to the strains of their band
Their moths and sweethearts and sisters also,
And you'll find out their feelings regarding the foe

Boasting or bragging was heard from no man,
"They're bearing it well" through the crowd quickly ran
You may talk of those Uhlans, and the great Prussian Guard
But to beat those young fellows their job will be hard.

When the big ship moved off, and the shore became dim,
From many a heart came a prayer unto Him,
To protect and to guide those leaving their home
To go to a war that was none of their own.

It's not often, thank God, that we witness such scenes,
Except just in fancy or perhaps in our dreams;
But may He who has said *"On Earth Peace & Goodwill,"*
The hearts of those brave lads with courage may fill.

The War Alphabet
By Michael Dwyer

A for Australia we're leaving behind,
B for Berlin where peace will be signed.
C for the Colonials, the boys who can fight,
D for The Day when our wrongs we shall right.
E for old England, to where we are bound,
F for the Flag we've all rallied round.
G stands for Germany, of honour bereft,
H for his Highness King George V
I for his Indian troops on the fields,

J stands for Justice we'll have e'er we yeild. [sic]
K for the Kaiser, who's fighting in vain,
L for the Losses his army sustain.
M for Montenegro that brave little state,
N for our Navy that's doing first rate.
O for "Orvieto," the best troopship of all,
P for the Patriots, who answered Kitchener's call
Q for the Queenslands, who'll fight by our side,
R for the Russians, who are with us allied.
S for the "Sydney," which made the "Emden" a wreck,
T for the Time, when again we'll come back.
U for the Unity, amongst us you'll find
V for Victorians, all bear in mind.
W for the War, to which we all go.
X is the only one Mic doesn't know.
Y is for You to try and find out,
Z for Zam-Buk, for the Kaiser we'll shout.

## To Mother, 28 Nov 1914

This short note was written on a postcard of 'Quarantine Island' in Aden, a British-controlled port near the entrance to the Red Sea.

## To Maggie, 14(–17) January 1915

George Tilley was most likely a member of a Melbourne family that George knew from his time at Brighton, thereby explaining their concern with his property. It points to the hurried nature of his signing up, and the relative rapidity of the mobilisation. In a later letter George reported being with George Tilley when he heard that war had been declared, furthering this connection.

George also makes several connections with Dimboola in this letter, and with the social circle of his wider family. He mentions meeting several people known to his sister Maggie, for instance, and comments on the comfort fund pudding that he enjoyed—a small taste of home. And, perhaps because of her particular interests, George made several musical allusions in this letter. Songs the troops sang while marching capture the aural bellicosity of the training regimen and growing *esprit du corps* among the Australian troops. Harry Lauder, whom George quotes, was a popular Scottish singer and comedian. In Melbourne during the start of the First World War, Launder avidly supported the British cause through fundraising and recruiting events. 'Fighting the Kaiser' was an irreverent ditty to the tune of 'Waltzing Matilda'. 'It's a long way to Tipperary' was a recent British song, which soared in popularity among troops during the war.

Similar sentiments were also expressed by George's general language usage. By 'Wilhelm the Mad' George means Kaiser Wilhelm II. In part this is fostered by the 'official' German atrocities he is told about. His comments about 'dum dum' bullets referred to the use of bullets designed to expand on impact and thereby cause extensive wounds. This was, he and his readers would have understood it, an especially egregious choice of weaponry—seen as being uncivilised and unsporting.

George's letter also reveals a growing use of Biblical allusion and referents. The childhood song 'Oh! Who will slumber in his bed' was probably based on Proverbs 6:9. Clearly aware that he was in Biblical territory, George's comments about seeing Sinai, the Ten Commandments, 'Pharaoh's daughter ... bullrushes ... Moses' were all obvious references to Exodus, but perhaps also reflect on his own sense of exile. The clipped quotation from John 14:2 concerned Christ's assertion of his imminent death and Resurrection in a wider section about the doubts of the Apostles Peter and Thomas.

Cardinal Newman's 'Lead Kindly Light' was originally a poem titled 'Pillar of the cloud', written in 1833 by the Anglican cleric John Henry Newman, a prominent intellectual and leader of the Oxford Movement, who converted to Roman Catholicism and was later made a cardinal. It became a well-known and popular hymn once set to music in

1865 by the English vicar John Bacchus Dykes, whose tune *Lux Benigna* was probably that to which George referred. In the context of the war, the recognisable tune may have given pause for reflection, especially if George followed the music with the familiar but unsung words.

> Lead, Kindly Light, amid the encircling gloom, lead Thou me on.
> The night is dark, and I am far from home; lead Thou me on.
> Keep though my feet; I do not ask to see the distant scene, one step enough for me.
>
> I was not ever thus, nor prayed that Thou shouldst lead me on.
> I loved to choose and see my path, but now lead Thou me on.
> I loved the garish day, and, spite of fears, pride ruled my will: remember not past years.
>
> So long Thy power hath blest me, sure it still will lead me on, o'er moor and fen, o'er crag and torrent till the night is gone; and with the morn those angel faces smile, which I have loved long since, and lost awhile.

## To Mother, 20 Jan 1915
A postcard. The Image is of 'The Pyramid of Gizeh'.

## Henry (D'Alton) to Mr Martindale, 27 February 1915
Prominent among the Dimboola recruits, Henry's response to Mr Martindale highlights a wider corresponding network. Henry was reacting to Charles Bean's account of Australian misbehaviours in Egypt, reported in the Australian press.[7] Bean's comments about 'bad 'uns', 'wasters' and untrained officers was taken as an affront by many of the soldiers.

Mr Martindale won the Dimboola rifle shooting trophy in December 1914. H.C. Budde came second.[8]

### To Mother, 28 February 1914

Charles Bean proved a source of commentary for George, just as he had been for Henry D'Alton. Referring to articles by Bean in the Melbourne *Age*[9] and *Argus*[10], George was responding to assertions that some Australian soldiers 'have damaged their country's reputation'.

'Byers' is Harry Alston Byers. The Rechabite movement was a Temperance movement, and Byers was a 'Methodist', which could explain the association. George's comments in this regard reflect a common anti-Semitic stereotype, both the explicit one and an allusion to Byers' 'seed forever'—a term used Biblically in scenes of both promise and curse.

Not all of George's cultural referents were Biblical or Australian, however. George quoted from Thomas Babington Macaulay's *Lays of Ancient Rome* ('And how can man die better?'), which was also quoted by Mr Martindale at one of the Dimboola recruit send-offs.[11]

George Reid was the Australian High Commissioner to London during the war, and a former Prime Minister.

### To Maggie, 28 February 1914

Maggie's news about 'Harkins youngsters have come to grief' referred to the death of Iola Rose Harkins's death on 26 January 1915 from 'burns sustained through her clothes catching on fire whilst ... she was playing with matches.'[12]

Clarence Jaehne was in the AIF and died of pneumonia while at sea on 14 January 1915 on HMAT *Themistocles*.[13] George's letter suggests that it was via news from home that he learned of Clarence's demise.

George's comments about forthcoming action reveal the general perception that Australian forces would be part of an assault on Turkish territory.

### To Dad, 28 March 1915

'Young Wallsgott' was an otherwise unidentified member of a Dimboola family. Fred Gersch was active in the Dimboola Farmers' Co-operative

# EXPLANATORY NOTES

Society. George Hoffman was a Dimboola Shire Councillor. Gustav Petschel was a local farmer. George's referents in this regard generally seem to be responding to his father's news. In turn, George conveys news of contact with a number of the Dimboola boys in Egypt.

Mr Martindale did make a 'trip to Keith SA & to the Little Desert' and an account was published in the *Dimboola Banner* on 19 February 1915.[14] It was part of an information-gathering mission to explore the possibilities of further settlement on the Dimboola Downs. That George made anticipatory reference to this in late March indicates the delays of communication through the post. Note the contrast with George's opening references to postcards from later in February having already been received.

George's comments about the value of rifle clubs are interesting in light of their prominent role in early recruitment, and the strong association between rifle shooting and the Martindale family.

George's 'poetry' quotation, 'We know whereon our hopes depend, we serve the hour, and wait the end!' has not yet been identified, but could be a mixing of two hymns. His other quotations are clearer: 'His foes at best are knaves confessed whose malice from envy springs' and 'And great & small, down down they fall 'neath the storm of his iron hail' are both from 'The British Lion', a patriotic song by Henry Walker, c. 1880 (quoted below).

**The British Lion**
Oh, the British Lion is a noble scion,
And proud in his conscious might,
The terror of those he has made his foes,
For ever he defends the right.
And yet so mild that a timid child
May approach him, and need not quail,
And may pat him on the crown and stroke him down,
But beware how you tread on his tail.

Oh, beware, have a care; :|| Oh, beware how you tread on
    his tail.—(Repeat in Chorus)

'Twill much require to rouse his ire,
For he's fond of quite a snooze;
No idle vaunt, or threat, or taunt
Will provoke him his strength to use;
No bliss he thinks like forty winks,
Yet his vigilance ne'er doth fail!
For he sleeps with but one eye-lid shut,
So beware how you tread on his tail.—Cho

His foes at best are knaves confest,
Whose malice from envy springs;
And it oft betides that his tawny sides
They pierce with their gnat-like stings,
But he merely yawns, for the thought ne'er dawns
Such pigmies to assail:
Till grown more bold, his sloth to behold,
They venture to tread on his tail.—Cho

Then, up he bounds, and his roar resounds
As he lashes each foaming side;
His warlike breath hurls fire and death,
And scatters them far and wide!
Down, down they fall, both great and small,
'Neath the storm of his iron hail!
And repent, to their cost, when all is lost,
That they trod on the Lion's tail.

Chorus—And repent, to their cost, when all is lost,
So beware how you tread on his tail.

# EXPLANATORY NOTES

'Blucher' is probably a generic reference to Germans, courtesy of association with the Prussian General, Gebhard Leberecht von Blücher, who fought with Wellington against Napoleon at Waterloo in 1815.

### To Mother, 16 April 1915
Walter Gamble was a resident of Dimboola.

Adolph Suhr, 'old Suhr', was a German-born resident of Dimboola. He died in 1917, and his obituary notes he had a nephew in the German navy.[15] Mrs A. C. Bennett and Mrs Deneys were wives of Dimboola businessmen, and were quite socially prominent in their own rights.

George likely thought 'Bert [Hurbert Wilson] … should make a good soldier' because of his intellect. Bert was a teacher in Melbourne. Sam (Wilson) was well known in Dimboola as a crack shot, hence the comments about shooting. The same applies to Henry (D'Alton).

Mrs Brown is probably the late wife of Dimboola chemist W. T. Browne, and Val her son, the same people referred to in George's first letter.[16] Gus Petchel lived at Katyil.

### To Mother, 13 May 1915
George's first surviving letter from Gallipoli, in which he is a little reticent about the fighting. 'Jack Johnsons' was a slang term for 15 cm artillery shells. George's comments about his hand being hurt in an accident, and causing him difficulties writing, does not appear in his service record, suggesting he largely kept it to himself. The photograph of George taken by Bean survives in the collections of the Australian War Memorial.[17]

### To Mother, 6 Aug 1915
Writing 'just crouched ready for a swift spring', this postcard is dated the first day of the August Offensive, an Allied operation designed to try to break through the Gallipoli stalemate. George was presumably writing it in advance of going 'over the top', hence the comments about putting it in

DODGING THE DEVIL

his pay book. Stawell is about half way between Dimboola and Ballarat. Arthur Ladner was a plumber from the Dimboola–Stawell region.

**To Dad, 10 Aug 1915**
The poem George added at the top of this letter was from the last verse of 'Mother-Country', a poem in *The Windsor Magazine*.[18] George later recalled seeing it on a grave marker. It diverges from the original slightly in the third line:

> Mother-Country, land and sea
> Yield strong sons who die for thee;
> Through the years God grant that we
> Worthy of thy fallen be.

In the original the 'Mother-Country' was explicitly identified as England.
The 'big prolonged battle' was the Battle of Lone Pine, a drive to break the stalemate on Gallipoli.

**To Dad, 26 July(–25 Aug) 1915**
'Young Watkins' was Percival James Watkins who was killed in May 1913 by a train.[19] The incident concerned the train hitting a 'tricycle', a small vehicle that ran along the railway tracks. Watkins was roadmaster clerk at Dimboola at the time and was travelling with the yard porter, A. E. Bunting. Both jumped away when they saw the express train coming, but Watkins then unsuccessfully attempted to get the tricycle off the tracks before the train struck it. Apparently the incident was unnoticed by the train driver until it arrived in Dimboola and the cattle guard was seen to have been damaged.[20] Jim Bond's 'firing' on the train meant he was working as fireman, not that he was shooting at it.
Lloyd St was one of the main streets in Dimboola, indicating the ship's size. The suggestion that the *Queen Elizabeth* 'could demolish Horsham, Nhill, W'Beal [Warracknabeal] & Jeparit without moving'

was a comment on the range and capacity of its guns, as these were all towns in western Victoria.

Maidos and Chanak were towns near Anzac Cove, which were shelled by the British fleet.

'The Queen of Battles' was a euphemism for the infantry. This, like other comments George made, reveals his interest in and familiarity with British military history. The battle of Inkerman to which George refers is another instance. It occurred 5 November 1854 during the Crimean War.

George's quotation, 'With never a speck of crimson perhaps it would make us vain', is a paraphrase of part of 'The Song of the Sparrow', a pious children's poem of the late nineteenth century based on Matthew's Gospel (Matt 6:26). It's the kind of thing George may have had read to him as a boy.

**What the Sparrow Chirps**[21]
I am only a little sparrow,
A bird of low degree;
My life is of little value;
But the dear Lord careth for me.

He gave me a coat of feathers;
It is very plain, I know,
With never a speck of crimson,
For it was not made for show.

But it keeps me warm in winter,
And it shields me from the rain;
Were it bordered with gold or purple,
Perhaps it would make me vain.

Pte Cameron, Geo Barmby's cousin, is possibly Donald Cameron.[22] George Barmby was a Dimboola carpenter.

DODGING THE DEVIL

### To Mother, 17 Sept 1915
This was a pre-printed postcard that George sent to his mother, scratching out the irrelevant options. He disobeyed the strict instruction slightly, by adding a '4' and an 's' to turn 'parcel' into '4 parcels'.

### To Dad, 23 Jan 1916
Adela Pankhurst was a prominent pacifist activist whose speeches often met with hostility from crowds booing and suchlike.[23] Brigadier-General McCay's speech commented publically on the need for more men to constantly replace the toll taken by 'modern warfare'.[24] A growing discourse about the need for recruits fostered a referendum on conscription later in 1916, which was defeated.

'Sox' probably means 'socks'. Lam Buk was a healing balm for cuts, burns and aches.

In this letter and the one following, George makes several comments that situate the success of Australian soldiery within a longer British tradition. His comments on known regiments required no immediate explication for his audience, indicating that Mr Martindale probably shared George's passion for British military history. George's references to Tel-el-Kibir and Sir Garnet Wolseley, for instance, refer to a battle that occurred in 1882. Arabi Pahsa had led a nationalist movement in Egypt against English and French rule. His defeat by Wolseley's force, however, ensured continued English control of the Suez Canal, and of Egypt.

By 'just as he's catching the bear' George seemingly refers to the tendency of book chapters to end on 'cliff-hangers'.

The 'Cape Helles' stunt was part of the Dardanelles campaign, where George was taken from Anzac Cove to support the English attack. He gives a longer account in a subsequent letter.

### To Dad, 3 June 1916
Joffre was Joseph Jacques Césaire Joffre, Commander of the French armies on the Western Front 1914(–16), and the famed 'Victor of

## EXPLANATORY NOTES

the Marne'. The quotation is, however, 'Endure and Fight', and was a phrase from the French President's Proclamation of 3 September 1914 in response to the German threat against Paris and widespread panic. It was widely reported in the British press. In translation, a 1915 pamphlet version runs:

> Endure and Fight! Such must be the motto of the Allied British, Russian, Belgian, and French Armies.
> Endure and Fight, while at sea the British aid us, cutting the communication of our enemy with the world.
> Endure and Fight, while the Russians continue to advance to strike the decisive blow at the heart of the German Empire.[25]

Once again in this letter George situated his service within a longer sweep of British tradition. John Moore's victory at the Battle of Corunna, for instance, concerned an English victory of 1809 in the Peninsula War.

By 'my first stripe' George meant Lance Corporal. His military records put his appointment as 9 May 1915, not 19. This could refer to the appointment's confirmation, which is not recorded in his file.

'Swanee River' was a song by Stephen Foster also known as 'Old Folks at home'. From America, it is about pining after home:

> Way down upon de Swanee Ribber,
> Far, far away,
> Dere's wha my heart is turning ebber,
> Dere's wha de old folks stay.
> All up and down de whole creation
> Sadly I roam,
> Still longing for de old plantation,
> And for de old folks at home.

DODGING THE DEVIL

The reference to 'Henry V' was to Shakespeare's play *Henry V*, Act III, scene 4, in the King's speech: 'We would not die in that man's company/ That fears his fellowship to die with us.'

'Hope on, Hope ever' was a hymn by Rev. I. Baltzell, the first lines of which capture its essential message: 'Hope on and hope ever, our watchword shall be, While sailing o'er life's troubled billows, We'll never despair tho' the clouds may grow dark, Or hang our bright harps on the willows.'[26]

George's comments about the Ten Commandments, 'Lot's wife's elbow' and 'the extra Commandment "the baksheesh one"' again reveal his familiarity with and recourse to Biblical allusions. The 'extra' commandment was, of course, Christ's message to his followers to 'Love one another' (John 13:34). By 'baksheesh' George was using a Persian term for giving charity. The English word 'charity' derives from the Latin 'caritas', itself meaning 'love', and deriving from the usage in John, perhaps implying a pun was being made.

### To Mother, June–10 July 1916

'Who dies for England sleeps with God' comes from the final verse of 'Spartan Mothers' by Alfred Austin, written in 1900:

> Should Heaven decree that he once more
> Unscathed return to home and rest,
> She will be standing at the door,
> To fold him to her trembling breast.
> Or, should he fall
> By ridge or wall,
> And lie 'neath some green southern sod—
> "Who dies for England, sleeps with God"

The original quotation 'For honour, not honours' probably refers to Gordon of Khartoum.[27] For the details of the D'Altons see their entries in the next appendix.

EXPLANATORY NOTES

The 'big "push" going on now' was perhaps the Somme, or early preparations for Fromelles.

### To Dad, 18 July 1916

The battle of the Marne was a major turning point in the early stages of the war in Europe, and an Allied victory. In September 1914 British and French forces stalled the German advance towards Paris, and with a major and successful counterattack, were able to repulse the Germans towards the sea. While saving Paris, the attack also effectively compelled the two sides to dig in across an extended frontier, creating the conditions for the Western Front.

The Moulders were a local family in the Dimboola region. Billy was clearly one of George's other correspondents. Miss Clements came from another local family.

Brigadier General 'Pompey' Elliot was a prominent Australian military officer, who served on Gallipoli and in Europe.[28]

George's account of the Battle of Fromelles is fascinating in its narrative clarity and his own actions. But it is also remarkable that George's writing helps place several other participants within the action. See in particular the entry for Norman Marshall in the next appendix. Note also the shift in tone from that portion of the letter written before the battle, focused on acknowledging letters, apologising for the lack of writing, making clear his location, ensuring money affairs were in order, and thinking of his mother and 'spiritual' matters before going over the top.

### From Mr Martindale to George, 16 May 1916

This letter is included here to fit with the patterns and chronologies of George's reading and writing in response.

The 'cause celebre' concerning Gooding and Schneider was a trial brought by Gooding against Schneider for an assault on 6 April 1916 in Wall's Hotel in Dimboola. The trial (court of petty sessions) was held on 16 May, the day of Mr Martindale's letter. The source of the fight derived in part from hostility to the speaking of German. Alcohol was also reportedly a factor.[29]

**To Maggie, 21 Oct 1916**
In this letter George gives an account of the action that saw him wounded and evacuated to England. He describes the hospitals at which he spent time and the nurses who attended him. Especially novel for George were the members of the Red Cross Society, which formed in Britain with the war, the Scottish Women's Hospitals movement, which grew from a variety of organisations (notably including suffragist ones), and the Order of St John, which was a nineteenth-century development that looked to the traditions of the medieval crusading Knights Hospitaller (the British order is known now as St John Ambulance).

'The Maiden's Prayer' was a mid-nineteenth-century composition by Polish composer Tekla Badarzewska-Baranowska.

Charles Bean's *The Anzac Book* was a collection of stories, poetry and cartoons from soldiers about Gallipoli.[30] Ostensibly revealing a steady mob of Australians enduring Gallipoli with good humour, it was in fact a carefully selected collection designed to have a certain effect. Bean sought submissions that conformed to a certain image he wished to promote and deliberately excluded submissions that did not present the image that Bean had in mind or thought suitable for the book's intended purpose and audiences.

George's comment to turning 'Ananias green with envy' likely refers to Ananias from the Acts of the Apostles (Acts 5:1–5). This Ananias kept some of the common property of the Apostles for his own gain and then lied about it. Ananias was rebuked by St Peter for lying to God, before then falling dead.

Croesus was an ancient king of Lydia, recorded by Herodotus, who was known to be exceptionally wealthy. To have 'felt a bit of a Croesus' would therefore mean to have felt a bit rich.

### To Mr Wall, c. October 1916

For the context behind 'Who dies for England sleeps with God' see entry for George's letter to his mother, June–10 July 1916. That this quotation would be a fitting and well-received ending to a condolence letter sent to western Victoria says much about the sentiment's hold. It also highlights the persistence of a strongly 'Anglo' identity during the war years that firmly situated Australia within England's Empire.

### Mr Martindale to George, c. 22 August 1916

'Bert' was probably Bert Wilson.

John David Scott was buried on Wednesday 16 Aug 1916 in Geelong. Mr Martindale travelled to the funeral and was one of the pallbearers. Scott was for a long time the Dimboola miller.[31]

Dr Ingham ran a private hospital in Dimboola. The Grandstand refers to the Agricultural and Pastoral Show Reserve Grandstand, which in mid-1916 was in need of repairs. The National Bank was the National Bank of Australasia.

### To Dad, 23–24 Nov 1916

The *Britannic* was one of the White Star Line ships, sister to the *Titanic*. It was only completed as war commenced, and was used as a hospital ship from 1915 until it sunk by striking a mine on 21 November 1916. The Austrian Emperor, Franz Joseph I, died the same day.

'Australia Will Be There' focused on the righteousness of Australia coming to Britain's aid. Its refrain and final verse typify the message:

> Rally round the banner of your country,
> Take the field with brothers o'er the foam,
> On land or sea wherever you be;
> Keep your eye on Germany,
> But England home and Beauty have no cause to fear,
> Should Auld acquaintance be forgot

No! No! No! No! No! Australia will be there
Australia will be there.³²

'Heroes of the Dardanelles' similarly addressed the righteous cause, including a line that mentions 'All singing "Tipperary", and "Australia will be there"'.³³ The chorus explicitly connected the continuing conflict with events at Gallipoli:

They were Sons of Australia,
Steady and strong,
True to our Country, righting a wrong,
And they proved their bravery,
As History now tells,
When they fought and died like Heroes,
In that Charge at the Dardanelles.

George's instruction into Northern Hemisphere astronomy was not purely esoteric. Recognising the 'Great Bear' and the North Star meant being able to discern compass directions. This facilitated navigation at night—a useful battlefield skill.

The notion of being 'chief Anarchist to the Club' was a joke, predicated on the anarchist movement of the early twentieth century.

The *Braemar Castle* was another hospital ship damaged in the Aegean. It was widely reported to have been torpedoed by Germans, but actually struck a mine. Despite the damage, it was repaired and returned to service before the war had finished.

The comments about Northcote refer to endeavours to remove an 'anti-conscriptionist' clerk from serving in the defence department, if such an employee were eligible to enlist, and where returned soldiers could do the work. It produced a heated debate.³⁴ Councillor Cain was the clerk in question.

# EXPLANATORY NOTES

**To Dad, 30 Nov 1916**
Otto Liman von Sanders was a German officer advising and overseeing the Ottoman forces on Gallipoli. Enver Pasha was an Ottoman military commander, one of the 'three Pashas' who effectively ruled the Ottoman Empire during the war. George was referring to the major Ottoman counter-offensive, which commenced on 19 May 1915. The HMS *Triumph* was a British battleship, sunk by torpedo on 25 May 1915 while supporting the Dardanelles campaign.

Note that George still has his 'small note book', helping him to write his account.

The 'Fall of Warsaw' placard was remarkably up to date. The city was occupied by German troops on 4–5 August. German forces had been pushing back the opposing Russian lines since the commencement of a major offensive in mid-July.

'We all go the same way home' was another popular song at the war's commencement, written by Harry Castling & C. W. Murphy in 1911. The chorus ran as follows:

> We all go the same way home
> All the whole collection in the same direction
> All go the same way home so there's no need to part at all
> We all go the same way home
> Let's be gay and hearty, don't break up the party
> We'll cling together like the ivy on the old garden wall.

The Suvla Bay operation was another amphibious landing on the Gallipoli Peninsula by British, designed to correspond with the August offensive and help break the strategic deadlock. It failed in its objectives and was considered something of a debacle, hence George's dismissive comment.

### To Dad, 23 Dec 1916

In referring to 'An Australia stripped of its fighting males falling an easy prey to any covetous Asiatic nation', George was quoting and responding to coverage of the failure of the 1916 conscription referendum. George probably read the report from the London *Times*, and may have posted the report along with his letter.[35]

The 'Nunc Dimittis attitude of mind' referred to the Canticle of Simeon (Luke 2:29–32), where Simeon recognised in the child Jesus the promised Messiah he had long waited to see. George seems to be using it to mock ideas that it was righteous to 'wait and see' if an Asian nation threatened Australia during the European conflict.

The reference to hiding a light under a bushel is another Biblical reference, being one of Christ's parables (Matt 5:15, Mark 4:21, Luke 8:16). George's point is that Mr Martindale is speaking truth rather than hiding it.

### To Dad, 27 Dec 1916

This letter reveals some of the complexities involved in dealing with money and personal affairs between soldiers and their families, especially in the event of death. While service records often capture the formal dealings between next-of-kin and soldiers' personal effects, this letter reveals the way that wider social networks also came into play in ways where the documentation has not so neatly survived.

George's mention of Joe Bishop's prior service is a pointed indicator that the early recruits in the AIF often had prior military experience. Contrary to popular mythology, the Gallipoli landings were not entirely conducted by untried and youthful recruits.

### To Peter, 27 Dec 1916

This short letter to Peter, clearly written in advance of movement, is similar to those he wrote to his mother prior to combat. It is likely more such short letters were written than have survived.

EXPLANATORY NOTES

George's service record confirms he was in hospital with laryngitis between 12 and 21 December 1916.

**From Mr Martindale, 28 November 1916**
The ostensible quotation, 'He that shall live this day & come safe home shall stand a tip-toe when those days are named & rouse him at the word, Gallipoli', is in fact a play on King Henry's speech in Shakespeare's *Henry V*, Act IV, Scene 3: 'This day is called the feast of Crispian: He that outlives this day, and comes safe home, Will stand a tip-toe when the day is named, And rouse him at the name of Crispian.' The line follows on from that quoted by George in his letter of 3 June 1916, part of the same speech.

**From Mr Martindale, 5 February 1917**
George's letter to Mr Wall does not appear to have been printed by the *Argus*, but it was, as already seen, printed by the *Dimboola Banner*.[36]

**From Mr Martindale, c. 12–18 February 1917**
Hospital Sunday was an annual fundraising event in Dimboola. The sums detailed in this letter match those for 11 February 1917.[37]

**To Peter, 23 July 1917**
'HE' means 'High Explosive'.
　　At the time of this letter, Peter was in France.

**To Maggie, 14 Aug 1917**
In addition to the places George mentioned in this letter, he saw other sites of note in England. Within the family collection there is a ticket stub, which revealed he visited one of the Royal Castles: 'Admit the Bearer to the State Apartments, Windsor Castle, on Tuesday, 18th September 1917, between the hours of 11 a.m. and 1 p.m.'

221

## APPENDIX TWO:
# FAMILY AND FRIENDS

**Part A: Family**
    George Gowthorp Martindale (b. 1884)

**George's parents:**
    Robert Martindale (b. 1858)
    Marguerite Love Martindale (nee Harvey) (b. 1860)

**George's siblings:**
    Marguerite 'Maggie' Love Martindale (b.1885)
    Dorothy Fisher (nee Martindale) (b. 1890) (married to 'Warrack' in 1915)
    Robert 'Bob' Harvey Martindale (b. 1892) (married to Ivy Maud Hirth; their children are Florence and Nellie)
    Peter Martindale (b. 1897)

**George's English relations:**
    Reverent 'Uncle' George Gowthorp Martindale (b. 1857)
    Ellen 'Aunt Nellie' Martindale (b. 1861)

### Part B: The 'Dimboola boys' and other companions in arms

The following is a compilation of mini-biographies of soldiers mentioned in George's letters, or who mentioned him in theirs.

**Alexander Campbell Anderson** enlisted in August 1914. He was a 21-year-old 'male nurse' at the time.[1] Initially he served in the 4th Battalion on Gallipoli, where he was wounded in May 1915 and evacuated. When the AIF was reorganised after the Dardanelles campaign 'Mr Anderson', as George knew him, was appointed as a lieutenant in the 59th Battalion. In mid-1916 (recorded as 21 July 1916), Anderson was severely wounded in what his record variously puts as 'chest', 'hip' and 'l.foot'. He was returned to Australia in 1917.

**Arthur Anderson** was among the early Dimboola boys to enlist, signing up in August 1914, and like several others he was assigned to the 8th Battalion.[2] He was a 31-year-old unmarried farmer. Arthur was wounded in the back of his neck on Gallipoli on 28 June 1915, causing a compound fracture to his head. He was evacuated to hospital in Alexandria but died of his wounds at 9.45 am on 11 July 1915. On 15 July 1915 the Defence Secretariat cabled his father that he was 'dangerously ill July 9th'. The following day a cable was sent from Dimboola: 'Please cable Arthur Anderson all at home hope speedy recovery love from all Dave Anderson Dimboola'. A few days later the Dimboola Presbyterian Minister was cabled to convey news of Arthur's demise.[3]

**James 'Jim' Anderson ('Jim A')** was a 32-year-old farmer who was among the early Dimboola boys to enlist in August 1914.[4] First posted with the 8th Battalion, Jim was reported missing at Gallipoli on 25 April 1915, before being evacuated sick to Harefield Hospital in England. As well as George's comments about his poor health, Jim's illness was reported in a letter home by Dimboola boy 'Kirby' Wright, who gave a brief account of several other Dimboola boys including that 'George Martindale is still well and in the trenches. Jim Anderson is gone to England, sick.'[5] Jim was subsequently posted to the Camel Corp in 1916 and served in the Middle East. He was returned to Australia in late 1917 after another bout of illness.

**Henry Martin Armstrong** enlisted in July 1915 and was possibly the **'Harry Armstrong'** referred to by Mr Martindale in early 1917.[6] He was a 29-year-old painter whose father lived at Natte Yallock. Henry arrived in France in late 1916, but served only a short period of active service. In December 1916 he was hospitalised with bronchitis, and returned to Australia in 1918 as medically unfit for further service.

**John 'Jack' Armstrong** enlisted in September 1914.[7] Jack was a nearly 30-year-old farrier and blacksmith, born in Murra Warra. He served on Gallipoli and in France, and was promoted to Corporal Farrier. Officially unwounded by combat, Jack did nonetheless suffer typhoid and malaria during his service. He was returned to Australia and discharged in mid-1918.

By the **'Arthurs of Wail'**, George referred to two farmers with family connections in the small settlement of Wail (near Dimboola) and Mount Gambier in South Australia.[8] **George Arthur** enlisted in early 1916 and was 28 years old at the time.[9] He arrived in England in November 1916 and was killed in action in early October 1917. George Arthur's older brother, 32-year-old **Herbert John Arthur**, generally known as 'John', also enlisted in early 1916.[10] The two brothers took their oath of enlistment on the same day, 7 April 1916, and both were enrolled in the 38th Battalion. John wrote to his family after his brother's death, telling them 'that the fatality was caused by an enemy gunshot wound through the head'.[11] Before the end of the month, John too was killed in action.

**Raymond Venor Baldock** was one of the Dimboola boys who enlisted in August 1914.[12] He was a farmer nearly 21 years old. Assigned to the 8th Battalion, he served on Gallipoli until evacuated in August 1915 with sepsis in his hands and abdomen from shrapnel wounds. Raymond was sent to hospital in Egypt, where he caught Dengue Fever while recovering. He was sent to England for further training in 1916, only going into active combat again on 31 August 1917. He was killed a few weeks later in action in Belgium on 20 September 1917.

**Samuel 'Sam' Edgar Barmby** was nearly 40 years old, married, and worked as a carpenter when he enlisted in January 1916.[13] In 1917 he was invalided by a gas attack, but managed to recuperate sufficiently to rejoin his unit and continue fighting. He returned to Australia in 1919.

**Charles Edwin Woodrow Bean** was an AIF 'press correspondent' and, later, an historian.[14] Captain Bean served throughout the war with Australian forces in Egypt, Gallipoli and Europe between 1914 and 1919. He sent reports to the Australian press during the war, and subsequently oversaw the writing of the government-sponsored official history of the conflict.

**Joseph 'Joe' Bishop** was one of George's trench-mates on whose behalf George sent money to Mr Martindale's care.[15] Joe was a 38-year-old English-born brewer, who had previously served in the South African War, among other conflicts mentioned by George. He was returned to Australia and discharged for 'senility' in 1917. In January 1918 the *Warrnambool Standard* reported that 'Joseph Bishop, a dusty and travel-worn man, with the returned soldier's badge, walked into the recruiting depot at Geelong and offered himself for active service. He said he had seen 1,119 days service, and had stopped a considerable lot of Turkish and Hunnish lead, but felt well enough to go back again. He walked the 120 miles to Geelong from Warrnambool, and thought that was recommendation enough for his acceptance, although he was right on the age limit. He

FAMILY AND FRIENDS

went before the doctor and passed.'[16] The period between Joe's oath of enlistment in 1914 and discharge in Melbourne in 1917 was exactly 1,119 days. There is no evidence that he was again taken into the AIF.

**James 'Jim' Henry Bond** was nearly 27 years old when he enlisted in August 1914.[17] Originally from Ballan, Victoria, James was known in Dimboola because he worked at the railway as an engine driver. Officially, he was killed in action on 27 April 1915 on Gallipoli. George reported being 'certain it was our gun that killed him'.

**Albert Edward Bunting** suffered a bullet wound to his right leg on Gallipoli in May 1915 and was returned to Australia in November that year.[18] Aged 25 when he enlisted in August 1914, he worked at the Dimboola railway station, and was 'well known as an elocutionist, and often appeared at entertainments in Dimboola and elsewhere.'[19] His family was based at Ballarat.

'Byers' is certainly **Harry Alston Byers**.[20] Harry was a 23-year-old grocer when he enlisted in August 1914. He worked at 'Story's' in Melbourne and was fairly recognisable to customers as a 'curly headed lively young fellow'.[21] Initially, he served in H Company 5th Battalion, the same as George. He served on Gallipoli and in France, and died of wounds sustained in action in April 1918. Harry was a Methodist and his parents lived in Melbourne. This probably explains an association with a Victorian Rechabite paper.

**David 'Dave' Stanley Ormond Cambridge** was a 20-year-old clerk upon enlistment in July 1915. He was born in Dimboola and worked at the local Farmers' Cooperative.[22] He had tried to enlist on multiple prior occasions but been rejected for being insufficiently fit. Through intensive training Dave got himself into condition and was accepted for service. He was killed in action on 28 July 1916.[23]

**Edwin Charles 'Charlie' Chidzey** was a 29-year-old labourer who enlisted in early 1916.[24] Part of his service in England and France was in the 'Anzac Light Railways'. He was one of those to have a letter home to Dimboola published in the *Dimboola Banner*, and was returned to Australia in 1919 with no wounds recorded in his service record.[25]

**Thomas George Clements** was one of the Dimboola boys who enlisted in August 1914.[26] He was a 22-year-old farmer and was assigned to the 8th Battalion. Wounded on Gallipoli in May 1915, he then served briefly as a policeman in Alexandria, and was returned to Australia unfit for further service in late 1915. He subsequently became the captain of the Dimboola Rifle Club.[27]

**Charles 'Charlie' William Collard** enlisted in June 1915.[28] He was a nearly 24-year-old grocer with two years' experience with the Dimboola Rifle Club. Charlie arrived in France in early 1916 and was evacuated that July with 'Shell Shock'. He was returned to France in 1917, was promoted, and returned to Australia in 1919.

**Edward Clemens 'Clem' Cordner** enlisted in August 1914. He was a 32-year-old clerk[29] born in Warrnambool. He served as a driver in the Light Horse field ambulance on Gallipoli, and subsequently as a clerk in France. He returned to Australia in 1919.

**Joseph Alan Cordner** enlisted in August 1914, a few days after his older brother Clem.[30] Alan, as he was generally called, was a well-known footballer who played for Geelong and then Collingwood prior to enlisting.[31] A clerk like Clem, Alan was 24 years old. He was wounded in action on Gallipoli on the day of the landing, 25 April 1915, although this news was not conveyed to his family until October 1915. In the meantime, his anxious father corresponded with military authorities about his status and whereabouts, and in July 1915 was given an address so as to cable Alan directly. Mr Cordner had heard several stories, variously reporting Alan as wounded or killed. Officially, he was also listed as missing from 25 April, and was only officially declared killed in action after an enquiry, which concluded on 24 April 1916.

**Colin Forbs Cromb** enlisted in Dimboola in September 1914, aged 20 years.[32] He was a carpenter and served with the 3rd Divisional Mechanical Transport Company. During the war he suffered several bouts of illness, but no combat wounds. He was returned to Australia in 1919.

**Frederick William 'Bill' Dalitz** was nearly 28 years old when he enlisted in June 1915.[33] He was a blacksmith, and was in Egypt by early 1916. Gassed in France in 1918, he survived the conflict and returned to Australia in 1919. He was one of a number of Dimboola boys that wrote home in gratitude for comfort parcels sent from Dimboola.[34] Three of his brothers also enlisted for service, one of whom was killed in action.[35]

**Edward 'Eddie' Charles D'Alton** enlisted ten days after his older brother Henry.[36] The 23-year-old surveyor ended up serving in the 8th Battalion with Henry, and both formed part of A Company. Promoted to Lance-Corporal, Eddie was killed in action on 6 August 1915, the first day of the 'August Offensive'. He was, his Captain related, 'popular and beloved by all in the company'.[37] His Lieutenant, Robert George Leslie Taylor[38], in the same letter to Mrs D'Alton relating the death of Henry, added that Eddie had 'been recommended for a commission'. He closed his account by adding a personal note:

Your sons and I were always very good friends, having gone to school together at Dimboola. They were very popular with their comrades, all of whom join me in my expressions of sympathy.[39]

Like George, Eddie wrote home regularly.[40] Only two months previously Eddie had sent his mother a cable from Cairo after being hospitalised from an earlier wound: 'Quite recovered. Rejoined regiment. Do not worry. Love. D'Alton.'[41] Eddie and Henry were the D'Altons' only sons, and upon news of their deaths, as was the case with many of the Dimboola boys, flags were hung at half-mast around the Dimboola region.

**Henry St Eloy D'Alton** was one of the first of the Dimboola boys to enlist, a 26-year-old municipal clerk at the time.[42] He acted as spokesperson for the recruits on a number of public occasions prior to their departure overseas, as recounted in the introduction. As with several of the early Dimboola recruits, he served in the 8th Battalion. Even once overseas Henry was seen as a leading figure for the Dimboola boys, as illustrated by the way that Dimboola townsfolk addressed a Christmas cable message to him personally on behalf of the wider group, which was sent to Egypt on Christmas Eve 1914:

All Dimboola citizens unite in conveying hearty good wishes to the Dimboola boys, and hope they may enjoy a very merry Christmas and a happy and prosperous New Year. Crebbin and Martindale.[43]

George's father had proposed this idea.

By late April and early May 1915 the electrical wires around Dimboola were carrying messages of condolence to Henry's parents.[44] According to a letter from his Lieutenant, 'Henry on the day of landing [on Gallipoli, 25 April 1915] volunteered to go forward on scouting duty … he was hit by a sniper the following day.'[45] Reportedly, the wound was in the stomach. Henry's Captain also wrote home, relating that Henry:

… was next to me in the trench when he got hit. Turning to me, he said 'Captain, I know I shall not recover from this. I have tried to do my duty and am not afraid to die, and will you please give my love to all at home.' I promised to do so, and we shook hands and we tried to cheer him up. We got him back for treatment at once, but unfortunately nothing could be done.[46]

Henry's service record simply states that he 'Died on transport "Seang Choon" of wounds received in action near Dardanelles'. As George's letter relates, the two last had contact on the evening of 25 April 1915 in the forward positions on Gallipoli.

**Albert Louis Domeyer** was one of George's good mates, a one-time resident of Dimboola, and was mentioned in several letters. Domeyer enlisted in August 1914. He was a 37-year-old mechanical engineer at the time, and first served in the 4th Light Horse.[47] He subsequently served in the Australian Motor Transport and Australian Flying Corps, and was returned to Australia in 1919.

**Samuel 'Sil' Philp Eddy** enlisted in July 1916.[48] He was a tailor in Werribee, 18 years and six months old. He arrived in England in late 1916, served in France in 1917 and 1918, and was returned to Australia in 1919.

**Albert Gordon Elliot ('Young Elliot')** was a 23-year-old labourer from Antwerp (near Dimboola) who enlisted in January 1915.[49] Young Elliot suffered a wound to his right eye in France on 29 July 1916. He spent the remainder of the war in England and was returned to Australia in 1919. His even younger brother, **William Ewen Robert Elliot**, enlisted in September 1915 and was killed in action on the Sinai Peninsula in December 1916.[50]

**Edward Nathaniel 'Tony' Fisher** was one of the Dimboola boys who enlisted in August 1914, and was assigned to the 8th Battalion.[51] He was a 25-year-old barman. Tony served on Gallipoli, from where he wrote home to his sister—like George taking issue with reports of bravery and nonchalance being published in the Australian press.[52] In 1916 he was transferred to the Camel Corps, spending the remainder of the war in Egypt and Abyssinia.

**Henry 'Harry' Fortington** was a 21-year-old hairdresser when he enlisted in June 1915.[53] He arrived on Gallipoli in November 1915, not long before the withdrawal. Sent to France in 1916, he was wounded in action on 28 August 1916. He never served in the front again, instead spending the remainder of 1916 and early 1917 as 'Sick Mental'. He was returned to Australia in May 1917 and discharged for 'Delusional Insanity'. George's condolences to Mrs Fortington referred to Harry's mother.

**Alfred Ernest Hermann** was one of the Dimboola boys who enlisted in August 1914.[54] He was a 23-year-old carpenter. Assigned to the 8th Battalion, he served on Gallipoli before being taken out sick in July 1915. Alfred spent a great proportion of 1916 and early 1917 in England, either in hospital (151 days) or detention (144 days), and was returned to Australia in mid-1917, 'Services no longer required'.

**Norman Frederick Haines** enlisted in August 1914.[55] He was a 20-year-old plumber whose father signed a letter of consent (permitting overseas service for men less than 21 years of age), which survives in his military file. Norman embarked from Australia in October 1915, survived service in Europe, and was returned to Australia in 1919.

**Alfred 'Alf' Sydney Hirth** enlisted in February 1916, a few weeks after his younger brother Leslie.[56] He was a 21-year-old labourer. The brothers met in England, as reported by George and Leslie. Wounded in France on multiple occasions, Alfred was killed in action in October 1917.

**Leslie 'Les' Clarence Hirth** enlisted in February 1916 when 18 years old, and recorded that his current 'trade or calling' was as a 'student'.[57] He gave 'Senior Cadets' as his answer for the question pertaining to prior military service. Arriving in England in late 1916 he encountered George, as recounted in a printed account of his service.[58] He spent most of his first year overseas in England, only being sent to France in September 1917. In December he was evacuated with head wounds from an artillery shell, and returned to Australia in early 1918. He died of influenza in the 1919 pandemic.

**James 'Jim' Hook** enlisted in July 1916 when 29 years and nine months old.[59] He was a married commercial agent, living at Antwerp near Dimboola. He was killed in action in Belgium in October 1917.

**'Bill' Houghton**, George's former 'tent mate' at Broadmeadows, was likely **William Henry Houghton**, who had enlisted in August 1914 when aged 19 and a half years old.[60] He was a plumber. William served on Gallipoli with the 5th Battalion, where he suffered a head wound. He subsequently served in France with the 57th Battalion, which was in support during the July 1916 Fromelles attack, the context in which George refers to 'Bill'. William returned to Australia in 1918.

**Robert Hutchinson** was one of the Dimboola boys who enlisted in August 1914.[61] He was a farmer from nearby Wail and nearly 21 years old. Assigned to the 8th Battalion, he was wounded on Gallipoli in May 1915 and returned to Australia in October. 'I stopped a bullet with my right foot between the ankle and toes. It made a mess of the bone,' he wrote to his parents while in hospital.[62] In April 1918 he again enlisted, arriving in Egypt in October 1918. Robert again returned to Australia and was discharged from the AIF in 1919.

**Clarence Vincent Jaehne** was a 21-year-old grocer when he enlisted in September 1914.[63] He died at sea from pneumonia on 14 January 1915 while aboard the HMAT *Themistocles* en route to Egypt. His father, living at Rainbow, Victoria, repeatedly wrote to the authorities after Jaehne's personal effects. 'I cannot see why there should be such delay.' Mr Jaehne wrote in July 1915, adding that 'If he had been killed in action there would be some reasonable excuse.' A package of Jaehne's belongings was eventually sent to his father in 1916.

**Thomas 'Tom' Kent** was born at Nhill, near Dimboola. He enlisted in June 1916, when 33 years and six months old. He was married and lived at Echuca in New South Wales.[64] Tom arrived in England in late 1916 and joined his unit in France in April 1917. In May he witnessed George getting wounded at Bullecourt and seems to have conveyed information about the injury to George's family. Tom had the misfortune to suffer badly from a condition that frequently put him in hospital: haemorrhoids. He was returned to Australia in August 1918 as medically unfit.

**'Young Lauchs'** was possibly **Henry August Lauchs**, a nearly 20-year-old labourer when he enlisted in January 1915.[65] He was from Colac. Henry was appointed to the 5th Battalion (George's one) and served on Gallipoli from May 1915. He was subsequently transferred to the Police Corps, served in France and England, and returned to Australia in 1919.

**Edwin Wilhelm Lehmann** was Second Lieutenant in the Dimboola Cadets in June 1914.[66] The young, single bank clerk enlisted two years later, in June 1916, when he was 20 years old, getting both of his parents' permission.[67] Edwin was suffered a gas attack in April 1918. He returned to Australia in 1919.

**Aubrey Liddelow** was married when he enlisted in November 1914.[68] He served on Gallipoli in 1915 with the 7th Battalion, sustaining several

FAMILY AND FRIENDS

wounds during the campaign. In 1916 Liddelow was, like George, transferred to the 59th Battalion. On 19 July 1916 Liddelow was reported missing, then killed, in France, a casualty of the Fromelles attack.

**Norman Marshall** was a 28-year-old mill manager when he enlisted in August 1914. Marshall started the war as a private in the 5th Battalion, was Sergeant by the time of the Gallipoli landing, and was awarded the Military Cross for service in the Dardanelles campaign.[69] In July 1916 he participated in the Fromelles assault with the 57th Battalion. 'On the morning after Fromelles he was observed running with another officer,' the Australian Dictionary of Biography noted, 'half-way between the opposing lines, hunting for wounded soldiers.'[70] He had been promoted to Major shortly before the attack. The other 'officer' seen with Marshall seeking for wounded was quite possibly George. Marshall continued his notable service throughout the remainder of the war, returning to Australia in late 1919.

**Peter Martindale** was George's younger brother and enlisted in April 1916 when 18 years and eight months old.[71] He was a bank clerk. Peter arrived in England in late 1916, where he was able to meet up with George. In April 1917 he proceeded to France and was made Lance Corporal by mid-May. Peter was awarded the 'Military Medal for bravery in the field' in July 1918. The commendation ran as follows:

Near Villiers, Bretonneux, on 4th July, 1918, this N.C.O. was attached to a section of snipers. During the attack he discovered a gap of 200 yards in which a party of the enemy were resisting. In the face of heavy machine-gun fire he led his snipers into the gap, captured the machine-gun and cleared the trench. Pushing forward he bombed another section of trench, killed three Huns and took two prisoners. He disposed his snipers and held this portion of the line until the Infantry dug themselves in. His section commander

DODGING THE DEVIL

becoming a casualty, he took command and supervised very effective sniping throughout the day.[72]

Peter returned to Australia in 1919, married, and had a family. He resumed service during the Second World War and died in 1948.[73]

**Charles 'Charlie' McDonald** enlisted in April 1916 when nearly 27 years old.[74] He was a 'forman labourer' from Horsham. Arriving in England in September 1916, a little before meeting George, Charlie was sent to France in December. He was wounded in May 1917 and returned to Australia in 1919.

**Roderick 'Rod' George McKenzie** enlisted in April 1916.[75] He was a 21-year-old farmer whose father lived at Wallap near Horsham and Dimboola. Shipped to England in 1916, Rod was severely wounded in his face, arms and back on 31 January 1917. He died the following day.

**Murdoch McRae** enlisted in March 1916, when he was 28 years old.[76] He was a Dimboola-born farm labourer, whose family were in nearby Horsham. Murdoch arrived in England in October 1916 and was sent to France in November. On 16 January 1917 he was killed in action.

**Rupert Vance Moon** enlisted in August 1914, and initially served in the 4th Light Horse.[77] He was the son of a former Dimboola bank manager. He was a 22-year-old bank clerk at the time of his application to serve. He served on Gallipoli and in France, and returned to Australia in 1919. In 1917 Rupert was awarded the Victoria Cross for 'very conspicuous bravery', concerning an attack made the day after George was severely wounded by a shell.[78]

**Franklin 'Len' George Morrow** enlisted in August 1914, aged 21.[79] His occupation at that time was 'Operating Porter'. His service record documents time in the 5th Battalion, and specialised assignments with artillery, signals, railway, telephony and various headquarters, which make this identification likely. He returned to Australia in 1918.

**Harry Norman Richards** was a 20-year-old motor mechanic in Dimboola when he enlisted in August 1914.[80] Like many of the early Dimboola recruits he served in the 8th Battalion on Gallipoli. Transferred to the 60th Battalion, he then served in France, and was promoted to 2nd Lieutenant in August 1916. That month he was, his military record confirms, 'awarded D.C.M. [Distinguished Conduct Medal] for conspicuous gallantry during operations. When his officers became casualties he took command & displayed great coolness & bravery under very heavy fire. He also did fine work carrying in wounded.' Gassed in mid-1917, Harry suffered poor health throughout the remainder of the war and was returned to Australia in 1919.

**Wilfred Robinson** was a 32-year-old farmer from Murra Warra when he enlisted in September 1914. He was wounded on Gallipoli and returned to Australia unfit for service.[81] In a letter home dated 12 days after the Gallipoli landing he described things as 'not too bad', but added bluntly that 'War is hell. Dead in heaps four or five deep, and a fellow in perfect health drops in a second, a bleeding, quivering mass of blood and flesh.'[82] Wilfred re-enlisted in 1919 and served for a while in the Solomon Islands.

**Robert 'Rob' Alexander Ross** enlisted in March 1916.[83] He was a 27-year-old farmer from 'Dant Dant near Dimboola'. He was shipped to Europe in 1916, served in France in 1917 and 1918, and was returned to Australia in 1919.

**George Russell** was one of George's trench-mates, on whose behalf George sent money to Mr Martindale's care.[84] Upon enlistment in

August 1914 Russell was a 24-year-old gardener. Like Joseph Bishop, he was born in England. Russell served on Gallipoli and in France, being wounded at the former and killed in the latter in September 1916. His will, dated June 1915 and copied in his service record, states simply that 'In case of my death I leave all my belongings to my mother.' His mother, living in Hayling Island England, had to correspond with the Australian military authorities in Melbourne about his death and personal effects.

**Roy Llewellyn Sandow** enlisted in September 1914.[85] He was a 30-year-old baker and pastry cook who served on Gallipoli. He was wounded on the day of the landing by shrapnel, was evacuated, and spent the remainder of 1915 in Egypt. A mate of his described the moment in a letter home: 'My old cobber, Roy Sandow, got knocked out first day. He got hit with shrapnel and his both feet and legs were cut about. His injuries are serious, but I don't think he will lose his feet, although it looked as if his heels were pretty well blown off.'[86] Roy served in France in 1916, but suffered multiple bouts of ill health before being wounded in action in September 1917, with a compound fracture to his right thigh. He died of this injury soon thereafter.

**Colin 'Col' Wilson Taylor** enlisted in August 1915.[87] He was a grocer, nearly 25 years old. Wounded in both hand and leg in France in July 1916, Colin was returned to Australia in early 1917.[88]

**John 'Jack' Myles Thornburn** was one of George's trench-mates, both serving in the 5th Battalion on Gallipoli.[89] Jack enlisted in August 1914 when he was 28 years old, a sawmiller at the time. In August 1916 Jack was awarded the D.C.M. (Distinguished Conduct Medal) for, as his record states, 'conspicuous gallantry & devotion to duty during operations he worked incessantly rescuing & helping the wounded quite regardless of his personal safety'. In late 1918 he was returned to Australia, despite multiple public reports of his death in his home region.

FAMILY AND FRIENDS

**Charles 'Charlie' Frederick Wall**, a nearly 24-year-old grocer, joined the AIF in August 1915.[90] Sent to France to reinforce the 31st Battalion, Charlie disembarked in Marseilles on 25 June 1916 and was killed a few weeks later in early August. His personal effects, returned to his father, were typical of those returned for many of the Dimboola boys:

Identity Disc, Letters, Prayer Book, Pencil, Cigarette Case, Cigarette Maker, Coin, Writing Wallet, Photos, Watch, Razor Blades—in Case, Metal Ring.

Charlie was known as a keen sportsman and fireman.[91] News of his death was relayed to his family through a cable sent to the local Anglican minister. George wrote a letter of condolence to his father after hearing Charlie had been killed.[92]

**James Randolph Babbington Wall** was a nearly 33-year-old baker whose mother lived at Jeparit.[93] He enlisted in April 1916 and served in France during 1917. In April 1918 he was returned to Australia with 'Trench Feet', and discharged from the AIF.

**David Stanley Wanliss** enlisted in August 1914.[94] Wanliss was Lieutenant Colonel of the 5th Battalion at Gallipoli, before being transferred to the 65th Battalion in March 1917 where he served in France. In May 1918 Wanliss was returned to Australia.

The **'brother of A. W. Ward of Murra Warra'** could be either **James Ward**, who reportedly enlisted in Dimboola, or **Harry Ward**, who enlisted in New Zealand, both of whom were killed in action in mid-1917.[95] Their parents lived in England, and they had siblings in Murra Warra, New Zealand and England. It could also be another brother, **Eben Ward**, whose enlistment and service has not been further identified in Australian records, suggesting he may have served in other Commonwealth forces.[96]

**Conrad Egbert Williams** enlisted in December 1914 as a 30-year-old bank manager, and gave membership of the Dimboola Rifle Club as evidence of prior military service on his application.[97] Wounded on Gallipoli, he was returned to Australia and discharged as medically unfit in May 1916.

**Arthur William Wilson**, like the other Wilson boys, was born in Bradford, Yorkshire.[98] He enlisted in 1917 when 43 years old. Married, and the father of three children, Arthur sold the family farm as he went off to war.[99] He served in France in 1917 and 1918, but was taken sick to England and discharged due to 'disability and age' in November 1918.

**Hubert 'Bert' Ward Wilson** had grown up in Dimboola, although he was living in Brighton in Melbourne by the time he enlisted in March 1915.[100] Bert was a lecturer at the Melbourne Teacher's College, having left Dimboola to pursue further study and a career in teaching. Serving at Gallipoli then in Europe, Bert was rapidly promoted through the ranks, and was appointed Chemical Advisor in gas warfare because of his expertise and training. Mentioned in despatches, he reached the rank of Major, survived the war, and earned an Order of the British Empire.[101]

**Sam Wilson** was widely noted as a particularly good marksman and very active in the Dimboola Rifle Club.[102] Sam answered the attestation question about prior military service by mentioning the club. Born in Yorkshire, England, Sam was a 35-year-old joiner who, like many Dimboola boys, served in the 8th Battalion and the Gallipoli campaign. Like George and many Gallipoli veterans, he was then sent to the Western front, where he was killed in action in mid-1916.[103]

**Septimus John Kirby Wright** enlisted in August 1914 and was assigned to the 8th Battalion, like many of the other Dimboola boys.[104] He was nearly 22 years old and worked as a railway engine cleaner. He was wounded at Gallipoli, evacuated, returned to Gallipoli, re-evacuated sick, and eventually died of pneumonia in Egypt in July 1917. He wrote a number of letters that were published in the *Dimboola Banner*, including one that mentioned that 'George Martindale is still well and in the trenches.'[105]

Autographs gathered on the *Orvieto* as the first recruits sailed to the Middle East in 1914, their fate as yet unknown.

# NOTES

### Notes to letters and commentary
1. A. W. Keown, *Forward with the Fifth: the story of five years' war service, Fifth Inf. Battalion, A.I.F.* (Specialty Press, Melbourne, 1921)
2. *Dimboola Banner*, 25 Aug 1914, p. 1
3. National Archives of Australia (NAA): B2455 item 8216707. This file contains George's attestation papers and service record, and provides most of the information concerning his service referred to throughout this book.
4. *Dimboola Banner*, 25 Aug 1914, p. 2
5. *Dimboola Banner*, 25 Aug 1914, p. 2
6. *Dimboola Banner*, 18 Aug 1914, p. 3
7. *Dimboola Banner*, 21 Aug 1914, p. 2
8. *Dimboola Banner*, 14 Aug 1914, p. 3
9. *Dimboola Banner*, 11 Aug 1914, p. 2
10. *Dimboola Banner*, 21 Aug 1914, p. 2
11. *Dimboola Banner*, 25 Aug 1914, p. 2
12. *Dimboola Banner*, 25 Aug 1914, p. 2
13. *Dimboola Banner*, 28 Aug 1914, p. 2
14. *Dimboola Banner*, 1 Sept 1914, p. 2
15. *Dimboola Banner*, 28 Aug 1914, p. 3
16. *Dimboola Banner*, 8 Sept 1914, p. 3

DODGING THE DEVIL

17  *Dimboola Banner*, 8 Sept 1914, p. 3
18  *Dimboola Banner*, 15 Sept 1914, p. 2; 2 Oct 1914, p. 3; 23 Oct 1914, p. 3; 30 Oct 1914, p. 3
19  HMAT = His Majesty's Australian Transport
20  Australian War Memorial (AWM), F00160
21  *Ballarat Star*, 20 January 1915, pp. 1–2; *Gippsland Standard and Alberton Shire Representative*, 22 January 1915, p. 3; *Mercury*, 22 January 1915, p. 5
22  The name is heavily scratched out.
23  Territorials
24  The text is heavily redacted, making the original text underneath largely illegible.
25  This name, like the section above, is heavily redacted and difficult to read.
26  George inserted a hand-drawn diagram of the formation here.
27  This line was appended at the bottom of the page, but seems to best belong here.
28  This is printed on the paper but scratched out by George.
29  Redaction here, struck through: 'Sam is away sick also Eddie [fell?] with a sore hand.'
30  Latin: While I breath, I hope.
31  This line is added along the side of the postcard.
32  This letter was started before the previous one, hence the reference to Eddie D'Alton, but was completed later.
33  Added above
34  James Anderson
35  '(over)' written below
36  Victoria Cross
37  *Dimboola Banner*, 7 April 1916, p. 2
38  one 2lb loaf
39  '(over)' written below
40  'Wilderness of El Tih' written at top of page.
41  George inserted a diagram of the bullet here, mid-sentence.
42  George inserted a diagram of the effect here, mid-sentence.
43  i.e. Robert Burns, the Scottish poet
44  At the top of the page George wrote 'New Colors Enclosed' and a strip of blue fabric is pinned over a strip of red.
45  George inserted a drawing of his badge and stripes here.

# NOTES

46 The remainder of the letter is in a different coloured text.
47 *Dimboola Banner*, 25 June 1915, p. 3
48 This was 4 May 1915.
49 Précised in *Dimboola Banner*, 6 Aug 1915, p. 2
50 Text colour changes here.
51 Text colour changes here.
52 George inserted a two-part diagram here of the 'Side view' and 'End section' of this implement.
53 Norman Marshall
54 Cablegram, from a copy in George's military file
55 Copied in his service record
56 *Dimboola Banner*, 8 September 1916, p. 2
57 *Dimboola Banner*, 23 Feb 1917, p. 3
58 'fined'
59 George inserts a brief diagram here.
60 British Red Cross Society
61 c/p = cost price
62 *Dimboola Banner*, 26 Jan 1917, p. 3
63 The poems are at the top of each page respectively, the text at the bottom. They are arranged here as per George's original writing, for ease of interpretation.
64 In original poem, a line from Juvenal meaning roughly: For the sake of living do not lose the cause for living.
65 Text colour changes here.
66 Warsaw is buried, Russia is lost
67 Text colour changes here.
68 Latin, *pro tempore*, meaning: 'for now'
69 Latin: 'at pleasure'
70 NAA: A427 item 7877500
71 On paper with printed banner: 'Church Army and Church of England Men's Society Recreation Hut'
72 On 'Church Army and Church of England Men's Society Recreation Hut' paper
73 'son of Roderick' added above
74 'Blue Ribbon' added above
75 *Dimboola Banner*, 22 June 1917, p. 2
76 This survives in the family collection.

DODGING THE DEVIL

77  George inserts a sketch here.
78  *Dimboola Banner*, 18 January 1918, p. 3
79  *Dimboola Banner*, 18 January 1918, p. 3
80  *Dimboola Banner*, 25 January 1918, p. 3

## Notes to explanatory notes

1   http://www.parliament.vic.gov.au/re-member/details/1322-menzies-james
2   *Dimboola Banner*, 11 Sept 1914, p. 2; 15 Sept 1914, p. 2
3   A. W. Keown, *Forward with the Fifth: the story of five years' war service, Fifth Inf. Battalion, A.I.F.* (Specialty Press, Melbourne, 1921)
4   *Dimboola Banner*, 16 Oct 1914, p. 3
5   *Stratford Sentinel*, 16 Oct 1914, p. 3
6   *Dimboola Banner*, 30 Oct 1914, p. 3
7   See next section
8   *Dimboola Banner*, 8 Jan 1915, p. 2
9   *Age*, 21 Jan 1915, p. 6
10  *Argus*, 21 Jan 1915, p. 7
11  *Dimboola Banner*, 21 Aug 1914, p. 2
12  *Dimboola Banner*, 29 Jan 1915, p. 2
13  *Dimboola Banner*, 22 Jan 1915, p. 2; 26 Feb 1915, p. 2
14  *Dimboola Banner*, 19 February 1915, p. 3
15  *Dimboola Banner*, 27 April 1917, p. 2
16  *Dimboola Banner*, 16 Oct 1914, p. 3
17  Australian War Memorial (AWM), G00963
18  *The Windsor Magazine*, Vol. 41, Dec 1914–May 1915, p. 118
19  *Geelong Advertiser*, 17 May 1913, p. 3
20  *Horsham Times*, 20 May 1913, p. 6
21  Excerpt from *Friends' Review, A Literary and Miscellaneous Journal*, Vol. 22, 1869, p. 591
22  Donald Cameron, National Archives of Australia (NAA): B2455 item 3199712. His service record indicates a period of sickness (dysentery) at Anzac Cove Gallipoli, requiring transfer to hospital, but no self-inflicted wound. He was transferred to Machine Guns, however, which could have kept him actively fighting without the need for an actual trigger finger.
23  *Argus*, 20 Dec 1915, p. 8; *Argus*, 24 Dec 1915, p. 6

24 *Argus*, 1 Dec 1915, p. 9
25 *Endure and Fight* (London: 1915)
26 Excerpt from Rev. I. Baltzell, *Golden Songs: for the Sabbath School, Sanctuary and Social Worship* (1874), p. 97
27 Gordon Stables, *For Honour not Honours: being the story of Gordon of Khartoum* (Shaw & Co, London, 1896)
28 A. J. Hill, 'Elliott, Harold Edward (Pompey) (1878–1931)', Australian Dictionary of Biography, National Centre of Biography, Australian National University: http://adb.anu.edu.au/biography/elliott-harold-edward-pompey-6104/text10459
29 *Dimboola Banner*, 19 May 1916, p. 3
30 Charles Bean (ed.), *The Anzac Book* (Melbourne, 1916)
31 *Dimboola Banner*, 18 Aug 1916, p. 3
32 Walter Francis, *For auld lang syne, Australia will be there* (Melbourne, 1914)
33 Reginald Stoneham, *Heroes of the Dardanelles* (Melbourne, 1915)
34 *Northcote Leader*, 25 Mar 1916, pp. 2–3
35 *London Times*, 15 December 1916, p. 25
36 The *Argus* did not seem to publish it, but it was printed in the *Dimboola Banner*, 26 Jan 1917, p. 3
37 *Dimboola Banner*, 16 Feb 1917, p. 3; 2 Mar 1917, p. 3

## Notes to family and friends
1 National Archives of Australia (NAA): B2455 item 1974032
2 NAA: B2455 item 1974334; see also his brother, James Anderson
3 *Dimboola Banner*, 23 July 1915, p. 2
4 NAA: B2455 item 1977024; see also his brother, Arthur Anderson
5 *Dimboola Banner*, 29 October 1915, p. 1
6 NAA: B2455 item 3035522
7 NAA: B2455 item 3035580
8 *Dimboola Banner*, 23 Nov 1917, p. 3
9 NAA: B2455 item 3036472
10 NAA: B2455 item 3036502
11 *Dimboola Banner*, 21 Dec 1917, p. 3
12 NAA: B2455 item 3046607
13 NAA: B2455 item 3049767

14  NAA: B2455 item 4028768
15  NAA: B2455 item 3085781; see also George Russell
16  *Warrnambool Standard*, 14 Jan 1918, p. 3
17  NAA: B2455 item 3097468
18  NAA: B2455 item 3166672
19  *Dimboola Banner*, 11 June 1915, p. 2
20  NAA: B2455 item 3178454
21  *Ringwood and Croydon Chronicle*, 17 May 1918, p. 3
22  NAA: B2455 item 3191537
23  *Dimboola Banner*, 8 Sept 1916, p. 3
24  NAA: B2455 item 3243399
25  *Dimboola Banner*, 12 April 1918, p. 3
26  NAA: B2455 item 3255717
27  *Dimboola Banner*, 6 Dec 1918, p. 3
28  NAA: B2455 item 3270647
29  NAA: B2455 item 3420800; see also Joseph Alan Cordner
30  NAA: B2455 item 3420840; see also Edward Clements Cordner
31  *Winner*, 13 Dec 1916, p. 8
32  NAA: B2455 item 3466927
33  NAA: B2455 item 3483699
34  *Dimboola Banner*, 11 January 1918, p. 3
35  Alan Clarence Dalitz, NAA: B2455 item 3483692; Carl Walter Dalitz, NAA: B2455 item 3483693; Ernest Oswald Dalitz, NAA: B2455 item 3483696
36  NAA: B2455 item 3483997
37  *Dimboola Banner*, 15 Oct 1915, p. 2
38  George did not mention Taylor in any letters that survive. **Robert George Leslie Taylor** (NAA: B2455 item 1932327) was a 22-year-old draper. He was born in Dimboola and his father lived in nearby Stawell. Taylor was wounded in his wrist by shrapnel during the Gallipoli campaign. Several hospital stints preceded an eventual return to Australia in early 1916 as unfit for continued service once the campaign had concluded.
39  *Dimboola Banner*, 15 Oct 1915, p. 2
40  *Dimboola Banner*, 25 June 1915, p. 3; *Dimboola Banner*, 6 Aug 1915, p. 2
41  *Dimboola Banner*, 2 July 1915, p. 3
42  NAA: B2455 item 3484248
43  *Dimboola Banner*, 25 Dec 1914, p. 3

NOTES

44  *Nhill Free Press*, 4 May 1915, p. 3
45  *Dimboola Banner*, 15 Oct 1915, p. 2
46  *Dimboola Banner*, 15 Oct 1915, p. 2
47  NAA: B2455 item 3512667
48  NAA: B2455 item 3534257
49  NAA: B2455 item 3538209
50  NAA: B2455 item 3539850
51  NAA: B2455 item 3900372
52  *Dimboola Banner*, 15 October 1915, p. 1
53  NAA: B2455 item 4023381
54  NAA: B2455 item 5476428
55  NAA: B2455 item 4266420
56  NAA: B2455 item 5477303
57  NAA: B2455 item 5477305
58  *Dimboola Banner*, 23 February 1917, p. 3; see also *Dimboola Banner*, 1 February 1918, p. 3
59  NAA: B2455 item 5823418
60  NAA: B2455 item 5822454
61  NAA: B2455 item 6928451
62  *West Wimmera Mail*, 9 July 1915, p. 1
63  NAA: B2455 item 7372038
64  NAA: B2455 item 4420553
65  NAA: B2455 item 7379966
66  *Dimboola Banner*, 16 June 1914, p. 4
67  NAA: B2455 item 4377003
68  NAA: B2455 item 8202321
69  NAA: J1795 item 5223642; NAA: QX6290 item 4838989
70  A. J. Hill, 'Marshall, Norman (1886–1942)', Australian Dictionary of Biography, National Centre of Biography, Australian National University, http://adb.anu.edu.au/biography/marshall-norman-7498/text13071
71  NAA: B2455 item 8216662
72  *Dimboola Banner*, 20 Sept 1918, p. 2
73  *Horsham Times*, 8 Oct 1948, p. 2
74  NAA: B2455 item 1839366
75  NAA: B2455 item 1950606
76  NAA: B2455 item 1959913

77  NAA: B2455 item 8334258
78  *Dimboola Banner*, 22 June 1917
79  NAA: B2455 item 7988773
80  NAA: B2455 item 8029537
81  NAA: B2455 item 1905713
82  *Horsham Times*, 20 July 1915, p. 6
83  NAA: B2455 item 8038388
84  NAA: B2455 item 8073414; see also Joseph Bishop
85  NAA: B2455 item 8077163
86  *Seymour Express*, 2 July 1915, pp. 3–4
87  NAA: B2455 item 1928629
88  *Dimboola Banner*, 20 April 1917, pp. 3–4; Colin's brothers (Albert Henry Taylor, NAA: B2455 item 1927395, and Leslie Douglas Taylor) also served overseas and returned home, as did other Taylors from Dimboola.
89  NAA: B2455 item 8099432
90  NAA: B2455 item 8347097
91  *Dimboola Banner*, 8 September 1916, p. 3
92  *Dimboola Banner*, 26 January 1917, p. 3
93  NAA: B2455 item 8375196
94  NAA: B2455 item 8347893
95  *Dimboola Banner*, 6 July 1917, p. 3
96  *Horsham Times*, 6 July 1917, p. 4
97  NAA: B2455 item 1806073
98  NAA: B2455 item 1996290; see also Hubert and Sam Wilson
99  *Dimboola Banner*, 23 Feb 1917, p. 2; 9 March 1917, p. 2; 23 March 1917, p. 2
100 NAA: B2455 item 2011335; see also Arthur and Sam Wilson
101 *Horsham Times*, 4 Jan 1914, p. 7
102 NAA: B2455 item 2014757; see also Arthur and Hubert Wilson
103 *Dimboola Banner*, 14 July 1916, p. 3
104 NAA: B2455 item 3450166
105 *Dimboola Banner*, 2 July 1915, p. 3; 29 October 1915, p. 1